Perfect Unfolding

Seven Years of Life-Changing Solo Adventure,
One Year That Broke Me Open

Kristy Halvorsen

PERFECT UNFOLDING

First Published 2026 in USA by Coddiwomple Now LLC in partnership with IW Press Ltd

This book reflects the author's personal experiences and perspectives. It is intended for entertainment and informational purposes only and is not a substitute for professional advice. If you suspect you have a problem, you should consult a qualified professional.

Permissions:
#36: From "wandering in the cage", from The Last Night of the Earth Poems by Charles Bukowski. Copyright (c) 1992 by Charles Bukowski. Used by permission of HarperCollins Publishers.

#218: Society
Words and Music by Jerry Hannan
Copyright © 2007 Record High Publishing
All Rights Administered by Bike Music c/o Concord Music Publishing
All Rights Reserved Used by Permission
Reprinted by permission of Hal Leonard LLC

#442 "Not Anyone Who Says" by Mary Oliver
Reprinted by permission of The Charlotte Sheedy Literary Agency as agent for the author.
Copyright © 2015 by Mary Oliver with permission of Bill Reichblum

Map of North America drawing by Mehtab Khan
Author photo by Hannah Halvorsen
Cover graphic design: 1981D
Interior design: Chapter One Book Production

Library of Congress Control Number: 2025914642

ISBN-13 979-8-9915203-1-7 (Paperback)
ISBN-13 979-8-9915203-2-4 (ebook)
ISBN-13 979-8-9915203-3-1 (Audio book)

Coddiwomple Now LLC, 411 Walnut Street. #13299 Green Cove Springs, Florida 32043
IW Press Ltd, 62-64 Market Street, Ashby de la Zouch, LE65 1AN

To the wanderer in you.

Praise for Perfect Unfolding

"This is a beautiful memoir of solo adventure and personal awakening. Through minimalist living and self-reliance, Kristy discovers a quieter kind of freedom rooted in emotional openness and trust. *Perfect Unfolding* is filled with poetic insight and wonder, and it will stay with me long after the last page."

— **Eric McHenry**, Past International President at Airstream Club International

"Coddiwomple along with Kristy on this beautiful and surprising journey of life and love. It will make you question why we have all so readily, and mindlessly, adopted our modern consumer-laden lifestyles. This story just might inspire you to be brave and follow your own tickles."

— **Kim Ossi van Brecht**, Associate Director of Planet Forward

"Kristy lives a life that takes my breath away. Her honesty and openness to life in the moment are stunning. She will likely challenge everything you think about how life works."

— **Lorna Davis**, TED speaker & former CEO

"*Perfect Unfolding* is a hell of a story and very compelling. This is what true living looks like. It cuts past all the spiritual nonsense and gets right to the heart of what living fully and being open to what's possible really mean. There were moments when I laughed out loud, parts where I felt sadness, and times of pure hopefulness. It left me wanting more."

— **Al Kenney**, Live Into Your Brilliance Podcast host & Chief of Staff at Duel

"I absolutely loved *Perfect Unfolding*. In fact, it might be the best book I've read in a long time, both as a reader and an editor. The flow is so engaging and creative, and I personally found so much wisdom in Kristy's words and journey. I know this story is going to stick with me for a long time."

— **Rachel Small**, editor & consultant

"Kristy takes you on an exhilarating ride through her personal adventures with exceptional skill, bravery, love and common sense. Her message to me is that we all have what it takes to get through what life throws our way. This book should be on the required reading list for adults."

— **J. Polk**, retired public school teacher

"In Kristy's alluring writing we get swept up into her and her humanness and we don't want to let her go. There aren't many books we can say that about. Join the adventure, strap yourself in, and enjoy!"

— **Jack Pransky**, Author & Three Principles' mentor and coach

"Kristy's new book, *Perfect Unfolding*, takes you with her on an exquisite journey. This eloquent and honest book ranges from musings and poetry to on-the-edge of your chair stories of Kristy's travels to some of the most beautiful and remote places in North America. I came away feeling as if I had joined her in her wanderings and that the two of us had discovered important things about ourselves and each other. This book will stay with me for a long time."

— **Maria Parker**, CEO Cruzbike Inc. & volunteer
Executive Director for 3000 Miles to a Cure

"Kristy Halvorsen is one of those remarkable yet beautifully ordinary people who followed the tickles of her soul and went walkabout. *Perfect Unfolding* is a selfless expression of living authentically, expecting nothing in return, only to receive exactly what you were meant to."

— **Mark Bilbe**, fellow Coddiwompler

"You will be more in love with being alive when you finish this book. This story will hold you and entertain you all the way to a threshold, an opening, where fear can give way to your own wisdom, your own goodness, and your own wild heart."

— **Mer Monson**, author & poet

"I couldn't put *Perfect Unfolding* down!!! It captivated me and when a book hooks you, like this one did, there's no problem finding the time to devour it!!"

— **Joy Belonga**, mentor & coach

"With this book, Kristy invites you to join her and her friend Coddi on a deeply delightful adventure for the heart and soul. If I were you, I'd take her up on it!"

— **Mavis Karn**, counselor, educator, & consultant

"This book is about letting go of everything we know: free-falling into the wild, open freedom and inclusivity of being fully alive. I laughed, I cried, and I found myself aching to fully embrace the essence of coddiwompling in my everyday life."

— **Rhonda Abrose**, grandmother & author of *Beyond the Door*

"*Perfect Unfolding* is a fantastic read. Great insights into the life of a single woman going off-grid full time in an Airstream. But it's more than just a travelogue. The author gets deeply personal about the journey of life, love and love lost. Never preachy or political, yet not shy about sensitive topics and real life issues. I really enjoyed the wandering and pondering nature of this book. Highly recommended."

— **Steve Monson**, financial advisor

"An extraordinary story about an extraordinary woman on an extraordinary adventure. If you've ever wondered what it would be to live your life without fear (but with every other emotion under the sun at full mast), this book will call to something deep within your soul."

— **Michael Neill**, author of *The Inside-Out Revolution* & *Creating the Impossible*

Contents

Hebron
Nain
Natuashish
Makkovik
Hopedale
Goose Bay
Port Hope Simpson
L'Anse Meadows
LABRADOR
Labrador City
Port au Choix
Bishop's Falls
Woody Point &
Gros Morne
National Park
Cape Bonavista
St. John's
NEWFOUNDLAND
Lac Manicouagan
QUEBEC
Argentia
Baie-Comeau
PRINCE
EDWARD
ISLAND
Cape Breton Island
ONTARIO
NEW
BRUNSWICK
Antigonish
NS
Québec City
MAINE
Fundy National Park
Falls
Augusta
Carp
VT
NH
Thousand
Islands
Dover
Green
Mountain
Wilderness
WISCONSIN
NEW
YORK
MA
Boston
CT
Martha's Vineyard
MICHIGAN
RI
Guilford
Newark
PENNSYLVANIA
NJ
ILLINOIS
OHIO
Harrisburg
MD
INDIANA
DE
WEST
VIRGINIA
VIRGINIA
Louisville
Charlottesville
KENTUCKY
NORTH
Cherokee
National Forest
CAROLINA
TENNESSEE
Black Rock
Mountain
Columbia
t Jean State Park
SC
Fulton
Ball's Ferry Boat Ramp
GEORGIA
ALABAMA
Havana
MISSISSIPPI
St. Augustine
NA
Cape
San Blas
FLORIDA
Topsail Hill
Preserve
State Park

LABRADOR SEA

ATLANTIC OCEAN

One-Year Journey
Epilogue Route
Featured in the Book
Other Stops Along the Way

SCALE OF MILES

0   100   200   300   400

GULF OF MEXICO

Map copyright © 2025 by Coddiwomple Now, LLC

Author's Note

This book is stitched together from memories, journal entries, written correspondence, and a sprinkle of research. While Newfoundland and Labrador is a single province, I chat about each part separately to honor their distinct experiences. For simplicity, I converted all currency to US dollars. For privacy, I changed a few names.

Just as my journey taught me to live more intentionally, *Perfect Unfolding* is created with intention too. We've chosen paper weight, font and spacing that minimize environmental impact while bringing you this story of realizing what matters most.

Perfect Unfolding is crafted in a unique fragmented style: a mosaic of adventure, introspection, and reflections. This story, like life itself, does not follow a straight line. Release any expectations about how a book *should* be read and let yourself be surprised. Be open and present as we move in and out of moments. The spaces between the numbered sections offer natural invitations to pause and reflect. If the format feels unfamiliar at first, take it slow and allow the pieces to settle. Soon, it will click, and the journey will carry you. This is an experience like no other.

Now, grab a cozy blanket, perhaps a cup of something warm, and imagine we're sitting around a campfire sharing stories about life. Read this book as if you're my friend. Because you are.

Prologue

I lay sprawled in leaves and scraggly shrubs. With each quick breath I took, my bike rose and fell on my chest, its front wheel spinning. Birds chirped, a breeze rustled branches, I tasted iron, my heartbeat thundered in my ears. Darkness zoomed in like the closing credits of an old movie, edges first, then center. A high-pitched squeal drowned out all sound until all that was left was the ringing and the black.

Woozy, tingling, I floated, waiting for sight and sound to return. Thank God I'd landed flat on my back. That saved me from fully blacking out.

I wiggled my toes. *What a relief.* They still worked.

All systems seemed a go. No pain. A miracle. *Fan-friggin-tastic!* I sat up and pressed my right palm into the dirt, ready to push myself up. That's when I felt it—something was out of whack.

My right hand was in a black full-fingered glove. But the pinky finger jutted sideways in an S curve, like a snapped twig. *That is quite unfortunate.* I wasn't all that concerned about the finger. My biggest worry was whether this would spoil the rest of my Newfoundland adventure. Using my forearm, I pushed myself to my knees and stood. Leaves and dirt fell from my clothes. Bright-red blood dripped onto my yellow shirt from a gash on my jawline.

No cell service anywhere. I walked my bike toward the trailhead. Thirty minutes later, I met two hikers.

"Hi, do either of you have medical training?"

"Yes, I'm career military," the man said. We stood at the edge of a wooden footbridge. Water babbled over rocks below. Cottony clouds blanketed the sky. A crisp breeze fluttered his unzipped jacket collar. I held up my gloved right hand.

"Eww!" His face contorted as if he'd bitten into something sour. "Is it broken or dislocated?"

His wife inched closer, then gasped and looked away.

"I don't know. Can't fix it myself, so didn't see a reason to take the glove off."

The man watched and grimaced as I inched it off. His wife turned her back and gazed down at the river.

"Oh gee, sorry, I can't help with that."

His wife rejoined us. We stood in a circle, staring down at my hand as if it were a wounded bird. "I doubt the clinic can handle that," he said. "The closest hospital is a few hours away. Where is your partner? Or your friends?"

"I'm traveling alone."

His eyebrows rose and then sunk. "You don't have anyone to help?" He rubbed his forehead, his expression a mixture of concern and disbelief.

An hour after the crash, I made it to my truck and tried the door handle with my three good fingers. That confirmed my right hand was useless. Even the slightest movement of the deformed pinky finger shot pain up my arm. Still no cell service for many miles. I had no health insurance in Canada.

As I off-loaded gear onto the passenger seat with my left hand, my emotional center was blank and toneless. The military man's words replayed in my mind: *You don't have anyone to help*? The look on his face had said it all: *Who would come all the way out here alone?*

Part One:
Finding Myself Northbound

I became an expert at being alone the day I decided I was safer without love. I was thirteen. By my mid-thirties, I believed I'd perfected the art of loving no one.

The walls I'd built to protect myself from love, life, and loss had locked me in a cage of aloneness. They were my masterpiece decades in the making: reinforced with self-determination, insulated with toughness, and constructed from the jagged stones of past betrayals. Then Wade happened. He was the exception I made to my own rules, the crack I allowed in my armor. For four years, I convinced myself I could love without risk. I was thirty-eight when he snuck off to Kansas to be with his ex, taking our shared dreams with him. *This pain is why I stopped loving. See what happens when I open up. I'll never do that again.*

My hands didn't have callouses, but my heart did—raw and tender under invisible barriers. I didn't know then that every wall contains a hidden door, and I had buried the key beneath years of "I'm fine on my own."

1.

September 2017 – North Port, Florida
"He left," Mom said. "He's gone. Imagine he's dead."

I sat on my carpeted floor, naked except for panties, slumped against my unmade bed, my bare legs splayed out in front of me like a dried-up wishbone ready to be pulled. My phone lay face up in the center of the

5

wishbone tethered to a bud in my right ear. The other bud dangled. Only the sound of the rhythmic *click-click-click* from the clock in the kitchen filled my ears, a reminder that life was leaving me behind. The lights were out, the curtains drawn. Muted daylight snuck in from the large, bare windows of the living room and lit the floor in front of me in a dim swath. "What's killing you is you think he stole your dream."

Mom was right. My dream, the dream that for years I had planned and sacrificed for, the dream I was willing to give up everything for, my dream of traveling full-time with Wade in our Airstream … that had gone up in smoke too. My grief wasn't cut-and-dried. More than anything, my grief was for lost dreams.

"You think you can't do it on your own," Mom said.

My breath stopped. My heart stopped. My world stopped. The weight of ten thousand dumbbells crushed my gut.

I exhaled. The kitchen clock *click-click-clicked* through everything there ever was.

I inhaled strong and full against the gut punch of impossibility.

I hadn't considered the truth of a lie I had told myself in secret. The lie was a lie, even if that wasn't crystal clear yet.

The lie: I couldn't live my dream by myself.

The truth: The Airstream was in the driveway. My big, badass truck waited there too. The missing ingredient had been the woman who, until that moment, thought she could never do it alone.

2.

May 19 – Black Rock Mountain, Georgia
Almost seven years after I left everything and hit the road, thanks to that phone conversation with Mom, my family and I were wrapping up a week in a rustic rental cabin. Mom, my brother, my sister-in-law, and my two nieces and I had spent the week hiking in the Smoky Mountains, enjoying ice cream parties, playing board games, and frolicking in the mists of waterfalls.

Mom and I sat on the back deck and sipped tea while gazing out at the mountaintops peeking through morning fog. "It's time for my little birdie to fly solo again," Mom said. "I'm a big girl and can take care of myself now."

I knew she was fine. I also knew that when we parted ways, my heart would feel as though it were being ripped in two.

A year before, Mom had three brain tumors. She lost her driving privileges and needed a caretaker. For a year of my wander, Mom's house in a tiny two-light town in North Florida became my home base. Mom and I traveled quite a bit, and we also lived in her home. I took solo journeys, but stayed close enough to touch base. Whatever Mom needed, I helped with. It was a time of family life, spending weekends with my nieces, going to softball games, and living closely with my mom for the first time since I was thirteen.

We would all leave the cabin in a couple of hours. My whole family was heading home to Florida, and I was going somewhere else.

As soon as my tires hit the blacktop headed north, a guttural moan escaped from my throat. I missed my mom and family and cried so hard I could barely see the road. That drive into North Carolina was more gut-wrenching than any drive since my journey began. The darkest part of night is right before dawn. I kept going.

3.

May 21 – Highway 64, North Carolina

Two days after leaving the cabin, I was meandering through North Carolina.

"Nice rig!" said a guy through his truck window, as he eyed my dust-covered trailer and white Ram 2500 with a kayak strapped to the roof. We sat at a red light in a small town. Red-brick buildings lined the main drag, bright-colored flower baskets hung from light posts, and the scent of yeasty bread carried by a warm breeze wafted through my open windows.

"Thank you," I said with a nod and a grin as I muted the mellow folk music on my radio. This connection with a stranger felt comforting after a couple of days of mountain solitude.

"How long have you had it?"

I checked the light, still red. "It's been my home for seven years."

"Home, wow!" He smiled with his whole face, twisted his torso toward me, and leaned over his center console. "Are you headed to Davidson?"

"No," I said shyly, with a shake of my head. I had no idea what or where Davidson was. I was pretty sure this was still North Carolina.

"Where are you headed, then?"

The longing in his eyes made something twist beneath my ribs "North," I said, as if the word could carry both of us toward whatever we were seeking.

"North," the man in the truck said, softer. His head tilted a smidge. He half-smiled and pressed his lips together. He was lingering at the edge of something. I felt his longing to be free, his fear of losing everything if he did what he really wanted, and his twinkle of wonder about what it might be like to let go of what he thought he was bound by. The way his eyebrows tilted up in the middle suggested that the tickle of his soul had been nudging him toward his own "north." But he didn't think he could. Our eyes locked. Rumbles of idling engines filled the space between.

A southbound car rolled through the intersection. The guy and I exchanged smiles as we let off our brakes and eased north.

4.

My journey began when I drove off and said goodbye to who I was. I sold my dream house, left a career as a firefighter/paramedic that had defined me for fourteen years, and packed my life into a travel trailer barely bigger than my garage. As I pulled out of the driveway, part of me worried I was running from something. I didn't yet know I was running toward myself.

While winding through misty mountains and sun-scorched deserts, and sleeping under more stars than I can count, I've learned that home isn't a location. It's a way of being. I've spent seven years migrating with the seasons, with no set plan regarding where to go or how to get there, and shedding beliefs I didn't know were wrong. This book chronicles one pivotal year of that journey—May 19 to May 19—when everything I thought I knew about love, freedom, and letting go would be turned upside down.

Now, as I write from my tiny aluminum sanctuary parked beside yet another stunning vista, I understand what the day I left was really about: not an ending, but an awakening. This is the story of how wandering revealed that I was already home.

5.

"What's its name?" asked a freckled eight-year-old, gently touching the curved aluminum side of my trailer. His family had stopped setting up camp when they saw me back up my rig between two trees, just feet from a raging river. They'd walked over to investigate.

"Coddi," I said, unhooking the safety chains. "Short for Coddiwomple. She's the best travel buddy."

His mother smiled. "Coddiwomple? I've never heard that word."

"It means 'to travel purposefully toward unknown destinations,'" I explained, watching understanding bloom across her face. "'To be open to anything.'"

"Like wandering, but on purpose?" she asked.

"Exactly." I waved my arm toward the mountains surrounding us. "Yesterday I had no idea I'd be here tonight. Three days ago, I met a couple who mentioned this place in passing. A month ago, I was five states south of here."

The boy's eyes widened. "You don't know where you're going?"

"Usually I know the general direction," I said, while raising the tongue jack. "Sometimes I wake up and feel pulled north. Sometimes a stranger mentions a hidden hot spring or a canyon I've never heard of. Step by step, I follow the nudges, the tickles of curiosity."

"Isn't that scary?" asked the mom, genuine wonder in her voice.

"Not at all, and it's way less scary than wondering 'what if.' Coddiwompling has taught me that life flows when we stop trying to control every detail. All we gotta do is allow."

The boy ran his hand along Coddi's side again. "So she helps you coddiwomple?"

"She does. Though I only call her Coddiwomple when she's misbehaving." I winked, and they laughed.

As they walked back to their RV, I heard the boy asking his mom if they could coddiwomple someday too. I smiled, remembering how that word had first called to me—how it had named something I'd yearned for but never knew existed. Here's how it might look in a dictionary.

coddiwomple
verb | kod-DEE-wuhm-puhl|
1: to travel purposefully toward unknown destinations, physically, mentally, and spiritually
2: to remain open to limitless possibilities
3: to unpredict your journey

coddiwomple
noun | kod-DEE-wuhm-puhl|
a relaxed journey with no specific destination

coddiwompling: the act of one who coddiwomples
coddiwompler: one who coddiwomples

6.

May 25 – Cherokee National Forest, south of Damascus, Virginia
I passed a sign for Backbone Rock Campground in northwest Tennessee. No cell service or power, and a perfect spot to stop. It was a creek-side paradise that included nightly visits from a large black bear that figured out how to remove a backpack full of snacks from my neighbor's ice chest. The bear took a couple of bags of Cheetos and left the backpack in the woods nearby (unscathed).

On my first night, I met Mike, a singer-songwriter, at a campfire. His songs gave me goosebumps. Around 8:00 a.m. the next morning, there was a knock at my door. The sweet aroma of mountain laurel and wet earth flooded in as a morning breeze rustled the rhododendrons.

"Good morning!" Mike said. He wore green waders and a long-sleeved gray T-shirt, and held a fishing pole in one hand and two cleaned rainbow trout in the other. His white camping stubble framed a big, toothy grin.

"Good morning." I stepped down and the sound of water rippling over rocks got louder. "Well, you're up and at 'em."

"I'm headed home and thought you'd like breakfast." He bent his elbow to raise the trout.

"Wow, thank you," I said, as I pressed my palms together below my chin in a praying motion.

He handed me the trout.

"You're welcome." Mike held my eyes while nodding. "I really admire your zest for life and how you live." He took a deep breath. "Safe travels, my friend."

I thanked him again and wished him well on his travels. This reminded me why I trust this journey—these moments of unexpected generosity keep appearing. Fifteen minutes later, I sat with my forearms resting on a dew-soaked picnic table enjoying a two-trout breakfast right out of my cast-iron skillet. The creek babbled and birds chirped.

For three more days, I met new friends and listened to stories about grown kids, parents, lost love, and adventures. Young people shared their dreams, burly guys cried in flickering firelight as they bared their souls, and an older couple hiking the Appalachian Trail shared what they wished they'd done differently early in life, and why you're never too old to do wild things, like walk to Maine from Georgia! I'm still amazed by the human interaction that occurs when we leave "modern" stuff behind; the natural connection at the heart of who we are.

This was my north until I meandered north some more. I left with Mike's CD and the reminder that connection finds us when we least expect it, if we're present enough to receive it.

7.

For most of my life, I avoided get-togethers and parties, though I had close friends. From thirteen through my mid-thirties, I didn't allow myself to feel much or express deep emotions. I didn't know I loved to cuddle until my first boyfriend came along (when I was thirty-two). I had a lot in common with Spock from *Star Trek*.

This journey has taught me to give up control, take one step, and then take another in perfect time. I've left a trail of favorite places everywhere I've been. The idea that I am a separate individual hides the truth. I am one with everything and everyone. This is true for all of us. I never know when one simple gesture might entangle me with a soul family, the love of my life, or appear to shift the trajectory of the universe. Without judgment, expectation, or insecurity, there is only love. This wandering life has shown me how much I've sacrificed by protecting myself from loss.

8.

Carp, Ontario, was my one planned destination for the summer. Thanks to an engineering internship in 2002, I knew two special people who lived there, Samir and Tania. The three of us and their two beautiful girls have been on quite a journey together. Because of travel restrictions, we hadn't seen each other for over four years. We set a date for my arrival: June 17.

I meandered through Virginia, Maryland, Pennsylvania, and the Finger Lakes area of New York, boondocking almost the entire way. I crossed the border at the Thousand Islands Bridge on June 13.

9.

Boondocking is camping with no amenities, services, or designated campsites. It strips away everything unnecessary. No reservations, checkout times, or campsite boundaries means complete freedom. Whether parked by a stream in Montana or on Bureau of Land Management land in Nevada, I wake to birdsongs instead of generators. This solitude has taught me the difference between being alone and being lonely. In the wilderness, I'm never isolated—I'm in a deeper conversation with life itself. Plus, the occasional people I meet out in the wilds have wholesome hearts and a love for nature.

I usually boondock on public lands. In the US, that's national forests,

Bureau of Land Management areas, state forests, and other government-managed lands. In Canada, that's Crown land and provincial forests and preserves.

Sometimes I find my sleeping spots by word of mouth, when locals let me in on their secrets. More often, I find spots via iOverlander, FreeCampsites.net, or Campendium.com. When I'm driving through urban areas and need a place for the night, I prefer churches. If possible, I ask permission. Parks and public areas work too. In a pinch, I'll stay in a store parking lot after asking the manager. If I must stay in a campground, primitive campgrounds are more my style. They have designated campsites and usually a community outhouse, but no power or water.

I turned thirty-nine a week after I set off on my full-time RVing journey. Mom surprised me with a unique birthday gift: a three-year subscription to an RV community called Boondockers Welcome. Regular folks let you park your RV on their private property for one to five nights. Mom's gift was sweet, but I figured I'd never use it. Back then, rolling up and parking at the homes of strangers wasn't my idea of fun. It took me a year and a half to book my first Boondockers Welcome stay. I backed into Janet and Greg's driveway in Bend, Oregon, and stayed for two nights. Janet and Greg became family for life. They were the first of many. This is the most meaningful birthday gift I've ever received.

10.

June 13 – Perth, Ontario, Terry and Mary's place
"You get an intimate peek into homes all over the world, don't you?" Terry said. We were on their back deck under peach-tinged clouds.

I'd met them an hour ago, when I backed my rig up their driveway and parked beside their barn. I'd requested to stay with them through Boondockers Welcome a few days earlier. A plate of cheese and crackers sat on the wrought-iron table between us.

"I do," I said.

Terry and Mary's sweet friend Catherine sat next to me. She had dementia, and her porcelain face had a perpetual smile. A gold earring sat cockeyed on the windowsill behind her. We each had a miniature goblet in front of us, half-filled with garnet wine.

I reached for my goblet and took a sip.

As I swallowed, a silky blossom slid down my throat, and the warmth spread out from my chest. My arms and legs tingled. My face smiled big and warm, like Catherine's. The truth in Terry's words had us all smiling at once. The wonder in their eyes reflected my own.

11.

The Essence of Coddiwompling

The person who pauses and reaches uncomfortably for fresh words and ideas is playing at the edge of the known, toward a larger, unspoken understanding that lies beyond our memories and what we've been taught to be true. Something special happens here: We begin to notice barriers we didn't realize we had; we are invited to look past what we believe; we become explorers of everything. Life opens effortlessly and flows beautifully. We come alive.

12.

June 17 – Carp, Ontario

I rolled up to Samir and Tania's house and we fell back into each other's lives.

I was there the night Tania went into labor with their oldest daughter, Zarah, who is eighteen now. My heart ached knowing that I'd missed out on Zarah's important teenage years. Now she has her own life. During my visit, I had a great time with her younger sister, Mattea. We kayaked, swam, and played together. It felt so good to be "home."

On my second morning there, Tania and I were chatting in the kitchen when Samir's dad, Uncle, gently embraced me. He took a half-step back, one hand on my shoulder, and whispered "Good morning" with a nod and a smile. When he ambled back to the couch, Tania and I looked at each other, shrugged, and lifted our eyebrows, as if to say, *What was that about?*

The morning hug tradition had begun.

Each morning I'd leave Coddi, walk around a stand of trees up to the back door, slide it open, and stick my head in.

"Good morning," I'd say.

Almost always, there was a "Good morning, Krissy," from Samir, Tania, or Samir's mom, Popo. I'd step inside.

With a gentle grin, Uncle walked toward me in his loose blue-and-white-striped pajama pants and long-sleeved T-shirt, his white hair and mustache a stark contrast to his walnut skin. He was just over six feet tall and thin, so we fit together like two peas in a pod. Uncle was a kind, soft-spoken man, and for a few years he'd been in the grips of dementia. The more his mind let go, the more affectionate he became. Sometimes those hugs would bring tears to my eyes.

13.

Outside my window, a field of daisies bobs in a breeze. Halos of white ring their gold faces. Each flower points in a slightly different direction, all toward the rising sun.

I look for my mom like that. Always have, always will. Whenever we lose each other, Mom calls me with a fluty melodic whistle. She's done this since I was a kid. Its subtleness cuts through a crowd. I heard it a few months ago as I walked through Costco.

14.

Living in twenty-eight feet requires brutal honesty about what matters. My composting toilet, Berkey water filter, and solar panels aren't just practical choices—they're declarations of independence. When I sold almost everything to live in Coddi, I thought I was sacrificing. Instead, I found freedom. With 900 watts of solar panels and lithium batteries, I can live off-grid indefinitely. This is not stylish minimalism to look all cutesy. It's carrying simply what I need. It's liberation.

15.

As I sat with the daisies in Samir's backyard, I remembered the last time Mom and I were in Costco. Mom's fluty whistle grabbed my ear. I stopped dead in my tracks, mid-aisle. The low mumble of voices, beeping machines, and clanking carts sunk to the floor. I heard her whistle again. My neck stretched to the right, my head high like a daisy reaching for the sun. Bright florescent lights beat down on dazed shoppers. I was tuned in to find my one.

There she was, gray hair curled over a maroon visor, gaze searching the crowd. I whistled back with my snippy birdcall. Her eyes darted to mine. In the midst of hundreds of shoppers, we saw only each other. Mom's whole face smiled, and she walked my way. For over forty years, I've turned into a daisy the moment I hear Mom's wispy call.

It's been a month since I sat with Mom at the rental cabin in Georgia. Tears are flowing. With her health issues, each time I leave, I wonder if I'll ever see her again.

16.

June 20 – Carp, Ontario
I stood in Coddi drenched in sweat, palms on my wooden tabletop, hunched over a map of Canada. My index finger traced the Atlantic coast, leaving a slight smudge as I moved north past Nova Scotia, Newfoundland, and then to a pointed tip shaped like a Santa hat: Labrador. The word felt unfamiliar on my tongue when I whispered it aloud. I hadn't even known it was part of Canada.

In the center of that tip, near the northeastern edge of the continent, my finger stopped at Torngat Mountains National Park. I pulled up images on my phone. Snow-capped peaks rose from deep fjords, their reflections perfect in still, glacier-fed waters. Shadows of clouds moved across valleys untouched by roads or electrical lines. Something in my chest tightened, like a fishing line suddenly pulled taut.

Through my open window came the scent of Samir's grilling spices, but my mind was already filled with the imagined smell of Arctic air: clean, sharp, ancient. I closed my eyes and could almost feel the chill against my face, and taste the crispness of northern waters.

More than wanted, I needed to go. Not someday, not eventually. This season. This summer. My finger trembled slightly as I traced the route again, estimating distances, wondering what it would take to get there. The northern tip of Labrador called to me like a lighthouse beacon, promising something I couldn't yet name but somehow recognized deep in my bones.

I called Torngat Mountains National Park.

"Our shortest excursion is three days and two nights, all-inclusive, with travel to and from Goose Bay, Labrador," said the national park representative. "You'll stay in yurts at the base camp and you can take day hikes with one of our guides."

I was scribbling down notes and getting excited!

"Great, what's the cost for a three-day tour?"

"Six thousand dollars."

If I were a cartoon character, my eyes would have bulged out of my head.

"It's just me. One person."

"Yes, it's $6,000 per person."

Holy shamolee. That's not gonna happen. I wondered if the exorbitant fee was a moneymaking venture or a way to keep people away. For Inuit, the Torngat Mountains are a special place, spiritually and culturally. *Torngat* means "place of spirits."

After a few days of research, I found two Inuit government organizations in Nain, the northernmost community in Labrador. Someone there had to know a local guide who took people to the Torngats for a reasonable fee. They gave me Margaret Fox's number.

I called Margaret. She and her husband organized charters to the historic settlement of Hebron, just south of the Torngat Base Camp. Their boat, meant for large groups, was slow. Fuel for the trip was thousands of dollars. They had no availability for a single person to join another group.

"Do you know anyone else who would take me north?" I asked, sitting at my desk, pen in hand.

"There is a man named William who has a speedboat."

I stood up and did a fist pump, Tiger Woods-style. "Would you mind sharing his phone number?"

"I don't know his phone number."

"If I called you back in two days, would you be able to ask around and get his number in the meantime?" My shirt was wet under my pits, and I was surprised by how much the adventure in Labrador meant to me.

"Well," she said. "That may be possible."

"OK, great. I'll call you in two days. My name is Kristy. Thank you so much."

17.

After thorough research, I determined that an Airstream was the RV I wanted for my life on the road. There were two main reasons. Airstreams are like turtles—they'll outlive you if you take care of them. Most other RVs have a lifespan of about fifteen years. And Airstreams are fully customizable. During manufacture, everything inside an Airstream comes through the front door, so they can be stripped down to the aluminum shell and plywood floors, and rebuilt. I wanted a custom home that would last.

18.

June 26 – Carp, Ontario

The two-day wait to call Margaret did not pass fast enough.

"Hi Margaret, this is Kristy. I was wondering if you found William's information." I was sitting in Coddi and hoping beyond hope this would work.

"Yes, I have William's phone number and email. He's happy to speak with you."

I jumped up and did another fist pump.

I called William.

"I can take you to Hebron," he said. "An Inuit settlement. It's close to Torngat Base Camp, and better. It's private and peaceful. Inuit history, polar bears, caribou, icebergs."

Perfect! But the fuel alone to get to Hebron was still $750. It was another $600 per day for William and his boat. I was in no place to pay over $2,500 for a three-day adventure.

"Thank you, that sounds wonderful," I said, as I squinched my eyes and hoped to come up with a workaround. "Since it's just me, do you have any other tours I could join, so I could share the cost?"

"A man might take a trip around that same time. I will …" Wind blew on William's end, muffling his voice. "Call me next week."

19.

People often ask how I afford to travel full-time, and some wonder if I keep a budget. The key to my travel finances is a simple equation: income versus expenses. In 2015, I started my coaching and mentoring practice and within three years, it became sustainable. As far as outgoing funds, what it costs to live like I do is rather low.

I spend less money now than ever before in my adult life. I don't keep a budget, but I keep receipts for tax purposes. My biggest expense is diesel fuel, which is usually $3,000 to $7,000 per year. Living off-grid allows me to enjoy nature in locations that are free or inexpensive. Plus, I have no utility bills. I don't like shopping, rarely buy anything other than consumables, and keep consumables to a minimum. Other expenses include vehicle insurance, health insurance, propane, and repairs. A big difference maker: buying high-quality items that last.

Now, my total cost of living for a year is $20,000 to $25,000.

Back in "normal life," it was over $50,000 a year.

20.

June 27 – Carp, Ontario
I was beat and hadn't slept well in days. A heat wave was rolling through, and thick smoke from wildfires was choking me out. I was parked too far

from Samir's house to plug in to power. My back and thighs were sticky with sweat and I was frustrated that Coddi kept breaking. I couldn't fix all these problems on my own. I beat myself up and procrastinated. I felt exhausted from wasting my energy on frivolous things.

The biggest issue was that the solar charging system wasn't fully charging the batteries. After hours of Samir's help and days of phone calls with a solar expert, I gave up on fixing it and ordered parts to install a DC to DC charging system. It would use the truck's alternator to charge Coddi's batteries while driving or idling. I needed to install the system.

Have I already asked too much of Samir? I didn't want to be a burden. I wished I knew how my friends felt about my being there. *Am I overstaying my welcome?* I should have been with them, soaking up summer, having the time of my life. Instead, it felt as if life was beating me like a rented donkey.

A few hours later, Samir and I stood on his back patio watering his tomato and pepper plants.

"In the conservative part of Pakistan where Dad lives, men don't typically touch or hug women who aren't their wives," Samir said. He kept his eyes on the plants. They were wiggling in a warm wind. "Dad shouldn't hug you. It's a bit weird to see every morning."

This was news to me. Though as I thought about it, I realized I'd known Uncle for twenty years and we'd never shared a hug until last week.

"Yikes, should I stop hugging him?" My face flushed. I should have known better.

"No, no. Tania, Mom, and I think it's cute." Samir chuckled and then turned to me with a squinty look of inner mischief. "Either he's forgotten seventy years of Pakistani customs, or he's being sneaky and knows he can get away with it now."

I belly-laughed at the thought of Uncle pulling a fast one to steal hugs.

"Well, good for him," I said. "I enjoy the hugs too."

After that conversation, I worked on Coddi's solar system with Samir's patient help. I learned as much about accepting support as I did about electrical circuits.

21.

Uncle's unexpected tenderness shook something loose in me. For decades, I'd practiced a kind of emotional efficiency—feeling enough to function but rarely diving into the messy depths of human connection. I'd become so practiced at independence that I sometimes confused it with isolation. But here, with this kind man whose mind was rarely able to have coherent conversations, Life was revealing what happens when I let my guard down. When I allow myself to be touched, literally and figuratively, by someone else's generosity. Each morning, that simple embrace was showing me something my years of wandering hadn't: that strength isn't about standing alone, but about being brave enough to lean in.

22.

"God spoke today in flowers,
and I, who was waiting on words,
almost missed the conversation."[1]

– Ingrid Goff-Maidoff

23.

For most of my life, I lived by the pros-and-cons ticker tape that rolled through my brain like news headlines at the bottom of a TV screen. When I was twenty-three, God spoke to me. It was 2002 and I was a few months from graduating with a bachelor's degree in engineering, which wasn't my thing, but I didn't know what was. On a Wednesday afternoon, I met a firefighter in a laundromat. We talked while our clothes tumbled. I fell in love.

24.

According to the Environmental Protection Agency, the average American household uses more than 300 gallons of water per day.[2] Coddi's water tank holds 60 gallons and lasts about three weeks. That's less than 3 gallons of water per day for drinking, washing, bathing, everything. One big reason I can live off of 3 gallons per day is that my composting toilet uses zero gallons of water. It doesn't smell, and it isn't gross. I love my toilet. Is that proper to say? Can one love a toilet?

25.

It wasn't the guy in the laundromat that fascinated me. I fell head over heels in love with his job. In 2002 and 2003, over and over, Life told me in no uncertain terms to be a firefighter: I was laid off from my first engineering job in dramatic fashion, walked out carrying a box of my stuff, and found fire trucks in the parking lot; I had several serendipitous connections with firefighters; I was surprised to find out a close friend, a mechanical engineering student who graduated a semester before I did, was in fire academy and loving it; and more. I didn't know this was God speaking and didn't listen. By January 2003, I was a graduate assistant going for a master's degree. Eventually, I understood I was in conversation with God, but I thought I knew better.

26.

To me, the words "Life" and "God" are synonymous.

27.

July 1 – Carp, Ontario

I prepped Coddi and was ready to roll east. Everyone except Uncle and Popo had plans for Canada Day, so I said my goodbyes that morning.

Popo wouldn't let me go without lunch. She warmed up a plate of biryani and kebabs and sat beside me at the dinner table.

"They will miss you," Popo said, in a quiet monotone voice. She stared straight ahead. Tears welled up in my heart and rose to my eyes as I chewed and looked down at my plate. Popo was a strong woman. I didn't want to cry in front of her.

I swallowed my food and grief; grief over missing this beautiful family;

over being too caught up in repairs to spend enough time with them; and over asking Samir for too much help.

"I'll miss them too," I said. With those words, my floodgates broke.

For the second time in six weeks, I found myself driving away from a family I loved. The road blurred through my tears as Popo's words echoed: "They will miss you." This was new territory, actually feeling the ache of separation.

28.

When I was a child, my dad had trouble with depression and took his frustration out on the family. A few years after my parents divorced, Mom sent me to live at Dad's place. I did not want to be with Dad, and I loved Mom more than anyone. At thirteen, despite having a roof over my head, I felt like an orphan. Alone and responsible for myself. I made myself a promise: never love anyone so much it would hurt if they left. I'd kept that promise for decades, building walls so thick I couldn't feel what lay behind them. The weight I'd been carrying wasn't grief—it was the absence of it, the numbness where love should have been.

Diane Sawyer once said, "I've always found a cure for the blues is wandering into something unknown, and resting there, before coming back to whatever weight you were carrying."

I was wandering, all right. But instead of escaping the weight, I was finally learning to carry it.

29.

I Plead My Case
I am not lonely when I am alone.
Judgment seeps in like a tide at night,
laps up on the rocky shore of what's proper.
Civilized rules muddy things up,
the haves and have-nots of this made-up place.
A lion is regarded as regal, but not the sea turtle.
She's a loner who swims halfway 'round the world and back

and never knows her young.

The masses don't get me,

beliefs and convention linger between words not spoken.

"That lady is traveling alone?" they say in questions and glances

on weekend trips with more junk in their trunk than an army needs.

I watched a lady today.

She sat at a picnic table while her husband set up camp.

She'd be eaten alive in the open sea.

The civilized world is a vise on my soul.

I am alone. I am not lonely.

I fend for myself and surf the waves.

Still, when people ask and imply,

I plead my case.

To myself.

30.

July 2 – Québec City, Quebec

"Go to Québec City," they said. "You'll love it."

Flanked by the St. Lawrence River, Old Québec City is a labyrinth of steep stairs and narrow cobblestone streets lined with colorful trinket shops, expensive eateries, and galleries.

Too many Gucci bag–carrying tourists and colognes, and I got a parking ticket because I couldn't read French. The win: I found a used Garmin GPS on Facebook marketplace, exactly what I'd need to find my way in no-man's-land.

31.

Going to bed dirty is a no-go. Since I live mostly in the bush and do laundry about once a month, clean sheets are at a premium. I enjoy my smooth, clean skin on crisp cotton. I go a day or two max between real showers, and at the very least I'll have a kitchen-sink bird bath.

Here's how I get by on just three gallons of water a day: I conserve water as if it were gold. In the evening I flip on the hot water heater, wash my full day's worth of dishes with soap and a moist sponge, and stack the soapy dishes in a pyramid in the sink. Then I rinse with a dribble of water, so the runoff also rinses all the dishes below. Hot water appears during the rinsing.

Then it's navy-shower time: A quick spritz. Suds up. Rinse off. Done.

Dishes and a shower use about a gallon of water. I might be stingy with water, but I don't skimp on cleanliness.

32.

Conversation is a wander. I dance with whoever I chat with and never know what will come next. I trust my lips will move and words will fall out. When I listen to a prepared speech, it's obvious there is no soul in it. The words feel un-alive and I lose interest quick.

33.

July 4 – Les Escoumins, Quebec

I continued northeast along the coast of the St. Lawrence River and stayed at a beautiful boondocking spot by a river with rapids. For a few days, I enjoyed biking, hiking, kayaking, working, dips in the river, and having conversations with other campers.

A man arrived one afternoon. We sat at a weather-worn picnic table between Coddi and his car. He was on a weeklong sabbatical from his troubled marriage. As he spoke about his longing for solitude and self-discovery, his voice quivered with a mix of desire and uncertainty. He hoped to find the space in his heart to fall in love with his wife again. We talked about love and loss, being alone and not feeling lonely, and who we are without all the made-up stuff we think is true about ourselves and others. From my desk window, I saw him at his campsite. He seemed more relaxed as he went about his evening; he smiled more. In the morning, as we visited for a short goodbye, his smile reached his eyes.

I meandered on, and turned north on Route 389 in Baie-Comeau, Quebec.

34.

Life is the same as conversation. The aliveness is sucked dry if I choreograph every step in permanent ink, and assume I am living.

35.

The more I remember *I am love*, the easier it is to love everything and everyone. Including myself.

36.

> "people are strange: they are constantly angered by
> trivial things,
> but on a major matter
> like
> totally wasting their lives,
> they hardly seem to
> notice ..."[3]
>
> – Charles Bukowski

Yes, Chuck! We work for the man, "someday" the best years of our life away, and make excuses for being stuck in front of a screen doing other people's busy work for peanuts. The world is full of trained monkeys. Humans are the strangest of all primates. Willpower is our most overused muscle. Even monkeys in captivity climb trees and play with friends.

If I could get on a megaphone the whole world could hear, I'd scream, "For Pete's sake! Live, people. Live! Do what bows your back with sheer delight. Forget the money or power. Let go of your made-up fear and projected shame. Forget what your mom, dad, and teachers said. Forget it all! Live in the joy of being alive."

37.

Life is living me, always, even when it seems the other way around.

38.

Quebec Route 389
QC-389 is a 350-mile road. It runs north from Baie-Comeau, Quebec, then east to the Labrador border. It's the only way to Labrador that doesn't involve a plane or boat. When I drove QC-389, over 150 miles of it was dirt or gravel, and many paved sections were so full of ice heaves and potholes that the gravel portions felt like heaven. Now and then a big rig semitruck flew by, throwing rocks and pea gravel. There were hardly any other vehicles. Besides a tiny wood building with a single gas pump in Relais Gabriel (200 miles north of Baie-Comeau), it's a winding, dusty road through a labyrinth of green hills and shimmery lakes, a couple of huge dams, and a whole lot of nobody.

39.

July 8 – Daniel-Johnson Dam
On my first night on QC-389, I slept in a dirt pull-off by the world's largest arched buttress dam. I left at sunrise. After about thirty miles of gravel, I felt the urge to stop and check Coddi, but I kept driving.

40.

Follow the tickles of your soul. They take the whole universe into consideration.

41.

Summer 2003
"You're young, no kids, no bills. This could be the best chance you ever take," said Uncle Troy, who spoke on God's behalf. We sat alone in the kitchen at Fire Station 1 in Tallahassee, Florida. I wasn't close to Uncle Troy, but he was the only firefighter I knew. I'd confessed that my heart wanted to fight fires, even though logically, it made no sense. "You can go back and finish your engineering degree." Whiffs of brewing coffee and leftover chili mingled with the stale scent of decades-old paint and plaster. "There won't be a better time than now."

"OK, OK," I said. "I'll do it."

Life kept nudging me until I couldn't not listen.

I also couldn't tell anyone that Uncle Troy's sage wisdom was the nudge that sent me tumbling over the edge.

On a Monday morning, midsemester, I walked into the mechanical engineering office at Florida Atlantic University and asked for the dean. My hand trembled as I reached for the dean's office door. The safe path beckoned me to turn back.

Thirty minutes later, I pushed open a large glass door and walked into fresh air. I had given up my scholarship, a grad-assistant position, and a paycheck of $300 a week (which was enough for rent and food). I skated the thin line between safety and risk. I was twenty-four years old without a fallback or income. For the first time, I felt as if I was living my own life. Emergency medical technician training started on Thursday. Fire academy began a couple of months after that. Like a schoolgirl, I skipped and bounced down the sidewalk. *I will be a firefighter!* I let out a yip and a "Yes!"

Everyone thought I was nuts for giving up my graduate-assistant position. Well, everyone but God, me, and Uncle Troy.

My time at the fire academy and at emergency medical technician school was the most fun I ever had in pursuit of an education. I lived on a shoestring and went into debt for the first time in my life, but never felt as though I missed a thing. I graduated top of my class, and for the first time I was officially in love with my chosen path. I had found my way.

While I applied for firefighting jobs, I took an engineering position and moonlighted as a volunteer firefighter in the evenings. What excited me about firefighting was purpose. As an engineer, I worked on fighter-jet engines: killing machines. As a firefighter, I helped people on their worst days. Also, the physicality appealed to me, a lifelong athlete and adrenaline junkie. From day one, "work" felt like going to summer camp and doing cool things with my friends.

42.

"We don't get to choose what or whom we love, I want to say. We just don't get to choose."[4] – Maggie Nelson, *Bluets* #13

43.

Life speaks in tickles.

44.

July 8 – QC-389, north of Daniel-Johnson Dam
While I drove the endless gravel road, a deep ache kept gnawing a bit below my sternum: "Check Coddi."

I stopped at the crest of a hill, where eighteen-wheelers could see my rig from either direction. I'd driven forty-four miles north of my sleeping spot. The rumble of my Cummins diesel drowned out everything except the crunch of gravel under my feet. Ahead was an ocean of emerald hills, a big swath of blue a few miles north, and the beige track of QC-389, which disappeared over the next hill.

I opened Coddi's door and craned my neck inside. It was a disaster. Shoulders slumped, I turned the truck off and climbed inside Coddi. My food pantry door had popped open and drawers had slid out. Stuff was strewn everywhere, as if someone had joggled Coddi like a cocktail shaker. I found screws on the floor and scoured walls to find empty holes. On the outside, everything was OK except half my center awning support arm was gone, and it had left gnarly scratches on Coddi's aluminum as a parting gift. The last time I saw that arm attached was back at the dam.

Shhhhit!

I grabbed a crescent wrench, ratchet, and step stool and removed the top half of the awning arm that dangled from Coddi's side. As I worked, the ratchet's rhythmic *click-click-clicking* interrupted the gentle wind that licked the leaves in the trees.

Holding the three-foot-long metal tube, I walked to Coddi's rear bumper and looked down the gravel road in the direction I'd come. The rest of the arm was back there somewhere. There was no ordering of new parts in Labrador, and I couldn't imagine going the rest of the summer without shade.

A quick fuel calculation showed I could go back to look for the arm, but only if I didn't tow Coddi. This road felt like the Wild West: untamed land, isolation, and gambles. The thought of leaving Coddi alone on the road made my stomach churn. Anyone could haul her off into oblivion. A couple of miles north, I found an old rock pit, where Coddi wouldn't be visible from QC-389. I chocked her wheels, unhooked the hitch, stood with my hand on her dusty aluminum, said goodbye, and hoped she'd be there when I returned and that I'd find her needle in the gravel-road-haystack.

45.

When I leave something behind, I gain something too.

46.

The Wanderer – "He who has attained intellectual emancipation to any extent cannot, for a long time, regard himself otherwise than as a wanderer on the face of the earth—and not even as a traveler toward a final goal, for there is no such thing."[5] – Friedrich Nietzsche

Intellectual emancipation is becoming free of control or suppression, developing the ability to think independently, and letting go of beliefs. I can confirm, with firsthand experience, Friedrich is right.

47.

July 8 – QC-389
I was flying south at 40 to 50 mph on the gravel road with my eyes peeled, scanning, looking, hoping to find Coddi's awning arm. My truck shuddered over washboard ripples, and the dash rattled as if it might come unhinged. In the curves, I drifted as though I were on ice until the tires caught hold of the gravel again. A dragon's tail of dust snaked down the road behind me.

There!! About fifteen miles back, a slender silver bar on the left side of the road caught my eye. Gravel crunched and tires slid. I threw it in reverse and backed and hoped and backed. I opened my window in a cloud of dust. There it was, just down the bank, the rest of the awning arm. A bit scuffed, but it'd do! Woohoo!

48.

I've been "different" my whole life. Even before I yanked myself out of the grips of societal rules and started coddiwompling, my "normal" life wasn't all that normal. Although, I did buy a big house at twenty-six because that's what responsible adults do.

If I had the right to pen a new definition of normal, it would be this:

Normal (adjective) : to seal yourself inside acceptable boundaries; to be a good little cog in the grand machine of the rich and powerful; to erect barriers between your heart and what might hurt it; (noun) : one who falls in line and knows their place; and trades vulnerability for security, just like the rest.

Before I sold almost everything and hit the road, my backyard was on a wild freshwater canal with untamed forest on all sides. I'd lie in my hammock imagining I was in the Amazon or Outback, dreaming of freedom while remaining safely in my manicured life. Bobcats, sand-hill cranes, alligators, snakes, and even walking catfish (no joke, they breathe air and waddled across my driveway) meandered through my little oasis. The mortgage, the expectations, the unwritten rules: all invisible bars I'd willingly installed. When I finally sold that house, I wasn't just selling property. I was dismantling a wall I'd built to protect myself from the wilderness of fully living.

49.

2005 – North Port, Florida
I was the first female on my shift at North Port Fire Rescue and boy was that fun. I felt like everyone's kid sister, was a natural prankster (the

guys loved that), and tough as nails. During my first year, the crew was heckling me at dinner. One fact about firefighters: the more they pick on you, the more they like you. I was taking their jeering like a champ when my lieutenant's deep voice, with a slight Southern twang, thundered through the room. "You can't hurt her feelings," he said, with a hint of a smile. "She doesn't have any feelings." I felt the honor beam from his eyes, the pride in his voice, and the wonder in everyone's silence before they erupted in laughter. Laughter is the salve of the fire service. I too was proud I had no feelings. I'd been perfecting that trait for fourteen years, and it's one of the reasons I was great at my job.

A few years later, I became a lieutenant.

As a station officer, I made decisions on scenes and in the firehouse, trained my crew, took responsibility for their actions, ensured mental and physical preparedness, and listened during tough times. I also loved getting my hands dirty no matter the situation.

Being the first female station officer had repercussions. Good ol' boys don't like being told what to do by girls. My first battalion chief spread false rumors about me to damage my reputation. Thankfully my crew and I were close. They told me about it and defended me, but the damage was done.

Firefighting was my dream job, but after my promotion, things went to hell in a handbasket. I tried my best to become a leader my crews loved and respected.

Several years later, I was drawn to life and executive coaching. In 2015 I went back to college for coaching, got certified, and hung my shingle. This process changed how I lived, led, and experienced life's ups and downs. I fell in love with guiding people through their own awakenings.

I saw the writing on the wall: In coaching, I helped people find their peace, happiness, and health, and let go of beliefs that kept them stuck. At the firehouse, more often than not, I scraped people's drunk asses off the interstate and put out fires, metaphorically and literally.

One night after treating two drunk drivers and their victims, a question slapped me: *Would I rather point people toward fertile ground for life-altering realizations, or keep delivering Band-Aids and quick fixes?*

The "bandages" I applied to broken bodies were physical versions of my own emotional walls. Could I help people tear down those walls instead? The answer grew clearer each day.

50.

July 8 – Lac Manicouagan, Quebec

Mountains, the color of billiard-table felt, towered over a lush forest, which ended at a sandy cliff, where I parked. The cliff dropped to a tan cobblestone beach. Coddi's front door opened to an enormous expanse of water dotted with islands and mountains. I wanted to kayak to a large island dead ahead and asked a guy camping nearby to help me carry my kayak down the cliff to the lake. "That water is like the sea," he said. We stood beside my truck, looking out. The sun was straight overhead in a cloudless sky.

"What do you mean?"

"I mean it's dangerous. That island?" He pointed. "Further than it looks. Much further. In no time, this lake goes from flat to waves that will flip a kayak."

We carried my kayak to the shore, but he insisted I stay in the bay.

Lac Manicouagan is an impact crater lake. 214 million years ago, a meteorite three miles in diameter slammed into the center of present-day Quebec. It created a crater sixty-two miles across and sent earthquakes across most of the continent. Lac Manicouagan is often called the eye of Quebec. The lake's unique eye-shape on maps and satellite photos sucked me right in. I had to see it with my own eyes, paddle on it, and bathe in its water.

The guy's warning made me think twice. Instead of a paddle, I took a swim. Through goggles I saw driftwood, a rocky bottom, and trout large enough for a meal, which I tried to catch with my bare hands. It got so deep, so fast, that the temperature dropped to frigid and the darkness gave me the willies. My mind raced with thoughts of what might be down there. I'm not usually frightened by what-ifs, but that lake commanded a respect I could feel in my bones. Its jet-black nothingness kept me close to shore. After the swim, I needed to warm up. I hopped in my kayak and paddled around the bay for about an hour, hauled the kayak back onto shore, and walked up the cliff toward Coddi.

"Mademoiselle!" a man yelled. "Mademoiselle! Mademoiselle!"

I stopped, my back to the lake. His voice echoed off cliffs as he babbled on in French. I thought mademoiselle was someone's name, but no one else was in earshot. I didn't know a lick of French.

"Mademoiselle!"

51.

The more I understand that life will play out as it will and I am not in control, the more I let go and wander in every part of life.

52.

There was a boat drifting toward shore. A man with bushy white hair stood on the bow. He stretched his arm in my direction and held a fish by the gills. It gasped as he rambled on.

"Sorry, I don't know French," I yelled.

"Do you want a fish?" a woman shouted in a thick French accent. She stood behind the wheel.

"Oh … yes," I said, as I stepped down toward the lake.

53.

If I am persnickety in one area, it's food. Most grocery stores have a poisoned section and a nonpoisoned section. The poisoned section is huge, the whole middle of the store, except for a few organics here and there. Most nonpoisoned food is on the perimeter walls. Even then, chemicals are still sprayed on most of that. I eat clean and organic. Processed foods are not my cup of tea. I enjoy cooking and don't eat out. My fridge and freezer are full of fresh fruits and veggies and wild or grass-fed meats. My pantry is two small baskets under my bed: oil, nut butters, wild rice, dried coconut milk, vinegar, and a few condiments.

54.

July 8 – Lac Manicouagan, Quebec

I waded to their boat. The man, Fabien, continued speaking in French. Daniele tried to translate and apologized for her English while I apologized for not knowing French. Fabien cleaned the trout on the side of his boat. Streaks of dark-red blood dripped down the shiny, jet-black hull. He tossed the innards, which landed with a cascade of *plops* a few paces to my left. He grabbed a hose, rinsed the fillets, and handed them to me. He gestured for me to move back and sprayed the blood off his boat.

"Goooood! Goood!" Fabien said, with a kind smile and a thumbs-up. The sun was bright and low in a clear-blue sky. An evening chill was settling in. Except for the ripples rolling out from their boat, the lake was a mirror.

"Thank you," I said.

I walked to shore and hiked back up.

A family was setting up camp near Coddi. The husband introduced himself as I strolled by.

"We're gonna have a fire, cook, and watch the sunset," he said. "You're welcome to join us."

This is the story of my life. While seeking nothing, I wander into the unknown. Food is given. Just as I'm about to gather sticks to cook my fish, I'm offered a place at a fire.

Some might call this lucky. I call it Life.

55.

I laid the trout in a cast-iron skillet, piled fresh dill, garlic, and lemon zest on top, and cooked it over an open flame while chatting with Darren, Heather, and their son. As the sun set over the mountains, the lake turned every color of the sky—pale blue to burnt orange to red to violet. Stars bloomed, fire crackled, and the surface of the lake went dark as the mountains faded into the sky.

This pattern kept repeating: the more I opened myself to strangers, dropping my guard about who was "safe" to trust, the more abundance flowed in. No amount of self-sufficiency could have created this connection. That one night felt as if it could have been the pinnacle of my entire summer. I had no idea about the life-changing, soul-lifting, death-teetering, love-struck kind of year I was in for.

56.

I've had two boyfriends, and both bloomed from friendships and bicycling. Jack was first. We met in 2009 on the Brotherhood Ride, a 600-mile charity bike ride that turned into a yearly event. We were close friends for two years before becoming a couple. He was twenty years older, though he looked much younger and was a kid at heart. We were an excellent match. He was a firefighter in Naples, Florida, and a sweet man who is one of the best people I've ever known. We are still close friends.

Next was Wade. We met during a twelve-hour ultra-distance cycling race. A friend introduced us midrace while we were cruising at 25 mph. He became my cycling coach. A year later, we were a couple. Wade lived in Los Angeles. We'd meet every few months—sometimes in exotic places, other times in California. We'd explore the West Coast and race bicycles in covert nighttime crit races in the Los Angeles area. We'd zoom through city streets cloaked in darkness, right alongside pro cyclists. Talk about an adrenaline rush! Wade was an engineer and a kind man who'd been abandoned as a child. He held on to a lot of baggage. After a couple of years long-distance, he moved to Florida, and we lived in my house for two years. Other than work, we did *everything* together.

57.

Wanting security and feeling insecure are the same thing. If I want to protect myself from what might happen, I am trying to be separate from

Life. It's this idea of separateness that makes me feel insecure. Everything that seems like an obstacle is divine. Nothing is in my path to trip me up. When I surrender to what is, true wellbeing takes center stage.

58.

March 2014 – North Port, Florida

"You have an autoimmune disorder attacking your nerves," my doctor said. We were in an exam room. She sat on a rolling stool, hands folded in her lap. "Your nerve function is that of an eighty-five-year-old. You are thirty-five, right?"

I nodded. White paper crinkled under me as I crossed my legs.

She looked down at the floor and then back up at me.

"You'll need to get blood tests every three months because this may attack your internal organs, and those may fail too."

I was sick from a chemical exposure. The nerve issue was one of many side effects. I got exposed to the chemicals while fighting forest fires, where people illegally dumped tires, appliances, paints, and chemicals. My job was killing me. This was the ultimate proof that all the things I thought provided security—a stable career, health insurance, retirement plans— were no guarantee of safety. Sometimes what we cling to for protection becomes the very thing that harms us.

Less than a year later, I had an accident at work and destroyed my right knee. I had knee (ACL) reconstruction. Eighty percent of my meniscus was gone. My doctor sentenced me to at least nine months of desk duty. That was the last straw. Time for an exit strategy.

59.

July 9, 2:00 a.m. – Lac Manicouagan, Quebec

Stars are pinpricks in a jet-black stillness, broken solely by the drifting shimmer of meteors. The Milky Way is like fairy dust in a swath, cradled between the jagged blackness of mountain peaks. I'm in the bottom of a bowl of those black peaks, a wide-angle 360-degree frame of the heavens. Standing naked under this vast sky, I feel both vulnerable and safe. The universe that holds these stars also holds me. My slow breath and the distant crackles and pops of a campfire are the only sounds. Zero light pollution, zero anything but Mother Nature, and she is putting on a show. This is how it was before civilization. Thank goodness I woke up for a pee. Life knew I'd be in awe, outside.

60.

I coddiwomple so I can journey into nothingness where everything else is left behind.

61.

July 9 – Lac Manicouagan, Quebec

4:30 a.m. – At sunrise, I woke to a lake so still it mirrored the sky all the way to the island. No matter what that guy said about this lake being like the sea, I wanted to paddle to the island. I threw on a bikini, pants, and a long-sleeved shirt, tossed some snacks and my GPS in a dry bag, and scampered down the rocks to my kayak. When the bow broke the pastel-painted surface, it felt like a sin. I paddled hard for forty-five minutes to leave the bay and hit open water. By that time there was a good chop. Thirty minutes later, the wind picked up. My GPS showed I still wasn't halfway to the island. It was further than it looked. Waves forced me to change my heading to keep from capsizing.

6:15 a.m. – I pointed my kayak into the surf and stopped paddling. Shit! My gut told me to float for a moment. My shoulders ached, knots tightened in my back, my wide-brimmed hat fluttered, and the waves breaking on the bow soaked my arms and chest. To the north and south was open water. Not a boat or evidence of humans anywhere. To the east was the cove where I parked Coddi on the cliff. It was too far to see her. I was halfway to the island but had to turn around. *Can I make it back?*

6:45 a.m. – I paddled to stay alive and had two choices: paddle directly into the waves or with the waves. Coddi was due east. "With the waves" was north-northeast, toward the mainland, so I headed that way. I paddled with all my might to hold my direction perpendicular to the waves to keep from flipping. The nose of my kayak dipped, and I felt the sensation of surfing for a second or two as each wave rolled under me. The nose of the kayak pointed up for a brief lull as each wave passed under me. This let me catch my breath, till the next wave, and the next, over and over. The hat, which I'd cinched with string under my chin, flapped over my eyes. I ripped it off and it landed in a wet heap in my lap.

62.

"The true test of love is how we respond in conflict. Do we turn away or turn toward?" – Marlene Mier

Run or embrace. Toss up a blind eye or dive in together. Love or blame. Meander through loving discussions or assume my ideas are best. Hug it out or kick dirt in the wound.

63.

2015 – North Port, Florida
A dream sprouted: leave normal life and live full-time.

Wade and I planned to quit our day jobs, grow our businesses, and travel the world together. We prepped for two years, and I worked seventy to ninety hours a week (full-time as a firefighter and almost full-time to build my coaching practice). Wade was laid off and couldn't find a job, and for over a year he took over all the household chores. I worked too much and wasn't present. In August 2017, Wade thought it was a good idea to drive to Kansas to get back with his ex from eleven years prior. I wasn't innocent and had tossed up a blind eye well before he ran. We'd both turned away.

64.

July 9, 7:00 a.m. – Lac Manicouagan, Quebec
I knew if I let my kayak turn away from the waves, I was a goner. Blisters lined the insides of my thumbs. Every paddle stroke was a stab through my shoulder, my lower back ached, and I hovered just above complete

exhaustion. Then the wind lightened. The waves were the same size, but no whitecaps. Spray soaked my back, and goosebumps covered my legs and arms. I was hungry, but I didn't dare stop paddling to snack.

The breeze shifted to my left and then increased. Within minutes, the lake transformed into a washtub of choppy waves. I spun right, and more right to keep my back toward the wind. The swells aligned until they were like soldiers marching in formation. This was a repeat of the last gale, and now I was pointing straight toward Coddi. I paddled with everything I had left. My shoulders screamed. My face stuck in a grimace, I grunted with each stroke. In the middle of a grand expanse of angry water, my fingers tingled and ached; the cold pricked my bare skin. All I could see in every direction was blue framed by green.

What a ridiculous thing to do. That guy warned me. Why am I out here? It's pointless. I wish I were warm and in my bed. If I flip, there's an ice cube's chance in hell that I'll make it to Coddi. No one will know I'm missing.

Forty-five minutes later, the cliffs and trees along the shore of the bay blocked the wind. I made it. I still had at least thirty minutes of paddling to get to the beach. *I can do it.*

65.

Out on that lake, with nothing between the elements and me, I confronted the truth: safety was never guaranteed. The real choice wasn't between safety and danger, but between being open to life or hiding from it.

As I see through my beliefs, I am freer. Ideas such as scarcity, separation, judgment, and the need for forgiveness fall away. This isn't a prescription to practice letting go of thoughts, not at all. It's an invitation to remember truth on such a grand scale that all the figuring out and practicing of self-help "tricks" seems silly.

Some of my stickiest bits are still hanging on. I constructed each bit to protect myself. For thirty years, I didn't love for fear of being left. I didn't want to feel. I poured my attention into being an A student and a determined Division 1 college athlete. I was taught sex before marriage was bad, and God would punish me for pleasuring myself. I believed I was a bad girl who wasn't loved. I lived under that shadow, and I am stepping into the light. The person I am today is a bright beacon compared to who I was seven years ago. I am no longer afraid of God and I'm done with "believing." Either I know or get curious. My body tells me when I'm skating on the thin ice of beliefs and assumptions. Knowing is clean. Knowing has no reason. Knowing is quiet.

66.

September 2017 – North Port, Florida

After Wade left for Kansas, I didn't want to travel alone and didn't think I could fix things on the fly or make ends meet with one remote income. I was going to do it anyway, and it was time. Within a week of the phone call with Mom I resigned from the fire department. For six weeks, I downsized my belongings and repaired my house. In early November, I put the place up for sale by owner.

On a Tuesday afternoon I received a cash offer. The buyers wanted to close that Friday, or they'd walk. No inspection, no survey, no nothing. They wanted my furniture, decor, and yard tools. I thought the closing date on the offer sheet was a typo and called to confirm. No typo.

"OK," I said. I sat in my office, my cell phone on the desk. My elbows rested on my knees as I leaned forward. My gut ached. *This is happening too fast. I'm not ready. Is it legal to close on a house in three days?* I gazed out at my backyard paradise, where a live oak shaded my vegetable garden. I was about to give away my whole life, with no lifeboat.

"Hello?" the buyer said.

"Ummm," I mumbled. This felt terrifying. I wanted to say *No! My house is off the market.* My neighbor, a twelve-foot-long alligator I'd named Max, sunned himself on the far bank of the canal. "I won't be able to pack all my stuff and be out in three days. I still have repairs to make on my Airstream. I don't have anywhere else to go—"

"Oh, that's fine," he interrupted. "We're leaving for Tennessee on Friday afternoon and won't be back for a month. Stay in the house as long as you need to get everything squared away."

I almost asked, but he continued. "Rent free. We trust you."

A wave of relief washed over me. This might work. In a matter of seconds, terror was replaced by a palpable sense of freedom.

67.

I am freedom. I am a leaf on a tree, and the tree. A tree doesn't conspire with itself any more than I conspire with my fingernails. I am along for the ride, and I am the ride. There is no rider. There is only living.

What is aware of the leaf, the tree, the journey itself?

I am that aware presence in which everything appears.

68.

July 9 – Lac Manicouagan, Quebec

I'd ventured out on a massive lake whose claim to fame is that it can get as angry as the sea. *Why?* By the end, all I'd wanted was to get back to shore and be done with kayaking forever. Sometimes it seems there's no point to anything. At times, this feels like total freedom; other times, it can feel as though I'm stuck on a hamster wheel with my legs spinning for no reason. I could lie on a couch in a tiny apartment in some average town and sleep my life away, or work my life away, or cry my life away.

I'll never do that again. This is why I paddle.

69.

Once back on land, I ate, licked my wounds, and then drilled out and replaced a couple of popped rivets on Coddi and prepped her for travel. The couple who gave me the fish were packing up, too. I rode my bike down to see them.

"Thank you, the trout was delicious," I said to Daniele. She was short, stocky, strong, and had a pixie haircut. I guessed she was in her mid-fifties.

"You are welcome! Looks like you are repairing your RV," she said, in her thick French accent, glancing up at Coddi and pointing with a quick bob of her chin. "You travel alone?" Her eyes were bright and engaged, and she wore a genuine smile.

"Yeah, I'm on my own and a full-timer. That road jiggled some things loose. Where are you from?" Our trucks were the same model, but Daniele and Fabien had a massive drop-in camper and towed a flatbed trailer. On the flatbed was a four-wheel-drive utility terrain vehicle that towed their boat. It looked like a golf cart on steroids.

"We live in Québec City. We are traveling to Labrador and Newfoundland."

"That's where I'm headed too!"

Daniele and I had a lot in common. She was a volunteer firefighter. Fabien owned a large RV repair company in Québec City, and they both were mechanics. They enjoyed boondocking and rarely stayed in campgrounds.

"Do you like to fish?" she asked.

"Yea, I do."

With a mischievous look, as if she were trying not to smile, Daniele looked toward Fabien, who was gathering a rope. "Wait here a moment."

70.

As I wander in wonder, I am never alone.

71.

July 9, 10:30 a.m. – Lac Manicouagan, Quebec
Daniele walked back toward me with Fabien following. "Maybe you like to come fishing with us today?" she asked. We stood fifty yards from the lake. Waves lapped up and tumbled rocks, which clicked and knocked like rhythmic background music. "We will drive north, maybe three hours, to boat ramp. The lake is good for rainbow trout. We will stay there tonight. Want to go? It will be fun." Daniele's smile crinkled the corners of her eyes. I'd planned to get some work done and drive the long stretch to the Labrador border. Instead, a couple of hours later, I was following Daniele

and Fabien's rig up a long gravel portion of QC-389, with their Motorola radio on my dash so we could stay in touch.

72.

In silence, each nudge is a demand. When I wander, there are no decisions.

73.

November 2017 – North Port, Florida
When I left normal life, there was no choice. My heart was lassoed with a rough rope made of twisted grass, and cinched so tight every beat was a scream for freedom. I was snatched out of my life and dragged down the dusty road kicking, screaming, and crying.

Two months after that fateful phone call with Mom, I had quit my job, sold my house and most of my belongings, prepared Coddi and my truck for full-time living, and said goodbye to the way I thought life should be.

November 30, 2017, was the day I left "the societal box," the day I drove off and welcomed the unknown, the day my love story began. Life had grander plans than I'd ever fathomed. My first month on the road was tame. I putzed around on the East Coast, mingled with friends and family, and got repairs and maintenance done on Coddi. I was in a safe harbor.

On January 1, 2018, things got real. Coddi and I ventured into the open sea, so to speak. Thrilled, full of piss and vinegar and hope for adventure, I left my mom's driveway in North Florida before sunrise and headed west on I-10. With no destination in mind other than "west," I drove from dawn till dark. Coddi has a special load-leveling anti-sway hitch. As I pulled into a parking lot in Katy, Texas, to rest for the night, the hitch popped and snapped somethin' awful. The thing was kaput. I tried to repair it in the blackness until my fingers froze. That hitch, which cost $3,000, was broke, and so was I.

I thought my love story had already failed me. I cried myself to sleep in an oil-stained parking lot, suffocating in a roar of interstate traffic. That parking lot is where my coddiwompling cookie crumbled. I cried a cry of brokenness and defeat. The cry was a sniffling, whiny little cry that soaked my pillow but didn't rattle the walls. I had much more to learn, in learning how to cry.

74.

I fell in love. Same as a river finds its way to the sea, one drop at a time.

75.

July 9, 3:30 p.m. – Lac Barbel, Quebec

I'd come a long way since crying in that RV park in Texas. Instead of broken hitches, Daniele and I joked with each other in broken English on the Motorola radio. After three hours of bumbling up that dusty gravel road, we parked at the boat ramp. Fabien brought Daniele over so she could translate.

"If you were a man, you would not come on my boat," Daniele said, and then Fabien rambled on in French. "If you were with anyone else, you would not come on my boat." We stood between our RVs. The golf cart on steroids and the boat were still on the flatbed trailer. "But you, alone. You are welcome on my boat." Daniele and Fabien both laughed as Fabien rambled then slapped me on the shoulder and held on tight, giving me a good fatherly shake.

"Now is the test: Can you catch fish?" Daniele shrugged her shoulders and giggled. With that, Fabien turned and motioned for me to help him with the boat.

It poured down rain while we were fishing. Between Daniele, Fabien, and me, we caught sixteen trout. While packing up, Daniele shared that Fabien had cancer. He'd received a grim diagnosis last year, given his business to his sons, sold their vacation home, bought the boat and trailer, and planned to have the adventure of a lifetime this summer. She said it was nice to have a third set of hands helping with everything, and they really enjoyed my company. Hearing about Fabien's cancer brought back memories of fishing with Mom. As I walked over to Coddi, I cried. I missed Mom. And my heart ached for Daniele and

Fabien, but boy they were living the guts out of life. Daniele's sharing felt like an invitation.

76.

Proof in memories, hah! Memories are silly stories I tell myself. Boy do I have stories to tell about love: what love is and isn't; what love does when it's ripped away; what true love means; how love has eroded the oxbows in the meander of my life like a flash flood through the butterscotch crust of a parched desert. Speaking of deserts (and desserts), I lived most of my life in a dried-up-love desert. I'd have given my left big toe to experience a sweet and rich love dessert—the kind of love I'd want more of until I passed out in an adoration coma.

77.

January 2, 2018 – Katy, Texas
The aftershocks of that broken hitch in Texas cracked the foundations of those walls I'd built around love. After that night of crying in the parking lot in Katy, I woke up and took apart the entire hitching system. It weighed 200 pounds, so I flagged down a couple of truckers to help me lift it into the bed of my truck. I dropped my Airstream on the ball, limped to an RV park northwest of San Antonio, and parked my not-so-happy ass for all of January and half of February. As I sat in Kerrville, Texas, and waited for a new hitch, loneliness grabbed hold and strangled me for over a year. Despair, tears, and regret consumed me, though I hid it well. If a big red Easy Button existed that would rewind time and undo my actions, I'd have tapped out in an instant. I wanted my house back, my job back, and my old life back.

78.

Love is a curious thing, always there, forever pulling, nudging, caring, and giving. The grass rope that cinched around my heart and yanked me out of normal life is made of love—for Life, myself, nature, for being of the world and in it, for giving and giving back, for receiving, for honoring the synergy and oneness of everything. Most of all, that tug on my heart was an invitation to live in the love of feeling alive.

79.

February 5, 2018 – Kerrville, Texas

I'd spent a month in the RV park in Texas, and sadness had wrung my soul dry. One morning, I sat in Coddi, loveless. I stood up. The same grass rope that had yanked me out of normal was still around my heart, tighter than ever, and it snatched me outside into the cold. I took one step, then another, stumbling as if drunk. I had no idea where I was headed. Then I was at the door of another RV. I knocked. It opened to a woman with long salt-and-pepper hair. She smiled down at me.

"Hi there," she said.

I opened my mouth to say hello. Blubbers fell out instead, along with instant shoulder-heaving tears I didn't care to wipe away.

"Oh honey, come inside," the woman said. "Come here, sweetheart." She wrapped me in hugs and kept me on her couch for a long while. What a wander. Boy, did I make up for lost time and tears. I learned to cry in that RV park in Texas.

80.

Wonder
Desire for something
is too much.
Wanting for nothing
is still wanting.
Just be
for no reason at all.
A beautiful emptiness opens.
Space for everything.
A quiet so loud.
A void always filled.
Pure wonder.

81.

My childhood theory: *If the L-word doesn't cross the lips, it doesn't exist.* I experimented with this for a quarter century. From thirteen to thirty-seven, I didn't so much as say "I *love* your sweater." No ma'am. Nope. No love. None.

82.

July 11 – Lac Carheil, Quebec
I sat on a beach south of Fermont, Quebec, writing my first journal entry ever. In our first two days together, Daniele and I had several intimate talks. She encouraged me to journal about my journey, the unique way that I live, and my philosophies on life. I'd told her about how I was going to catch a three-day ferry to the remote settlements of northern Labrador and hire an Inuit guide to take me further north on the Labrador Sea. She didn't think this was safe. Fabien didn't either.

On the drive the previous day, I'd pulled onto the shoulder of gravel road QC-389 to wait for Daniele and Fabien. White dust coated the trees like powdered sugar on a pastry. Three semitrucks passed. Each one slowed to a stop, their trailing dust clouds swallowing us whole. Each driver craned up and over to peer through the passenger-side window, checking to make sure I was okay. In the middle of a lonesome road, the human heart bursts open, and strangers become kin.

83.

Now I see there was much ado about nothing. In between birth and my falling into the great meander, I hid from love, the essence of everything. Like a kid who hides in plain sight behind a sapling. What a jolt out of my stories. What a surprise. What a wild ride these forty-five years have been.

I was a world-class hider, but no one is perfect.

84.

If I had only a month to live, would I live any differently?

85.

I would not change a thing.

86.

Coddi is female. I'm not sure why, she just is. I am her caretaker and she is mine. She's also my time capsule, my safe space, and my beautiful adventure partner on this incredible journey of Life. My truck's name is Casper the Friendly Beast, but I usually call him Casper, Caspy, or the Beast, depending on my mood. Sometimes I make up playful diatribes between Casper and Coddi while rolling down the road. The GPS lady, Thelma, often gets involved too.

"Coddi, gimme a break!" Casper says, as his exhaust brake groans and his engine screams on a long descent down a winding mountain road. "What a freeloader. You're either shoving me down a mountain or expecting me to haul your ass up. I can't catch a break around here," he mumbles.

"Quit your moaning," Coddi says. "We all know you like being pushed around for a change."

"Well, it wouldn't hurt if you dropped a few pounds," Casper says. "Speaking of dropping weight, I've been working all day and I'm thirsty. It's time for a pit-stop and thirty gallons of diesel to wet my whistle."

87.

Coddi was built in 2001. She's an old gal and things wear out. In seven years on the road, I've repaired or replaced all the appliances and systems (fridge, water heater, furnace, water pump, stereo, range, plumbing, wiring, solar, toilet, cabinets, front door, air conditioner, vent fans, hitch, etc.). An ounce of prevention is worth ten pounds of repairs.

Here's a list of Airstream regular maintenance:

- Inspect all seams, lights, windows, and vents yearly and reseal every five to eight years, or when leaks pop up.

- Lubricate window gaskets, awning arms, door hinge and latch, hitch bearings, hitch ball, steps, hinges, and clasps, and repack wheel bearings yearly.
- Wash the exterior regularly, especially when exposed to salt.
- Torque lug nuts and check tire pressures.
- Clean solar panels and check panel bolts; tighten connections between the solar panels and batteries/inverter/charger.
- Keep the humidity below 50 percent inside.

I do all the maintenance listed above, as well as most repairs. The first few years of learning about Coddi were rough. The more I know, the simpler it gets.

88.

Inside, a steady fire burns with gentle, warm intensity. I tend it with images, senses, and wonder. For it burns in my heart, you see. Lit by one miracle delivered in divine time like prayer, a love song.

89.

Remember
I never know what will be.
There is delicious enjoyment remembering this.
I forget.
I remember.
… And repeat.

90.

July 12 – Fermont, Quebec
Daniele, Fabien, and I finally made it to the end of the gravel road. I'd traveled QC-389 for seven days, between Baie-Comeau and Fermont, and never once had cell service. I had no music, podcasts, or anything downloaded. Thanks to Mike (the singer/songwriter I met camping in

Tennessee in May), I had one CD. When I got the hankering for enter-tainment, I listened to Mike on loop in Coddi.

Daniele got us tickets to tour the iron mine south of Fermont. My stomach churned and my heart ached as I looked out over a scar the size of a city and as deep as the deepest canyon—a colossal pockmark on Mother Earth's once-pristine face. The earth bled as a steel monster chewed through her skin. Hundreds of ginormous dump trucks crawled up and out of the mine, pregnant with precious rock. Trains slinked in and out.

"Each dump truck takes approximately 1,600 gallons of diesel a day to operate," the tour guide said. We were standing on an observation plat-form above one of the mines, which had to be five to eight miles from end to end. *1,600 gallons each?* That's not counting all the other machinery and vehicles. My stomach somersaulted with remorse. She also mentioned we shouldn't eat fish out of the nearby lakes. I felt ill.

What if we didn't need high-rises, each family had only one car, and we bought only what we needed? Nothing more. I wish everyone could sit beside immaculate lakes, breathe the crisp air, listen to birds chirp and hear wind rush by their feathers when they flap their wings. I need less as nature seeps into my bones.

After the tour of the copper mine, Daniele and Fabien set off solo. I parked by a free laundromat while I worked. The nicest laundromat ever: shiny new washing machines and comfy leather recliners so the miners can do their civilian laundry, but open to all. Score! It's the little things in life. There was just one road for the next 750 miles. I'd find Daniele and Fabien, eventually.

Part Two:
Love Unveiled in Labrador

As I drove that last stretch toward the Labrador border, I realized how much had changed since leaving Mom and my family at the cabin in Georgia: the emotions I'd let flow with Popo, the budding friendship with Daniele and Fabien, the gentleness I was holding myself with. I was letting in more light and more life. Even after all those years of wandering, I was still learning that the real adventure isn't out there on the road. It's inside, in the dismantling of my armor, piece by careful piece.

91.

July 12 – Quebec–Labrador Border
In the rain, at 4:50 p.m., I rolled up to a blue sign the size of a broad side of a barn. It read:

Newfoundland

Labrador

Welcome to the Big Land

Behind the sign, four soggy flags on tall silver poles tried their best to flap. I threw on my raincoat and hauled my A-frame ladder out of my truck, climbed up, and snapped a photo of Casper and Coddi, caked in dust and mud, in front of the sign.

On a side note, Coddi and Casper sat on *pavement*! The entire Trans-Labrador Highway is paved. Thank you, Labrador! Quebec's 150-plus miles of gravel road were plenty enough for me. Like for forever.

This wasn't just another border crossing. This was the threshold to somewhere I'd been dreaming about, and perhaps unconsciously moving toward for years. I'd been driving north for months, each mile taking me further from the familiar and deeper into something I couldn't yet name. Somehow this moment felt like the true beginning.

92.

Summer 1987 – Wakulla Springs, Florida

Where I Begin
I first became dazzled by depth on a rickety three-story tower.
Ridges of rough-cut timbers notched the soles of my bare feet.
My bathing suit dry from waiting,
drips from strawberry-blonde ringlets rolled down my back.
Breathe.
A forest of cypress and oak circled me and the spring, like wise elders.
Spanish moss dangled from outstretched arms.
They watched as I looked down into turquoise fangs.
A funnel of cliffs 185-feet-deep stared up,
asked me to trust, to come, to dive in.
I was eight years old, scared to jump and petrified not to.
My mortality was my bargaining chip.
A roll of the dice, a leap into the unknown.
To take my last breath is my only birthright.
Sink into wonderment.
It will come, that final inhale, today or in a hundred years.
Death is more alive than that.
I want to touch the submerged stony edge, to grab hold,
pull myself down, inside, underneath, to a space most are too afraid to go.
Dying in the act of living, again and again, this is a life well lived.
My toes wiggle at the edge, tips free, soles still, held by timber,
hair wafting in a breeze, dry from deliberation.
There is power in doubt. I befriend where I stand.

I inhale deep for the last time, and let go.
Head first, tiny fingers reaching, wanting.
And this is where I begin.

93.

Labrador, Canada, is one of the last untouched frontiers on the planet. Most of the province is pristine nature: dense boreal forests, bogs, lakes, lakes, and more lakes, roaring rivers, hills, mountains, and waterfalls. Gas stations, stores, and cell service are nonexistent between towns, and it's three to six hours of nothing but nature between each community. The province of Labrador is so remote that the government offers drivers on the Trans-Labrador Highway (the only road through Labrador) free satellite phones on a first-come, first-served basis. These phones are pre-programmed to call the police in Labrador City.

94.

July 12, 5:15 p.m. – Labrador City, Labrador

I stopped at the Labrador welcome station, got a map, bought a trout-fishing permit, and continued on. The lady at the welcome station was expecting me. Daniele told her I'd be passing through and to be sure I purchased the correct fishing permit. Gotta love family!

Next, I rolled up to the Wabush Hotel, the first location offering the government satellite-phone program. It's a crapshoot whether a phone will be available, and I planned to stop at each of the designated sites until I found one. A set of wooden stairs led me to a hotel lobby that felt frozen in time. It was silent except for the creaking floorboards. It had hardwood everything, worn forest-green carpet, and an empty desk with a silver-domed bell.

I rang the bell.

A few minutes later, a lady came out of a back room.

"Hi, do you have any satellite phones?" I asked. She looked confused for a moment, then I saw the lightbulb go on.

"We haven't had any in a while, but one came in yesterday. Let me see if it's still here."

I stood there in the silence looking at grainy black-and-white photos on the wall from back before there was even a road and my mind began to wander.

All my research, all those phone calls and planning—it would have been easy to give up. But something about this place kept pulling me, like a compass needle finding true north. I'd left behind so much in my old life. Here, nearing the edge of the continent, I found myself willing to spend a small fortune and take considerable risks just to witness something few ever see. Maybe what I was really seeking wasn't just an unspoiled landscape, but proof that places still existed beyond the reach of convenience and compromise. Places that demanded everything of you just to stand in their presence. After years of shedding what no longer served me, I felt ready for that kind of sacred ground.

CLUNK!

I jumped. Startled, I looked back at the desk.

The lady was thumbing through a stack of papers. A beat-up yellow watertight safety box, about the size of a kid's lunch box, sat beside the stack. She handed me a form.

"You need to fill this out. State where you'll return it, how long you'll have it, and your credit card number, which we *will* charge if you do not return it."

YES! Score again! That made me even more at ease with traveling this wild land.

95.

Live life. Be. Be free. Simple enough.

96.

For internet, I rely on cellular data. I have a Verizon hotspot (which didn't work in Canada), and an AT&T phone. I use cell phone boosters when signals are weak. If there's no service where I'm camping, I drive Casper to find service and work from the truck.

Working was tricky in remote places like Labrador. I dedicated two days a week to client Zoom calls from towns with strong cell service, and was available via text and email the rest of the week. I love when my phone goes silent in the bush. When there's no urge to check emails or scroll, every cell in my being relaxes in a deep exhale. Even with my off-grid living, I rarely spend more than a few days beyond cell range.

97.

July 13 – Boondocking between Labrador City and Churchill Falls, Labrador, with Daniele and Fabien

I love the way the lake and cool breeze dance together to create a living painting of the trees and a blue sky dotted with puffy clouds. A bee buzzes from bud to bud on bright-pink flowers as I inhale the peaty scent of algae. I wonder if he appreciates the beauty and sacredness of his home. I forget too. Then there are moments like this, when Life hugs my heart, takes my cheeks in her palms, tips my face up, toward all of this, and says, "Look, breathe, feel." My brows lift with awe. I take in the majesty of the entire work of art, down to the gnats buzzing around my face. A tear clings to the corner of my eye. I am in heaven.

98.

All I want is to be loved and to love with my heart wide open, unafraid, and undomesticated. Unaware of the lie that says I could ever be harmed by the depths of this raging river of love that satiates my soul.

99.

July 14 – Boondocking between Labrador City and Churchill Falls, Labrador

Daniele, Fabien, and I enjoyed chatting, sharing stories, teaming up for meals, and fishing. Beyond all that, they loved me. And I loved them. After I left camp that morning, I'd need to drive several hours to get to Churchill Falls, where I'd do some work. I told Daniele and Fabien I'd be too tired to find a nice campsite in the bush for the night. I'd sleep in Churchill Falls and hoped to meet up in Goose Bay in a few days.

As I packed up, I found myself moving slower than usual, lingering over goodbyes. Seven years on the road had taught me to release attachments easily, to places, routines, even people. But something about this couple, the way they'd welcomed me without hesitation, felt different. It reminded me of my little family (my brother's family and my mom) and that sense of belonging despite all differences. The recognition that under every story we tell about ourselves, we're all just looking for the same warmth. Daniele caught me staring off at the lake, lost in thought.

"What's on your mind?" she asked.

"Just thinking about how certain people feel like family right away," I said.

She smiled and nodded. No explanation needed. We both understood.

In the first two hours of driving, I saw one abandoned car missing a wheel, one bicycle rider, and four other vehicles.

100.

July 14 – Churchill Falls, Labrador

I found a hose bib and washed at least ten pounds of dirt off Casper and Coddi, a delightful morning at the spa for them both. I pulled forward one hundred yards into an empty parking lot, opened up the awnings on Coddi, toweled her off, and had lunch. After that, I began session one of a three-day Zoom immersion with a new client. After the session, I found two texts from Daniele.

> Hello! We found you a nice home by a sweet little lake
> [photos of sweet little lake]

> Come, here is our position
> [coordinates]

She knew I was working until 3:00 p.m. and preferred wilderness over towns. This is love, though her invitation surprised me. Most travelers were protective of their perfect spots and solitude. I'd known Daniele and Fabien less than a week, yet they were treating me as if I were family, saving places, sharing meals, checking in. It was the kind of connection I'd once thought impossible while living this wandering life.

> Sweet! Leaving Churchill Falls now
> [kissy face emoji]

> Perfect! Drive safely

> [kissy face emoji and hearts]

Even her small gestures, a simple "drive safely," felt like love. Thank goodness they had Starlink and could text no matter where they were. As soon as I left each town, I had no connection.

I arrived at the sweet little lake at 5:00 p.m. Daniele and Fabien did their own thing while I set up camp. By then we knew the help the other needed and didn't need.

There was a knock at my door.

"When you finish setting up, come right over," Daniele said. "We have something to show you."

I'd been parked for less than ten minutes. As tired as I was from a long day that began at 6:00 a.m., I wouldn't miss a short hang-out with them for the world. Five minutes later, I was at their RV.

Fabien opened the door. "Mademoiselle," he said, as he invited me in with a sweep of his hand, like a French maître d'. They had set their table for three, complete with wine, candles, grilled vegetables, baked potatoes, and fondue. *Who travels cross-country with a fondue set? My goodness gracious, a surprise Michelin Star meal with a lake view.* My lower jaw must have been on the floor.

"Come. Come, my friend," Daniele said. She sat at the table grinning and patted the seat next to her.

How do I get so lucky? Loving friends and delicious food on a day I'd have otherwise collapsed in bed. Life couldn't have scripted this any better.

101.

What exactly do you do for work?

I don't separate work from life: it's all following the tickles of my soul. I guide people who want to live more authentically through deep, transformative conversations.

Everything changed for me in February 2019 during what I call "the Poof," a profound realization that shifted my entire understanding of life. I discovered that what we think of as our separate self making choices is actually the whole universe expressing itself through us. This understanding dissolved fear, worry, anger, and the need to control outcomes. It showed me that all our experiences, even struggles, are expressions of life itself.

People come to me seeking specific things: success, less stress or anxiety, more confidence or creativity, better leadership skills or relationships, or to simply feel alive again. But when we look beyond the surface, what we all truly desire is peace, contentment, love, and happiness. I help people uncover this for themselves through understanding our true nature (who we are at our spiritual core). These conversations are enlightening regardless of belief systems or religious backgrounds.

I'm like a stripper (not the pole-dancing kind!) who helps people shed beliefs and conditioning that keep them bound up. I know this intimately because I've lived it. My nomadic journey has deepened these insights, but this freedom goes far beyond travel.

Clients begin with a three-day immersion. We meet for a few hours each day, go deep, and time flies. In three days, people realize truths that would take months in traditional weekly sessions.

The process is simple: we see through what isn't serving them, and they experience life with fresh eyes. Play replaces struggle. Worry and the need for constant willpower melt away. Life becomes stupid simple. Clients discover their true nature, learn to trust Life again, and are forever changed. From that space, everything shifts, and they naturally receive far more than they originally came for.

Simply put, I help people get out of their own way so they can live their fullest expression. I love what I do, and it doesn't feel like work. That's what I wish for everyone.

102.

Our honoring of each other and our honoring of This is the ultimate honoring of the sacred, most of all.

103.

July 15 – Sweet little lake between Churchill Falls and Goose Bay,
Labrador

At 8:00 a.m. Saturday, I prepped to drive to Goose Bay for day two of my
client's immersion. Daniele and Fabien knew I'd be on the ferry Sunday
afternoon. They weren't feeling too warm and fuzzy about the idea of me
jumping on a boat with a man I didn't know. They insisted I text or call as
soon as I had service, keep in touch, and tell them when I was back in Goose
Bay. We said our farewells and promised to rendezvous in Newfoundland.

Once I arrived in Goose Bay, I called William. He didn't have any
other charters during my time frame, so if I wanted to go, I'd have to pay
full price. He shared the name of another guide, Richard, who also took
people to Hebron and might have a less expensive tour.

After work I set off to find a nice sleeping spot. At 4:00 p.m. I saw
Daniele and Fabien's empty rig parked near a trailhead in Goose Bay.
I texted them my location. They drove by an hour later. I stood at their
driver's-side window and we made small talk for a couple of minutes.
Fabien made fun of my sleeping spot. They were going to a paid campground with more privacy. No hugs or sweet farewells. We had no clue
that was the last time the three of us would be together.

104.

For years, I'd convinced myself that true freedom meant complete independence. I'd built my life around the ability to leave at a moment's notice,
to need nothing and no one. But here in the wild, I was discovering an
unexpected truth: teaming up wasn't the opposite of freedom—it was
another form of it.

Daniele and Fabien moved through the world with the same
unattached curiosity I did, yet they'd found each other. They'd created
a partnership that expanded their worlds. I watched them together, how
they anticipated each other's needs without losing their individuality,
how their shared experiences enhanced their joy. Was there room in

my nomadic existence for this kind of connection? For the first time in years, I found myself wondering.

105.

I am of God and infinitely connected to everything. There is no good and bad, there is only what is. Sometimes people get so confused and caught up in fighting against Life they do things that inflict mental and physical pain on themselves and/or others. I will no longer live in fear of being harmed, robbed, or anything else. Life tests my resolve in this in subtle ways. For instance, with ferry clerks.

106.

July 16 – Ferry dock, Goose Bay, Labrador
Midday Sunday, I parked Casper and Coddi at the ferry dock in Goose Bay, which was almost as far north as roads go on the east coast of North America. After securing everything, I walked to the ferry office window and waited in line.

"You don't have a return-trip ticket and the southbound ferry is sold out," the clerk said. "How are you getting back?" This was a two-and-a-half-day ferry trip to Labrador's northernmost community, Nain. Once in Nain, the ferry turns around, and it takes another two and a half days to make the trip back.

"I'm not sure yet."

"Do you have plans to stay in Nain?"

"Not yet, but I'm working on it."

"Nain isn't the kind of place you go without plans. If you get stuck there, you'll have to wait a week for the next ferry. You need to get on the waitlist."

People were lining up behind me. This lady was the only one at the ticket counter.

"I'll probably stay in Nain a few days. I don't need a ticket back."

"Do you know anyone there?"

I shook my head.

"Listen," she said, lowering her voice and leaning closer to the glass window that separated us. "A single lady isn't safe there. You need a ticket back. I'm putting your name on the waitlist."

I didn't want to be on a waitlist and I told her so. She thought I was nuts. In the end, I let her put me on the list, but only for her sanity. I would not ride two and a half days on a ferry just to turn around and come straight back.

107.

Time and again, by grace, special families have loved and welcomed me in. Chosen families. Though I never felt as though I chose them. They chose me. Through these close relationships, I've come to see the world through the eyes of the oppressed and the privileged. My heart has felt empathy for all, shaped as they are by the beliefs they hold as truth. The wealthy have welcomed me into their homes and loved me. I now understand why they feel compelled to live as they do, and I've done my best to support those who serve them. I've also lived in the homes of those who serve and experienced how love and kindness matter far more than money. I know what it's like to feel at home anywhere, and to love (and be loved by) anyone.

108.

There are many places where I end up, and there are those special places where my heart sings, days seem like weeks, and sleep no longer seems important. On my meandering seven-year journey, there have been a few places where, without knowing it, I'd been waiting lifetimes to be. The northern coast of Labrador is one of these special spaces.

109.

The world is meant for you and me to figure out our destiny.

110.

July 16, 12:30 p.m. – Goose Bay, Labrador
I hopped on the *Kamutik W* ferry with only a backpack and the giddiness

that comes with setting off on an adventure. The ferry stops at five Inuit communities (overseen by the Nunatsiavut Government) and one First Nations Innu community. Scattered along the shores of the Labrador Sea, these communities are accessible only by air, sea, or, in winter, by snowmobile over frozen land and water. Once the ferry leaves Goose Bay, there is no cell service for the entire two-and-a-half-day trip. Nain is the one place on the northern coast of Labrador that has a cell tower. When I was on the ferry, there was no Wi-Fi. Thanks to lobbying from the Nunatsiavut and local Inuit community governments, there is now free Wi-Fi on board.

As we motored out of Lake Melville toward the Labrador Sea, I watched the sun set over the hills and paint a shimmering orange swath on the water. While taking in the views, I chatted with a sweet family, the Dysons, from Makkovik (our second stop). I wish I could wiggle my nose and forever be a part of their clan. Perry Dyson, the father, knew almost everyone in the northern-coast communities, including William and Richard, the two guides I was considering hiring to go to Hebron. He vouched for both of them. *My mom and Daniele will be thrilled!*

"Who would you recommend going on an adventure with?" I asked. We were standing on the top deck of the ferry, leaning on the railing. My jacket fluttered in the wind and Perry was in a T-shirt and shorts.

"Richard organizes a nice tour." Perry gazed off toward the horizon before looking back at me. "William will take you on the adventure of a lifetime."

111.

My life is better than I ever dreamed, but a part of me feels like a neglected houseplant, leaves wilted and thirsty. I'm ready to drink love in big, satisfying gulps that curl my toes and wet my lips. Not average love. I mean the kind that springs up from the corners of my eyes and dribbles down my chest. I'm ready to dive into a pool of this and drown in its caress.

112.

July 16, 9:00 p.m. – Rigolet, Labrador

Seven hours after we left port, we arrived at our first stop: Rigolet (population 320). I explored each of the communities on our "layovers." We had two hours in Rigolet, so I set out in the dark to hike part of the longest boardwalk in North America (nine kilometers long) and met a man from Quebec. He was eighty-two and flew to Goose Bay to make the five-day ferry pilgrimage. We walked as far as we guessed was "safe." If we missed the ferry, we'd have to wait four days to be picked up. Once back on the ferry, the rumor on the top deck was that we'd be in prime iceberg territory around 4:30 a.m. *Time to take a nap.*

113.

The ferry to Nain ($75 per person) is the lifeline for northern Labrador communities. It carries people, food, vehicles, and supplies. I booked a $190 economy room for the journey: a windowless space with two beds and a small sink. The darkness and engine vibrations lulled me to sleep.

114.

July 17 – Labrador Sea

7:30 a.m. – The same iceberg has infinite faces. Some are dull and dark, others silky smooth and shimmering. Some have cracks on one side but glossy, wavy-striated ripples on another. I find looking at icebergs is like looking at clouds. My mind plays with what I see: a cat frolicking, a top hat, an old lady's face. All are ever-changing.

8:45 a.m. – The Dyson family is on the top deck again. They're showing me photos of their harbor packed full of icebergs a few weeks ago. They harvest the icebergs each spring and save chunks in freezers to use in drinks all year long. Perry claims the best ice is the clear ice from an ancient stream. It's 10,000 years old! But the white ice and turquoise ice are good too.

They've lived in Makkovik (population 360) for generations. Their entire family is loving, free-spirited, and kind. Selena, their ten-year-old daughter, fishes and hunts pheasants on her own. Winter is their favorite time of year, which seems to be the consensus. Each community is isolated and has only two to six miles of road. After it snows and the water freezes over, everyone can zoom around on snowmobiles all over northern Labrador to hunt, explore, and play. What took us eight hours by ferry will take two and a half on a snowmobile. I'd like to stay here all winter someday.

115.

My heart always knows the answer, the next step, the truth. But my brain tries to take over. It's repetitive, loud, lacking, scared, and convinced it knows best. The heart is still in its knowing. Just like with people; the quiet ones are often the most enlightened. Give space for the soft-spoken to share truth.

116.

July 17 – Labrador Sea

10:00 a.m. – After thinking it over, I decided *not* to hire a guide to go to Hebron. It was too expensive. Since I had no way to connect with the outside world, I wrote a note to give to Perry so he could call William and let him know.

I went to find the Dyson gang.

"Is the trip to Hebron worth it?" I asked Perry.

"No doubt it's worth it," Perry said. I had my "no thanks" note in my hand, but my heart still wanted to go. "The mountains, they grow as you go north. You'll see polar bears on shore." He went on. We sat on the upper deck. Icebergs floated here and there.

"Even for $2,000 for two days? Is it still worth it?" The thick morning air rippled his shirt as he gazed up in contemplation. Then he looked me in the eye.

"It's worth it." He shifted his whole body to face me. "You don't know what you're missing, but if you knew, it's something you'd regret for the rest of your life."

We sat on a cold metal bench at the front of the top deck, eyes locked.

The other people and their conversations faded away. A warm, expanding feeling rippled out from my chest. I didn't know the details, but I was going to Hebron.

Perry's mouth turned up in a big smile. He knew I knew. I brushed my windblown hair out of my face with one hand and crumpled the "no thanks" note inside my pocket with the other.

"If I write William a message, would you call him for me?"

"Yes, of course."

I reached into my backpack to get a piece of paper, scribbled a message, and gave it to Perry.

A few minutes later, Perry returned. "Selena asked, 'Why don't we take Kristy to our house to use our internet?' I think that's a great idea!"

11:00 a.m. – Once inside Perry's place, he offered me a glass of water with iceberg ice. *Yes, please.*

I told William I wanted to hire him and that I'd be there Wednesday morning. I wanted to get a hike in, so Perry showed me the local boardwalk and hiking trail, then drove me past each trail intersection so I could find my way back to the ferry. He dropped me off at the trailhead, and we said our goodbyes.

117.

I fell in love without my own permission. I rebelled. My conditioned brain said, *Hell no. This will not work. I won't have it, not me.* I love this soul like I've never loved before, but the situation, the circumstances, and the body are all wrong. Sure, everything may be perfect now, but one day ... And what will people say?

118.

"Intelligence is the door to freedom and alert attention is the mother of intelligence."[6] – Sri Nisargadatta Maharaj

Alert attention, that's an interesting idea. When all is well, being alert and attentive is effortless. But in the midst of a really shitty shitstorm, it's not as if I can push pause and have a little Zen moment where I intend to be alert and attentive. When I'm fine with feeling everything, every rogue turd of a feeling or ray of sunshine, and I feel the emotion with no desire to make it go away or change—that is alert attention. Many of my foundation-shaking aha moments about Life have come either in the middle of, or shortly after, a painful shitstorm. Deep down, I know this. My door to freedom seems plastered with the knowing that even the shittiest situations are a divine gift in the grand meander of living.

119.

My biggest challenge living on the road has been when things break and I have to figure it out. I wish someone could fix it all or at least be there, hand on my back, to remind me everything is OK. Being out in the wild with limited resources is tough. If someone else had repair knowledge or I could reach a skilled mechanic, I would relax. My knuckles wouldn't bleed. But no one is coming. I have two choices: step up or wither into a useless puddle of goo. Even though I sometimes kick and scream, I step up.

In December, I was visiting my mom and got frustrated while repairing Coddi. I started at 7:30 a.m. and by 1:00 p.m., I had completed only one repair out of fifteen. Things snowballed into pure frustration and dead ends. I said fuck, shit, and ass in front of my mother several times. I walked off, had a change of scenery, found a glimpse of hope, and returned. The tides turned. By 7:00 p.m. I had completed more tasks than anticipated and learned a lot.

I think I find the way. Truth is: the way finds me.

Through breakdowns and repairs, I've learned that anything can be a love story or a tragedy. It's my choice. This lesson became clear early in my journey. Initially, it applied only to Coddi. I had a choice when something went wrong: get closer to her, learn how she works, and fix her myself, or wallow in self-pity and wish someone else would fix it. This applies to everything in life.

All frustration is a misunderstanding. We do our best given our physical, mental, and spiritual state. When I choose to love life, humans, and Coddi, I become more forgiving, creative, and open to new ideas.

120.

On the pathless path, the way is waiting.

121.

This journey has also shown me people are naturally caring and giving. People act unkindly when they're stressed, fearful, worried, or experiencing lack. Many people are in a state of fear, worry, or lack. Catch my drift? We all experience our heart being drawn to things that seem unusual. However, sometimes we're too afraid to do something new, or we think we can't. If we're afraid of the unknown, we'll tend to go against our heart's desire and keep the status quo. This leads to the stress, conflict, and insecurity rampant in society today. We have lost sight of who we are: a shared, infinite, and eternal being. It's unnatural to hurt someone while living in this space of love and understanding.

122.

July 17, 5:00 p.m. – Postville, Labrador
While in the third community, Postville (population 160), a lady told me there'd been a fire in the cultural center in Nain that afternoon. Two people suffered smoke inhalation, and there was major smoke damage. The Cultural Center was a brand-new multi-million-dollar structure and the pride and joy of the entire north coast.

As I absorbed this news and continued exploring the community, I kept being amazed by how kind, caring, and helpful everyone was. It was as if everyone knew the secret: we are leaves on the same tree. I'd been there a day and a half, and *here* was relative since I'd been in three communities in that time. There didn't seem to be any racism. I'd chatted with locals who were Indigenous, locals who looked European, and with many who were mixed heritage. Everyone got along, helped each other, smiled with their eyes, and seemed to be swimming in love and peace. There wasn't any stress or tension. In this place, there were no strangers, only family. And we were all family even if we weren't neighbors.

After leaving Postville, the ferry came to a stop in a stunning cove surrounded by mountains in all directions. A ferry staff member shared that it's expensive to moor at the dock, so we'd stay in the cove until early morning. An incredible sunset, water like glass, a tiny white cabin on the shore of a nearby island. It was like something out of an adventure novel. *I can't believe I get to be here. I can't believe a place like this exists.* Good night. Gorgeous night.

123.

I am not this jumble of thoughts and ideas. I am the mystery and I get to live the mystery. Nothing is what it seems. Everything is.

124.

On my first day in Labrador, I met a local man wearing a shirt that said "Dildo, Newfoundland." What a name for a town! There were six tourists on the ferry (including me); the rest were locals. Three of the tourists had Dildo trinkets or T-shirts. I despise tourist traps. I vowed to avoid it like the plague.

125.

July 18 – Labrador Sea, north of Hopedale, Labrador
I felt heartbroken after our last stop, Hopedale (population 590). This was the first community that had a palpable sense of poverty and despair. Workers at the dock were unloading six tall pallets of beer from the ferry, perhaps to drown the sorrows of the oppressed. I met a man named Jason while on a walk.

"The church is over three hundred years old," he said. Jason walked up as I was reading a sign in the church window. He was missing several teeth, and his skin folded in crow's feet around his eyes. At 7:45 a.m., the sun was already high over the sea behind him. "It's strong like my people."

We walked down a dusty dirt road lined with run-down houses. Jason had overcome his addictions, but lost his family. He shared the story of his people being forced to leave Hebron in 1959, twenty years before he was born. He'd never been. I *wished* I could take him there. The more he spoke, the more my heart broke and the smaller he appeared. I *wished* I could remove the sad stories from the forefront of his mind. I wonder who he'd be without them. Jason lifted his tattered yellow T-shirt to wipe his eyes, and I noticed several scars, like dark snakes across his hairless abdomen and chest.

"From fights," he said. "I used to be an angry man." He drank his way into battles. Battles with himself, the past, and other men. Each left a mark. Some on his body, some on his heart.

Houseflies buzzed around us and landed on the smoked Arctic char (fish) he'd brought out of his house for me. We stood in a patch of dirt with garbage and broken machinery strewn about. The fish lay on a piece of wrinkled and stained cardboard with dog-eared corners. The longer we talked, the more flies came to feast. I was tempted to take a piece. Now I was thankful I hadn't.

Jason rattled something in me. Our lives were different, but not all that different. I'd lost my family and dealt with addiction, too. But my privilege let me be addicted to sports and school, which put me on a fast track to being "successful" in the eyes of the world. What if alcohol or drugs was my only option? Take away my privilege, and ... I can't even imagine. Jason and I were more alike than not. I *wish* it were different for him.

126.

Sometimes I wish, and don't take action.

127.

After speaking with Jason, I hiked to Hopedale's highest point, a former military base. The heat was intense, and I climbed to the summit wearing my sports bra and pants. I was surprised to find more islands and water to the west, as far as I could see! I'd assumed Hopedale was connected to the mainland. The ferry horn sounded, signaling departure in thirty minutes. From the top of the hill, I wondered if I had enough time to get back.

128.

Living on the edge is something I enjoy. That space crackles with excitement. It's the thrill of pushing limits and experiencing life fully that makes the risk worthwhile.

129.

My not knowing where I'll sleep for the night raises eyebrows. On the ferry, people were shocked I'd travel to Nain without concrete plans. Most modern travelers plot every detail, but I've embraced an ancient ease that echoes how the nomadic Inuit once lived: comfortable with not knowing, free from the anxiety of needing everything secured in advance. In Coddi, I usually head in a general direction, north for summer or south for winter, but I'm open to something tugging me toward a different route. Sometimes it's difficult to find a place, and sometimes my sleeping spot just shows up. No fear, worry, or pleading with the universe. Even when I'm excited about a particular destination and plans change, I remind myself: I only thought I knew where I was going. What will be, will be.

I still hoped to go on the Hebron expedition, but that hinged on the weather. A guy on the ferry suggested I join the Nain Flea Market Facebook Group and ask to rent a room from a local when I arrived. I needed Wi-Fi or cell service to put the plan into action.

130.

I don't feel like a grown-up yet. Then again, what does a grown-up feel like? There's one me, one soul, one ageless energy. Animals and trees don't know how old they are or how they should act.

131.

July 18, 12:00 p.m. – Labrador Sea, north of Hopedale, Labrador
As we traveled north, the ferry population dwindled. The forward top deck was my usual hangout, with its stunning views and interesting people. That afternoon there was only one guy: George. He stood at the railing in

an oversized blue hoodie staring out, relaxed and deep in thought. Wind tousled his dark-brown hair.

I walked over and asked, "What's it like to live here?"

He leaned against the railing with me. The wind was so strong that, when my mouth was open, air rushed through my nose and down my windpipe. A sensation I'd never felt before.

"It's heaven," George said. "I never want to live anywhere else."

During our chat, I noticed George saying "the Inuit" a few times, which caught my attention.

"Why do you say 'the Inuit'?" I asked, as I cocked my head to the side. "Aren't you Inuit?"

George shifted his weight to face me. "I'm Innu."

I was surprised there were two distinct groups. George seemed pleased I'd asked. He explained that the Innu live more inland, and travel to coastal areas in summer to fish and hunt water species. Inuit live on the coast. He also mentioned that the Innu are a First Nations group, while the Inuit are not. George lived in Natuashish (population 875), the fifth ferry stop. He had a boat and traveled north in the Labrador Sea for hunting and to be in nature. Through his work for the Innu government, George aimed to improve Innu lives. He was a happy man who loved his family, his home, and his job.

132.

When I explore with curiosity and wonder, I come alive. There is a fireball in the sky that nourishes my cells, grows plants, and heats the earth and water. It never explodes. It just hangs there. *That's magic!* Nature restores, dazzles, and mystifies. The more I notice the magic all around me, the more grateful I am. It's as if I'm seeing the world through a child's eyes.

133.

My heart radiates the magnitude of all I feel for you and the sun delivers it.

134.

July 18, 2:30 p.m. – Natuashish, Labrador
A couple in a pickup saw me walking from the ferry dock toward town. They asked if I'd like a driving tour, and I hopped in. Our trip included the community, a historic river used for transport and migration, and a visit to the dump, where at least twenty brown bears feasted on garbage.

Natuashish is an Innu reservation, the newest of the six communities in the region. Because of early European influence and more recent government relocation, Innu were forced out of their natural way of living. Rows of cookie-cutter houses stood in grids along gravel roads. Dense forest surrounded the area, but the land had been clear-cut to build the community, so there were no trees. Dirty dogs roamed free—freer, it seemed, than the people. Most of the residents I saw had sad eyes and long faces.

The couple drove me around for about forty-five minutes. They owned the convenience store and ran an organization that supports troubled youth. They said many in Natuashish struggle with depression, drug addiction, and alcoholism. Their organization takes young people deep into the forest for weeks at a time. After a few days in nature, the youth come alive: happy, talkative, helpful, and creative. But when they return to Natuashish, the same youth often fall back into depression, lethargy, and addiction within days. It's a pattern the couple has witnessed again and again.

I felt heavy with sadness for the people here, and ashamed of my white skin.

135.

Trading nature for blacktops and busyness is a shock to the system. When I land in a city or the suburbs after being out in the wilds, there's a sorrow for society that seeps in. I miss nature's quiet rhythms and feel suffocated by the blight of buildings, concrete, and traffic. What weighs even heavier is witnessing how many of us have unconsciously adopted patterns of endless consumption, handcuffing ourselves to work that often serves systems rather than souls. We give our days to an economic machine that rarely benefits the common good, while the natural world we were born to live in grows ever more distant. In cities, I often sleep in parking lots of big-box stores because it's illegal to stay overnight in parks or quiet neighborhoods.

Tuesday Morning in the City
Back by the dumpsters and loading docks.
8:30 a.m. sun sneaks in behind the shades.
A semi idles outside my window.
This is where I work, live, and cook meals.
Where I snuggle under my covers on a chilly night.
Where, after dark, I wish kids in shiny cars
with no mufflers would turn down the music.
Where I wake up at 2:50 a.m. when deliveries roll in,
and read poetry until my eyes get heavy again.
Where the hum of a six-lane highway
almost sounds like ocean waves.

136.

Inuit who live in Labrador are descendants of Inuit who traveled across Canada from Alaska. They, along with their Thule ancestors and earlier Indigenous cultures, have called the north Labrador coast home for over 7,000 years. Most Inuit didn't come into contact with Europeans until the Moravian missionaries set up settlements in the 1760s. Before the influence of the missionaries, Inuit lived a nomadic lifestyle, hunting on land and sea.

Innu lived nomadically in the interior of the Quebec-Labrador peninsula. They followed the caribou migration and lived free. In the 1940s, Innu were forced by the Catholic Church to settle in coastal areas and assimilate into a Canadian culture. Today, some Innu travel to hunt caribou in late spring and fall, living a way of life similar to their ancestors.

There are approximately 2,600 Innu living in two distinct communities: 1,700 live in Sheshatshiu, near Goose Bay, and 875 in Natuashish. In 1978, Canada recognized an Innu Nation land claim covering about 70 percent of Labrador. The Innu are still in negotiations with the government regarding benefits, land claims, and rights such as those related to the provincial government's right to dam rivers for electricity. The challenge is that for over three generations, Innu have been forced to live on reservations. This disruption has weakened their traditional language, cultural knowledge, and practical skills for living from the land. Despite being "given back" their land in one of the largest land-claim settlements in history, the multigenerational disconnect from their traditional lands has eroded many aspects of their natural way of life.

137.

We are nature, yet we've boarded ourselves inside our forts, leading to bigger waistlines, weaker hearts, and bouts of melancholy. In normal life, the further I strayed from nature, the deeper my loneliness grew. There was a sense of losing something I couldn't put my finger on. I became accustomed to this disconnection, like a frog slowly boiled alive. I too lost touch with my true self and what naturally draws me. I am finding this again. Kids know this pull and are more apt to follow the lure of nature, as long as they haven't sat simmering behind their screens too long. When a forest, the ocean, or even a mud puddle calls, they dive in wide-eyed and giggly.

138.

July 18, 7:00 p.m. – Labrador Sea, north of Natuashish
I figured we'd arrive in Nain around midnight, so I planned to stay in bed until morning, hoping no one would bother me. That plan was foiled. The ferry left Natuashish early and was due to dock at 10:00 p.m. Only the five tourists with return tickets were allowed to stay on board, and I wasn't one of them. Luckily, a ferry worker I'd befriended and the captain came up to the top deck to watch the sunset. I asked them if I could stay. After some deliberation, they said yes.

139.

The Big Tease
A man in a fine suit walks a city street as if he's in a chain gang,
bent forward, brows furrowed, shoulders slumped.
He takes quick steps to keep up with photos on billboards.
He gives his all, decades of days and nights,
gives up on love and a family, gives away his fantasies.
It's all a big tease. I am him.
My dreams crushed
like a lipstick-stained cigarette butt in the crack of a sidewalk.
I have lost my way.
I smile with my lips, but my eyes tell the truth.
There is darkness in the windows.
Too many know-it-alls,
with dollar signs for spectacles, publish how-to books.
Puppeteers peddle the bestseller:
"Ten steps to sell your soul," but with a rosier title.
The unaware quote the quotable and line up.
If I stay in work that kills my spirit because I fear change,
I am a prisoner.
I know not what I do.
Melancholy Sunday afternoons are an early precursor
to a mass grave dug in plain sight.
I take a look at my reflection.
The twinkle of my toddler's eyes died long ago.
I am spellbound by a promise I hope is true.
If I work hard for long enough, I'll finally get to rest.

140.

What is one thing in your Airstream you may not need but are surprised by
how much you enjoy it?

My Big-Ass Pillow (also known as the BAP). Coddi has a permanent
queen bed in the "everything room," which is the whole front half of my

Airstream. It's the bedroom, living room, kitchen, dining area, and office. The bed serves as a lounging area with pillows for backrests. Mom found it uncomfortable, so she bought a massive backrest for the bed. I didn't want more clutter.

"Mom, please return it." We stood in her living room. The monstrosity covered the entire couch. "It's just a big-ass pillow."

"You don't get to decide," Mom said. "I'm giving the pillow to Coddi. You can thank me later."

When moms have their mind set on something, they win. I lugged it into Coddi. Now, the BAP is one of my favorite things. It's so comfy. I'm leaning against it while typing these words!

141.

Nature has begun to rewild me. The farther I step away from the noise of "civilized ways," the cleaner and simpler life becomes. I joke around that I am feral: I'd rather pee outside; prefer bare feet over shoes; lick my plates, burp, and fart; wear clothes until the seams are threadbare; wash my hair maybe once a week, do nothing to style it; prefer wild game and fish over store-bought meat. I'd rather eat vegetables right out of the ground but no longer have a garden, nor know how to forage. I can clean fish but have no clue how to dress an animal. Drop me in the wild, without tools or technology, and I wouldn't survive long. Nope, I'm not wild at all.

142.

You move me in this timeless time.

143.

July 18, 9:44 p.m. – Labrador Sea
Nain (population 1,200) is less than five miles away. The glassy water sparkles in neon pink, flanked by mountains that resemble treeless Appalachians with patches of snow. They fade into shades of mauve before blending with the crimson and purple sky. I've stood on the upper deck for the past hour, leaning into the icy wind. Next to me is Jonathan, a young

Inuit man. We struggle to hear each other, so we move close and speak in fits and starts. Jonathan's words are succinct and strong. Untouched wilderness surrounds us; a warm, fiery sky stretches in all directions. With wind against my chest and sky pulling me forward, no words can do this justice.

I snap a photo of Jonathan gazing into the sunset and offer to email it to him. He doesn't have an email address or a phone number. He asks me to message him on Facebook.

As the almost-empty ferry turns left and the lights of Nain twinkle, I feel a sense of coming home. I say a few goodbyes. The ferry docks with a *clunk*. Jonathan walks up.

"Can I give you a gift?" he asks. His one bag is a small black backpack. Since he mentioned being an apprentice rock carver, I figure he might give me a little statue. I don't keep trinkets and would rather he sell his pieces. His eyes wait for my answer. I do too.

"OK."

He smiles and extends his right hand, as if ready to shake. In his handshake, there is something small, thin, and sealed in plastic. I look down at my palm and find a condom.

144.

Europeans stripped the wildness and wisdom from Indigenous cultures across the world—without permission, without thought for the consequences, without care for those whose lives and lands they disrupted. In just a few centuries, fear and greed choked out so much of what was beautiful, sustainable, and whole. I wish there were a way to undo the harm. I long for a time when people lived in deep relationship with the land, in communities rooted in reciprocity and reverence, in harmony with the natural world.

145.

July 19 – Docked at Nain, Labrador

6:15 a.m. – I gaze out a window on the ferry. Guys fish at the dock below. A German tourist couple, Heike and Eckhi, sit with me and share their favorite spots to visit in Newfoundland. They will head south on the two-and-a-half-day return trip, along with the other three tourists. Of all the people on the ferry who know I don't have plans beyond this point, the white folks think I'm nuts, though they still respect my spirit of adventure. The Inuit? They don't think anything of it. That says a lot.

8:00 a.m. – As soon as the *Kamutik W* ferry drops its ramp, I walk off and call William.

"Welcome to Nain," William says, as he steps out of a rusted red pickup. He's wearing a faded navy-blue T-shirt, sweatpants, Crocs, buzz-cut dark hair, and an ear-to-ear smile. His tawny face is sprinkled with salt-and-pepper stubble. Thin pale stripes stretch from the sides of his eyes back to his ears—tan lines from sunglasses.

William tosses my bag in the truck bed and motions for me to hop in beside it. I sit on the tire hump as we bumble up a gravel road past small wooden houses, each about 800 to 1,000 square feet. Their dirt yards hold a few tufts of grass, and most have snowmobiles out front. Cars are rare, but dusty four-wheelers are everywhere.

146.

Here I sit. In Love. In the purity of complete freedom.

147.

If I could fall back, into Inuit culture in the 1600s, I'd go in a heartbeat.

148.

July 19, 9:00 a.m. – Nain, Labrador
William's primary boat wouldn't be back from Hebron for another day or two. He had a smaller aluminum boat, a 19' Silver Dolphin, but he was hesitant to take me to Hebron in it. We had a weather window the next day (Thursday), but Friday was iffy. He asked me what I wanted.

"I want to go to Hebron, and I'm fine with the small boat," I said. "I trust your judgment." We sat at his dining room table, which was against the wall in the living room, butted up to the refrigerator. A wood-burning stove stood in the middle of the tiny room. It felt kinda like Coddi's everything room. The three-bedroom house was maybe 1000 square feet.

"OK, we'll go in the morning. Leave at 6:30 or 7:00."

We hauled the boat to the town fuel pump and gassed up: twenty-five gallons in the tank, three red ten-gallon jugs, and a green fifty-gallon drum. William never invited me into the cab of his truck. *Maybe the passenger-door latch is broken?* Once back at his house, William asked where I was staying. I told him about my plan to ask for a room to rent on the Nain Flea Market Facebook Group.

"No, no, no, no," William said, as he shook his head, chuckled, and gave me a mischievous grin. "Come here."

He showed me his granddaughter's room. A twin mattress on the floor and some toys filled the small space. It was perfect.

149.

July 19, 11:30 a.m. – Nain, Labrador

I sit, bundled up, at the high tide line on an Arctic bay. The water's surface is as smooth as glass. I am surrounded by glacial mountains with jagged obsidian cliffs.

Love with nowhere to land sits like an iron weight on my gut, heavy and hot. It boils my insides and pumps tears from my eyes. The sweet release is what I've missed. I welded my relief valve shut. I've held a lifetime of tides inside. Waves of love and love lost have not soaked my shores. Fear of being hurt keeps my sandy beaches dry. Without storms, my rainbow hasn't been let loose to shine. I thought I was free, but my heart is still under lock and key.

Seagulls flap their wings and jump from rock to rock. Birds of prey grace the sky, dive, crash against the sea, and plunge deep. Then flap and flap and flap until they heave up and out of the water's grasp with their catch.

Yes, I am the bird of prey. I fly high and look deep. Fearless, I take the dive. I break the laws of the world above and plunge beneath.

This is it, my divine request, to bring back tales of forgotten ways from a place inside that begs to be set free. To find the words to bring to life the magnificence of all these stories alive inside. To release the tenderness I've buried. To stop playing love safe. This has been too much for far too long. I want to be brave enough to tell the truth, open up, love and be loved, and feel the rain.

150.

Let's allow and experience everything in sweet sips, just us and possibility.

151.

I lived in Florida until I hit the road. In September 2007, I flew to Montana to fight wildfires. When my hand crew of twenty firefighters from Florida checked in at the US Forest Service Cache in Bozeman, Montana, there was a pile of forest-green Government Issue sleeping bags waiting for us.

Here's the deal: When going on missions like this, we took everything we needed (a tent, a sleeping bag, daypacks, clothes, etc.). We didn't need another sleeping bag. The logistics officer whistled to get our crew's attention. "You folks from Florida don't get what cold is, and we don't have the time or manpower to haul you off that mountain because you freeze to death in your sleep," he said. "I have a direct order to issue each of you a sleeping bag. There is no negotiating."

When I unzipped my tent to take a pee at 3:00 a.m., frozen grass crunched under my feet. Who would have guessed it would be that cold in September??

152.

In fall 2018, I stored Coddi in San Jacinto, California, and jetted off to Europe with only a large backpack. I guessed I'd coddiwomple for three months. I ended up traveling with the items in that backpack for seven months. During cold weather, I layered my clothes under my Patagonia hooded puffer.

I was in Denmark visiting friends in November 2018, getting ready to fly to Switzerland. My friend, Natasha, stopped me as I was leaving.

"Don't you have a bigger coat?" Natasha said. We stood in her living room. A tall, thin white candle flickered on the coffee table.

"No, I have layers. This is all I need."

"But that's so thin." She tilted her head to the side and raised an eyebrow while pinching the material on the shoulder of my Patagonia puffer. "You're going to be cold."

"I'll be fine."

Natasha slid open her coat closet and pulled out a pink zip-up fleece. "I want you to have this."

"Oh, thank you. That's really kind, but I don't have room."

"You have room. Open that top zipper."

I did, and with a little effort, she stuffed the pink jacket in.

"You'll need this too." She handed me a purple-and-gold wool scarf. "Please, it'll warm my heart to know you're warm."

That was a long winter, and the scarf and extra jacket kept me warm. They both still hang in my closet.

People from Florida don't understand what cold is, and I'm still learning. William was about to save me from becoming a popsicle.

153.

July 19, 5:00 p.m. – Nain, Labrador

"Let me see your coat." William's voice startled me. He stood at the door. I was organizing all my stuff on his granddaughter's bed. I handed him my black Patagonia puffer.

"This is it?" William held the jacket between his thumb and forefinger, arm outstretched at eye level, as if holding a smelly diaper.

"Yes, and I'll wear layers under it. I have a wool shirt and these." I held up the three long-sleeved shirts and my thin nylon raincoat.

"No, no, no, no. Not good," he said, with a chuckle and playful head-shake. William's dimples emphasized his cute smile. "This is a sweater. You don't have a coat?"

"That's the biggest coat I own."

William's eyes dashed from right to left and back again. With a charming smirk, he held the "coat" in my direction, still pinched like a dirty diaper. "Come."

This was going to be a fun trip. Playfulness permeated the air.

154.

July 20 – Nain, Labrador

With all the excitement, I slept four hours. By 7:20 a.m. I sat in the bed of William's truck. Chilly sea air blew through my hair as we bounced down the gravel road to the boat ramp. I wore William's daughter's thick brown coat. Puffy white fur lined the hood and an Inuit design was stitched on the back. I also wore her insulated rubber boots, and waterproof winter gloves were clipped to my chest. William had played Arctic dress-up with me, and I felt as snug as a bug in a rug. After launching the boat and tethering it's bow to a boulder with a rope, William went to park the truck. I balanced step by step over boulders and loaded the rest of our gear into the boat.

"You're a hard woman!" William said, as he walked down the ramp.

"I'm not hard," I said, as I tossed the last bag on the bow. The weight of the gear made the boat drift away until the rope went tight. "I'm soft and nice, and stuff like that."

"Ooo-kay," William said, with a big dimply sideways smile, as if he knew better.

At 7:40 a.m. we stood looking over the dashboard of his 19' Silver Dolphin skirting over smooth waters into the still-rising sun.

155.

As mentioned, I used to be an ultra-distance bicycle racer. For example, in 2012 I rode my bicycle 259 miles in twelve hours. That was uncomfortable, to say the least.

"You're a world-class sufferer," Wade said. He was my cycling coach back then. "You take yourself to the knife's edge, where, if you pushed more, you'd bonk." Bonking is when someone pushes their body too far and collapses. "Somehow you hold yourself there, at the ultimate suffering point, longer than most pro racers can."

I sat at my desk in front of an Excel spreadsheet as we reviewed training data. I felt proud of myself for doing that. "I can't teach you or anyone else that," Wade said. "This is your secret weapon."

Being a world-class sufferer shows up in more than just bicycle racing. I live through being cold with subpar clothing. Against advice and without proper gear, I kayak into treacherous lakes. For goodness' sake, I'm writing these words while camped out in one of the most stunning places I've ever lived. A beautiful river is right outside my front door, and there are mountains in every direction. The downside? The closest grocery store is four hours round trip. I'm running out of food but want to stay. So what do I do? I ration food as if I'm on a life raft in the middle of the Pacific. No joke. I just ate a small portion of black beans with a few carrot slices for dinner. I'm still hungry. Jiminy Crickets! I'd never make someone else live this way, but I'm fine treating myself like this.

156.

July 20, 9:30 a.m. – Labrador Sea, north of Nain
A stranger, a drum of fuel, and I on a little metal boat heading into the Arctic wilderness. I never saw that coming, but it felt perfect. As we skirted through unimaginably spectacular seascapes and craggy cliffs, something subtle shifted. The walls I'd built around my heart started to creak. Mountains and islands grew taller and larger the further north we went: towering, bright-green-grass-covered mountains dotted with patches of snow; jagged cliffs the color of rust with marigold, tangerine, and bronze swaths of minerals flaunting themselves in the bright Arctic sun. And icebergs! Oh. My. Goodness! Their shimmering aquamarine color cannot be described. Several were humongous enough to house a small town! Seals, whales, polar bears, and caribou roamed the banks and swam in the waves.

I wore three shirts, my Patagonia "coat," the thick fur-lined coat, huge winter gloves, and my raincoat on top. I was still freezing! A ball of frozen crystals was growing on the relief valve of the ten-gallon gasoline jug next to me. The Labrador Sea ain't no Gulf Stream! I was in awe for six hours straight on that boat.

157.

We met. A captivating current wrapped itself around both of our hearts. Two strangers, who've known for lifetimes, but in those first moments, didn't fully realize.

158.

July 20, 11:00 a.m. – Labrador Sea, north of Nain

"Can I touch an iceberg?"

William tilted his chin up and looked at me side-eyed. "You want to touch an iceberg with your hand?"

"Yes!"

"You're a hard woman." He laughed and shook his head. "No one has asked me that before."

An hour later William spotted a sailboat on the horizon offshore, heading north. "You want to check it out?"

I answered with quick nods and a big grin.

After ten minutes of chasing, I asked, "What if they think we're pirates?" We were in no-man's-land in our aluminum boat with a rusted-up steel drum. William thought I was joking. We kinda looked like pirates. "Do you have a white flag?"

William shrugged and laughed at my silly questions.

Halfway to the sailboat, we cruised up to an iceberg. It towered over us like a five-story building, and it took a few minutes to circle. William nosed the boat toward a flat spot. When the bow was five feet from the ice, we both lurched forward as William jammed the boat in reverse.

"Too risky," William said, as we floated away from the turquoise wall. "The sea is moving too much. No touching today."

159.

I'm a migratory mammal and need little: a quiet and flat place to park Coddi; a clear view of the sky for my solar panels; a delightful view of mountains, the horizon, the ocean, a creek, river, or lake is a nice bonus too.

160.

The unknown is my drug of choice. Keep the liquor and pills and serve me up a goblet full of "Who the hell knows what's next?" Life is a rollercoaster, with ups and downs and surprising turns. I have complete permission to be high on Life and embrace *every* part of the adventure.

161.

July 20, 1:30 p.m. – Labrador Sea, east of Hebron
As we headed inland, William talked about Hebron, the polar bear guard stationed there, efforts to renovate the church and other structures, and more about the special land we'd soon be stepping onto.

Hebron was once an Inuit settlement called Kangerdluksoak, which in Inuktitut (Inuit language) means "the Great Bay." Inuit had always lived in and around this area as part of their nomadic way of being. The Moravian missionaries first arrived in 1830, renamed the settlement Hebron, and built a mission. A few Inuit stayed at Hebron year-round. Most continued a seminomadic migration and made journeys to Hebron to trade with the Europeans, and for celebrations.

This peaceful, powerful space, this paradise continues to be one of the most culturally significant places for Inuit in Labrador—a place of loss and forgiveness, and a place where ongoing healing endures. Thankfully, it's far enough from creature comforts that most tourists won't make it this far. The polar bears that frequent the beaches scare away the rest.

The Moravian mission wasn't only about religion; economy and trade played a huge part. Moravians relied on Inuit trade for furs and other goods. After one hundred years of missionary influence, the way of life at Hebron changed. With each generation, Inuit were more dependent on Moravian goods and services. In 1926, the Moravians transferred their trade to the Hudson's Bay Company. Then most of the Moravians left. In 1942, the Hudson's Bay Company withdrew from Labrador. The provincial government assumed responsibility for trade, social, medical, and educational services in Hebron, which was challenging and expensive. In

1959, the Canadian government forced all Inuit to settle hundreds of miles south in small villages, where most lived in poverty.

162.

The greatest sin of modern society is brainwashing the masses into materialism.

163.

July 20, 2:00 p.m. – Hebron, Labrador
As we motored inland, William gave me the polar bear talk: stay far away. The bear guard in Hebron carries a rifle everywhere and uses plywood studded with long nails to protect the sleeping quarters at night. William brought a rifle. Polar bears are serious business. I was excited to see one.

Soon I could make out a long white building, which was the church, a few more dilapidated structures, and some ruins. Two men were coming down a hill, one with an orange vest and a rifle, the bear guard I suspected, and a thin guy in a baseball cap. I had assumed no one else would be here.

164.

I've landed on my butt and got back up, time and time again. I've landed on my feet too, more often than not. I've landed on shores of distant lands and in my grandmother's kitchen.

165.

Through the Hebron Ambassador Program, the Nunatsiavut Government normally stations four seasonal employees in Hebron each summer to work on restoration, keep guests safe, and protect this unspoiled land and its artifacts. When I visited, there were three ambassador staff on site: Joas, the polar bear guard; Emily, the cook, who welcomed guests, shared history, and kept everyone warm and fed; and Steven, the jack-of-all-trades, who made repairs, helped Joas and Emily, and caught fresh Arctic char for supper. I was beyond touched by their warm welcome, care, and sharing.

In the small building that served as a hangout area and kitchen, there was a wood-burning stove and a large wood table. A thin wire fastened a one-inch-by-one-inch stick to the ceiling. Long strips of raw Arctic char and raw caribou meat hung over the stick like socks drying. The Arctic char's pink flesh was brighter than that of wild salmon. Its silver skin was still attached and its tail was intact. The tail made a perfect hanging point. The flesh was scored in one-inch sections. The caribou meat was the color of wine and had been drying for a couple of days but still had another day to go. Raw, wind-dried meats are the way of the Inuit.

I hesitated at the thought of eating uncooked meat that had been hanging in seventy-something-degree Fahrenheit temperatures for days, but I thought: *They've eaten this for thousands of years and look healthy. Guess I'll live.* Emily offered me some ready-to-eat pitsik (char). It was salty, hard, and satisfying: delicious fish jerky.

There is no power or well in Hebron. There's a stream for fresh water, and Steven turned on a gasoline generator a few times a day, but gasoline must be brought by boat from Nain in fifty-gallon drums, and that's not easy.

After a chat and shared chocolates, they encouraged me to take a walk around.

Joas gave me a Motorola two-way radio, with strict instructions to keep it on, and volume up. They insisted I stay within sight of the kitchen hut. "If you see a bear," William said, "even far away, say 'Bear bear bear' on the radio."

"Got it," I said.

When Joas and William speak of bears, they don't mean black bears or even grizzlies. Those are cuddly creatures compared to the polar bear. "They are fast and hungry," William said. "You are food."

"If I see a bear, I'll fire a warning shot," Joas said. "If I call you back on the radio, quickly come right back."

"Yes sir, I will. Thank you." And with that, I set off.

166.

Coddi is like a flower. All she needs to live and take care of me is water and light. On a clear day I can run my refrigerator, Vitamix blender, induction cooktop, computer, and everything else off solar. At night my fridge runs on propane and my batteries handle the rest. If it's cloudy for several days, I charge my batteries with the DC to DC charger connected to the truck's alternator. I can run my air conditioner on solar, but only for a few hours, or less if it's a cloudy day. This is why I migrate north in the summer. In high heat I cannot survive off solar alone. If it gets too hot, I'll find a campsite with power. For water, I fill Coddi's tank at gas stations, friends' houses, campgrounds, or in a pinch I've asked to fill at a fire station. I've never had a hard time finding water.

167.

July 20, 5:00 p.m. – Hebron, Labrador

I slipped off my shoes and set out barefoot. The ground was soft, dry, and spongy. After seventy-five yards I stopped and turned to look out at the rolling hills dotted with fuchsia wildflowers and a picture-perfect bay framed by layers of jagged mountains on all sides. The water was still, a mixture of sapphires, teals, and Arctic blues more striking than the tropics. My heart swelled with emotions, my forearms prickled. This paradise was someone's home; many someones. I felt the very soul of this sacred space. Tears streamed down my face. This paradise fed, taught, and took care of many beautiful humans.

I waded across a tidal flat about two feet deep. My ankles felt as if they had vises on them, my calves screamed, pain shot up into my hamstrings. I couldn't see icebergs, but they were out there. The seafloor was soft sand dotted with large boulders. Thanks to the falling tide, dry boulder-tops jutted through the water's surface. I stepped up onto land again. My legs were bright pink and numb from the knee down. I walked up a small hill; its soft grasses and freshly bloomed fireweed bent in the breeze. I could see out into the Labrador Sea again. My radio crackled. I turned and looked down at my right hip. Green light on, volume at ten. I took a long, deep inhale, head tilted up to the sky.

"Kristy." Joas's voice on my radio startled me out of the bliss moment. "Come back, please."

168.

Emily had shared some Inuit history. As she spoke of colonial policies and their aftermath, the weight of what had been lost in Hebron shook me.

In 1959, just days before the Canadian government and the remaining Moravians forcibly relocated all Inuit to southern communities, the relocation plans were announced during a church service. Church was a special place for Inuit. Out of respect, Inuit did not argue in church. In the spirit of trust and cooperation, Inuit packed their things and boarded boats. They were promised relocation to communities that offered a better life.

When the Inuit of Hebron arrived in their new communities, instead of housing, there were tents, instead of hunting and fishing, there was hunger. Most did not receive their promised education, work, or food. The impact of relocation on Inuit spans generations, resulting in a profound and enduring sense of loss.

William's mother and father lived in Hebron until they were eleven and twelve. On the ferry, I met a small, thin lady who had a big toothless smile. She lived in Hebron as a child and described the beauty and sacredness of it. She had been back to visit, but said it would never be the same.

Another alarming reality is that the Inuktitut language could face extinction. William's generation (those in their late thirties and forties) represents the last to speak Inuktitut daily. Though William addresses his children in Inuktitut, this practice has become increasingly rare. Most youth no longer use the language regularly. Much is being done to revive the language. Elders are providing guidance and there is a renewed interest from younger generations. Without this, Inuktitut may vanish within decades, taking with it centuries of cultural knowledge and perspective that cannot be recovered once lost.

As I listened to these stories of forced displacement, I couldn't help but see the paradox. I had voluntarily left behind my home, my career, and my conventional life to enjoy freedom in movement and impermanence. Inuit had their mobility and connection to land and seasonal rhythms ripped away. What I saw as liberation, they experienced as loss. And yet, I wished for something many Inuit had fought to preserve—a deep sense of belonging. Their loss cast light on the privilege in my wandering. I could return. They couldn't.

169.

Joas's plea, *Come back, please,* made my heart 'bout jump out of my chest.

"Bears go to those islands to feed," Joas said. "It's not safe." After I heard that, I relaxed. He was just being cautious.

While I reached for my radio, I looked out over the undulating hills of bright green and pink that carpeted the small island. Nothing white in any direction.

"Copy. Coming back," I said, as I looked toward the kitchen hut. I couldn't see Joas, but he saw me. I chuckled at my fire-department radio lingo, which was still so ingrained, and then said something I'd never say over a dispatch radio: "Thank you, Joas."

"You are welcome. Just keeping you safe." Joas's voice was kind and mellow with a hint of guilt.

"I really appreciate it. See you in a few minutes."

170.

A nudge opens a tiny crevice in the hull of my ship; a hairline fracture lets truth seep in. I sink to the seafloor. The knife of all things cracks open the clamshell of my soul. The pearl of knowing basks in an eternal light. I am that. I am the wander.

171.

I wander in words. That's how this book gets written.

172.

William knew I enjoyed fishing. He handed me a pole and pointed to a spot a hundred yards away.

"When the tide changes, char swim through that small channel between the pointed rock and the island. Cast there."

I did, then cranked the reel two or three times and BAM! It hit. I reeled in a large Arctic char, a delicacy in many parts of the world. First cast! *This place is a wonderland.*

I asked William to show me how to clean Arctic char the Inuit way. He taught me patiently, but still finished at lightning speed. I stood in awe. "From forty years of cleaning thousands of fish," William said.

We walked to a five-gallon bucket of salt water with a spigot and rinsed our hands.

"Do you want to sleep in the room with Joas, or a tent?" William asked. We stood in a grassy area between two small buildings. Joas slept in one, and the other was the kitchen hut where Emily and Steven slept.

"Either is fine." I squinted to see William. He had shown me the tent earlier. It was square, the size of a small bedroom, had three plywood sleeping tables in a U shape along the perimeter, and a cast-iron stove in the middle. The sun was bright and low behind William. The breeze was already chilly.

"With Joas is safer. He puts plywood with nails over the windows and on the ground in front of the doors at night. You need to know, Joas snores loud."

"Where will you sleep?" I asked. I'm a light sleeper, and I was exhausted.

"I go with you, whichever you choose."

"Let's do the tent."

William smirked. "You're a hard woman!" He laughed.

"Well, if Joas snores, I won't sleep."

"It could be dangerous. A bear can claw through the tent."

"I'll take my chances."

173.

Travel seeps into my bones and changes me forever. I've become a chameleon who blends with my surroundings. I am a bird, free to flit from branch to branch. An orphan with many homes, carried by wonder, wrapped in a blanket of love wherever I land. Each person I spend a moment with alters the hem and fit of my soul. Each landscape carves me like a glacier that transforms plains into lakes. With each breath of biome, fresh life takes root. Each forest and lake pulses through my veins. Each bird flutters my heart.

174.

I love you doesn't even come close to This.

175.

After dinner, William asked if I wanted to walk to the island together. The tidal flat between the island and us was as dry as a bone. He slung his rifle over his shoulder and checked the battery on my radio. We walked a few minutes, then William stopped.

"Where're your shoes?" William said, as he stared at my bare feet in the grass. I hadn't worn shoes since my first walk.

"In the tent." He stood upwind from me. His raw scent of rugged manliness had me wanting to sniff him like a drug dog sniffs luggage. At the same time, his presence stirred something deeper than attraction—a recognition that felt like coming home to what I'd never left.

"Why?"

"I love the feel of soft grass, and it's great for our health to walk in bare feet." We were halfway between camp and the tidal flat. This almost felt like a date.

"Good for health? How?" William tilted his head to the side, his blinking eyes fixed on mine.

"For most of human existence, we walked around on either bare feet or leather." I glanced out at the rolling hills and what was left of the original settlement. "I bet your parents didn't wear rubber-soled shoes when they lived here, right?"

William chuckled. "Yeah, that's right."

"Yeah, our bodies need connection with earth. We exchange electrons through contact with the ground. People used to be in contact with the ground for most of the day, every day and night." Seagulls cawed overhead. William's eyes were still focused on mine. "When we touch the ground, our bodies have less inflammation. We sleep better and we're more relaxed mentally."

We continued walking. William inhaled deep. "You're a hard woman," he said, with a loving grin and a shake of his head.

It had been twelve hours since William and I left the boat ramp in Nain. He'd said "You're a hard woman" at least ten times. The way he said it had shifted. The love and admiration in those four words lit a warm fire in my belly. The way he let me try difficult things, taught, looked after and protected me, and truly wanted me to have the experience of a lifetime ... I'd never been on the receiving end of anything so attractive.

176.

What I miss most about normal life are the simple things I took for granted. My life feels like a 20,000-piece puzzle. More often than not, the pieces fall into place, but it's a lot of work to fix things on my own, find water, find places to live, and find cell service to work. It's much easier to go to sleep in a bed at the same address each night, have access to unlimited water, electricity, internet/phone, and clean clothes anytime. And to have trusted mechanics, doctors, dentists, and grocery stores nearby.

What I love most about wandering is the freedom of being in awe of nature in ways I never imagined. I love connecting with so many people and cultures, and the life-changing insights that come through being open to remembering how little I know.

177.

The mosquitoes attacked as soon as the sun went down. At 9:45 p.m. William and I pulled out our sleeping bags and slipped inside. He took the bunk by the front of the tent, next to the zippered door, and fell asleep on his back with his rifle resting against his hip, the butt on the ground. I found his "guarding the door" chivalrous, though I doubted a polar bear would let itself in with the zipper. Still, a man sleeping with a loaded rifle, ready to protect me from a wild beast … that's pretty darn hot.

I slipped a mosquito net over my head and zipped up my sleeping bag until only my nose was sticking out. Those little buggers were still getting inside the bag. Their buzzing sounded like helicopters. William was already snoring softly.

By 3:30 a.m. I gave up on sleep, slipped out of my bag into icy air, got dressed, unzipped the door slowly, and snuck out. William kept on snoring. There was already enough light to see the whole settlement. I walked around the backside of the kitchen hut and looked for a spot that faced east.

178.

Polar bears are solitary animals. As adults, they prefer to be alone. The only exceptions are when they mate or raise their cubs. Translation: except when they love. They spend most of their life hunting. They will tolerate the company of another if they find food large enough to share, such as the carcass of a whale.

179.

July 21, 4:00 a.m. – Hebron, Labrador
I sat on stony, moss-covered ground and gazed at a sunless pastel sky, jagged mountaintops, and a glassy bay. My back was against a cold rock face; beyond my feet was a patch of still-fuchsia fireweed. Mosquitoes buzzed against the netting draped over my head. I took a deep breath of salty sea air. I wore two jackets, two pairs of pants, and gloves to protect myself from mosquitoes and the Arctic cold. Sand glistened between the mainland and the grassy islands.

Joas would have been worried if he'd known I was outside alone. I stretched my head up above the huge rock face like a prairie dog every few minutes to be sure no polar bears were sneaking up from behind. A colony of seagulls snacked on sea creatures in the tidal flat. A roar of flapping wings lifted the gulls in a unified wave. The flock squawked and fluttered south. Silence flooded in. I soaked in the historic settlement, and the towering Torngat Mountains to my left. Dead ahead, out beyond the safety of the natural inlet and bay, was the Labrador Sea, and beyond that, Greenland.

How did I end up here?

Since leaving the cabin in Georgia, it had been two months of coddiwompling, meeting people, and being given fresh fish—so much that Coddi's freezer was packed to the gills. Then an incredible boat journey into this rugged Arctic paradise. Luck, chance, divine nudging? I could have been working a regular job, living in a regular house, experiencing regular old things. Tears rolled down my cheeks as waves of gratitude and awe washed up on my shores.

180.

Cubs. Me? No, I never had a maternal urge for kids. And I would not force any living being to go through the torture of adolescence.

181.

Gazing at the predawn sea with tears dripping down my cheeks, I admired all this beauty, felt sad for the people who were forced to leave their paradise, and grateful for the kindness and wisdom of my new friends, who, after less than a day, already felt like family.

What I learned from my friends, and from reading about their history, is how Inuit received what they needed from nature. They didn't take like society does today. Indigenous peoples all over the world live in harmony with and learn from nature. They receive. And my goodness gracious does this place give. There were fish waiting to be caught, caribou, berries, and a freshwater stream. The daytime temperature was around seventy-five degrees Fahrenheit, but there was still a humongous chunk of frozen snow (the size of a small house) to use for chilling things too.

Inuit lost an entire way of being and their sacred connection to this place, and they were on a journey to find themselves again. Now I wondered if my journey was really about finding not just any belonging, but the one that called me with such clarity that my soul recognized its voice. Perhaps true freedom wasn't in perpetual movement, but in recognizing when to stop, when to say: here, this one speaks my name.

182.

The Journey
Rough seas whisper truth.
The lure of adventure tingles.
Sunrise brings realization.
I know no fear.

183.

Joas was the first to wake up. At 6:30 a.m. he found me watching the sunrise and invited me on a serene meander to see and hear more about their history. I was astounded by the love and generosity of everyone in Hebron. I wanted to stay to help, learn, and love the people and this land. I would have stayed until the winter sent me south. I hope to someday.

As William and I were in the tent packing up, I asked him, "Have you ever traveled outside of Labrador?"

He froze, one hand in his duffel. "Why? You gonna take me somewhere?" He looked at me with smiling eyes and a cheesy smile, like a little kid asking for a treat. I doubled over in laughter. My goodness, his cuteness!

"Who knows? Maybe." I continued to shove my sleeping bag into its pouch.

"I went to St. John's once for eye surgery."

"And that's it? Nowhere else beyond Goose Bay?"

"No, that's it."

This paradise was his entire universe. Oh, how I'd love to show him the world.

184.

Mating. Me? No. I'm a solitary animal. Sex is making love, thus I need to be in love. I've managed to have two boyfriends, who were both understanding. Jack was the first person I kissed who I also cared about deeply. This poem is about him.

Love Enough
My first real kiss was in my midthirties.
My sweet guy caressed my silken lilies,
as tears dripped down his face.
His eyes were full of affection.
His soft palms cradled my cheek.
We'd dated a year.
I liked him a lot, and wondered if I'd ever love,
let alone love enough to cry.

Wade made it three years in celibacy with me. Before we had intercourse, I wanted us to be in love together. I eventually fell in love with him. He wasn't in love with me and thought sex would help with that.

He popped my cherry when I was almost thirty-eight. Mercy sex. It was meh. He rolled over, lay a foot away, and happy exhaled.

"You wanna go ride bikes?" he said.

Still on my back, bare in the cold, my face flushed as a wave of embarrassment and heartache washed over me. *Bastard!* I dropped my head to the right to look at him. He stood beside the bed, limp dick flopped over, eyebrows raised with a silly smile.

Wade's silly smile was for his bike. *No! I don't want to ride bikes. I want to be loved!*

"OK," I said. *Fucking idiot. You are literally a fucking idiot.*

At least he saved me from being a forty-year-old virgin.

185.

People wonder if I have a house or home base. No, my home base is Coddi. In the US, it's illegal not to have a physical address. So there are domicile companies that cater to full-time travelers. I use a company called St. Brendan's Isle for my official domicile for my businesses and me, and my mail-forwarding service. They collect my mail (I receive ten pieces of mail a year, tops), and whenever I need it, they'll ship my mail anywhere in the world.

Little-known fact: the address on my driver's license is Coddi's license plate number.

186.

July 21, 7:30 a.m. – Labrador Sea, east of Hebron
The picturesque paradise shrunk smaller and smaller behind our wake. Wind howled and the outboard screamed. William stood next to me, hands on the wheel, eyes focused east. I ambush-hugged him. "Thank you for taking me here," I said in a shaky voice, tears welling up again. "Thank you."

Forty-five minutes later, we were flying south on the Labrador Sea when the motor's pitch dropped lower and lower. The boat slowed until our wake caught up, lifted the tail and rolled beneath us. The bow rose, then dipped. William idled to the right and eased us into a fjord. Up ahead, hordes of floating goliaths towered above their own perfect reflections. We motored between and around icebergs, like a slow dance in a ballroom of turquoise giants, their gleaming faces smiling up toward the heavens. In awe, I gazed up, my heart full.

187.

To wander in the wild is to love with reckless abandon.

188.

As we walk our meandering paths, my hand is always waiting for its next chance to hold yours.

189.

A nudge to my shoulder jolted me out of my iceberg ballroom daydream.

"Get your bottle and take this." William handed me his bottle. "Fill them up and touch your iceberg!" He seemed more eager than I was. I scampered to the front of the boat and pressed my hand against the giant. It was solid, slick, smooth, and wet. I leaned in and held my bottle in a crystal-clear icy stream. The deluge of water shoved my hand down.

"Cheers!" We clinked bottles and gulped down ten-thousand-year-old ice-melt.

"Oh me, oh my!" William said, as his eyebrows tilted together in pure delight.

He turned the boat back toward the open water, and we continued dancing with the turquoise giants while we meandered east.

"Give me your phone," William said. We floated beside the edge of another berg. "Go wash your face in that stream and I'll take a video of you."

William waited while I dug in my pocket for my phone.

See the video at: PerfectUnfolding.com/189

As the icy water dripped down my face, something inside me awakened. After years of calculated self-sufficiency, here I was, laughing like a child, fully present in my body, with this rugged and loving man. The last few walls I thought kept me safe felt less necessary, even foolish. What was I protecting myself from? This joy. This connection. This wild, beautiful, imperfect moment.

190.

We die slowly when we become slaves to habit. When we walk worn paths, avoid new colors, silence wonder. When we stop speaking to strangers, numb ourselves with screens, or choose safety over passion to avoid emotions that make our eyes glimmer … this is dying slowly.[7]

191.

William and I shared another seven hours of adventure on the boat ride south. Emily had packed us some pitsik (air-dried char) and nikku (air-dried caribou meat) for lunch. I felt like an honorary Inuit enjoying it.

The seas got rough, and for four hours we stood together, William behind the wheel and I next to him, bent-kneed. Huge waves threw us up and down, like a bucking bronco. Sometimes, my feet left the floor. It was a quad workout for the ages. Two hours into the wild ride, William's satellite safety device buzzed. He asked me to take the wheel. As the boat bucked, he motioned me to slide in front of him. He steadied me, hands on my hips.

"Aim between those two islands," he shouted.

I nodded, and wished he'd stay longer, hold tighter. He stepped to the back and didn't return. I was trying so hard not to smack my face on the wheel, to keep my balance, and to keep us headed straight that I didn't dare look back. After ten minutes, I snuck a peek and saw him leaning against the back seat, bright unblinking eyes on me, a soft smile on his face. I looked forward again. My tummy did a little backflip. I was turning into mush. He didn't come to the front. I imagined him back there, lovingly watching me.

The bow smacked a big wave, and the engine went from screaming to idle. I flew forward like a rag doll, my gut into the wheel, my face almost hitting the windshield. Immediately, William was behind me, left hand on my hip. He held me firm, chest against my back, as he pushed the throttle forward with his right hand.

"You are a hard woman," he said, softer and slower than ever before, his mouth inches from my right ear.

192.

Eating char and caribou is right up my alley. I cook 99 percent of my meals at home. Even on the move, fast food is a no-go. People have asked if I take my rig through drive-thrus. No, I'd end up jumping curbs and whacking Coddi on overhangs. Coddi has a full kitchen: three-burner gas stove, oven, induction cooktop (which my solar and batteries power just fine), full-size fridge and freezer, double sink, and a full complement of spices and condiments. A Corian countertop covers the three-burner stove when it's not in use, giving me triple the workspace. In the summer, the induction cooktop keeps the heat down inside Coddi, and I can use it outside on a folding table. I also use my Vitamix every day for smoothies, vegan ice cream, and more.

When I'm driving, I pull off in a park or parking lot, hop into Coddi, and eat. I wash dishes, leave the plate and silverware in the drying rack, and head down the road. When I'm invited out, I often offer to cook instead. Shared meals—whether cooking together, gathered around a table, or picnicking—foster better conversation and connection. Most restaurants are expensive and the food is disappointing.

193.

Society's got life ass-backward. If a horse breaks its leg, it's put out of its misery. When a dog is losing its functions, the family knows it's better to put it to sleep so it doesn't suffer. Humans; if we know one thing well, it's how to die slowly, in misery and pain. There is no love in this.

194.

To love beyond is to coddiwomple in every little thing: what I eat, what I do, who I share time with, how I play, or even what I wear.

195.

When even the mundane is a wander, there is no dying slowly.
When my body dies, let it go quick. This is true love.

196.

July 21, 3:00 p.m. – Nain, Labrador
The 19' Silver Dolphin floated up to the dock in Nain. I was a different person. I had seen a world I didn't know existed. Perry had been right (#116).

William and I hauled the boat back home, with me perched on the wheel hump in the truck bed. We unloaded our gear, both of us famished.

"We need to set up a website for you," I said to William. We sat at his dinner table with his adult daughter, Jade. His granddaughter, Cecelia, played on the couch.

"Why?" William asked.

"Well, it's almost impossible to find you. I bet your business would take off if people knew you existed."

"But I have a website." William grabbed his phone and thumbed to his Facebook page. "Jade set it up for me."

"Nice, but that's Facebook, not a website."

William looked confused.

In the northern-coast communities, I found that Facebook was the primary means of communication. Since most people outside of Nain didn't have phones, they relied on Facebook Messenger for all their texting, calling, and video calls.

CBC (Canadian Broadcasting Corporation) Radio was often the only source of news. Many people weren't aware of the internet outside of Facebook, which highlights the impact and limitations that a big tech company can have on a society. It was sad and concerning, but not the fault of the people there. William didn't own a computer, but Jade did. She was studying to become a mental health and addictions counselor.

Jade and I spent all Friday evening and Saturday morning setting up a simple website for William's business, AvaniAdventures.com.

197.

Choosing when and how to die is the ultimate freedom. Everything in us, our fabric, is made to keep us alive. To go against our nature, to let go of what we've been taught, and to, on purpose, quiet the body for the final time—that is serious. That is complete love.

No judgment, no sorrow. When darkness knocks, step into the dark.

198.

July 22 – Nain, Labrador

I didn't want to wait three days for the ferry, and then spend another two and a half days on the ferry back to Goose Bay. So, I treated myself to an hour-and-a-half-long direct flight. It cost me $375 and was well worth it.

Part of me wanted more time with William. I felt chemistry. Ever the gentleman, he never crossed any professional boundaries, but I sensed his eyes on me, his admiration and attraction in how close he stood and how he lingered. The knowing kept coming to me, though: *This isn't part of my journey.*

I went back and forth between wanting it to be and listening to my gut that said otherwise. On Saturday afternoon, Jade, William, and Cecelia drove me to the airstrip. We hugged, snapped a parting photo, and I was off. One of the hardest parts of my journey is saying goodbye. What a place to realize the strength of the human spirit and to be embraced by loving-kindness. Everyone's thoughtfulness blew me away, especially that of my Nain and Hebron family.

The plane to Goose Bay felt smaller than it was, as if the emptiness beside me had weight and substance. As Nain disappeared beneath the clouds, I felt an unexpected hollowness. I'd spent years learning to embrace the freedom of goodbye, but something about this parting felt unfinished, like putting down a book mid-chapter. I told myself it was simply the magic of the north, the spell of icebergs and ancient shores. But the truth whispered something deeper as I flew south, away from possibilities I hadn't allowed myself to fully imagine.

199.

To my brothers and sisters who suffer: I see and hear you. I love you. I am you. I am not a slave to the habits of the world. I am free. You and I, we are the same. We find peace as we leap into the darkness from which we came. My loves, we are the trailblazers, the true sages of our time.

200.

I will never die slowly.

201.

My life is a continuous dabble in newness. What a wild, glorious way to romp about in this nutty world. I've tasted the freedom of knowing I am along for the ride, and all I ever want to do from now until forever is saddle up the horses and hold on tight.

202.

Then there was the feeling, a knowing I tried to ignore. A deep sense of the familiar pulling our hearts together. Asking us to realize again, to admit the truth, to say *yes* to all there is. When all there is, is This: *Hello Love, there you are … So nice to see you again.*

203.

Places find me. I don't decide where to travel. I am on a great meander. The dots get connected. When I hear about places, or am invited to some-one's home or on an adventure, I am open. When I know to say "No, thank you," I do. Otherwise my answer is yes.

I follow the tickles of my soul. Some call that intuition. I am curious. When people notice my curiosity, they often share more than they normally would. Where to go next eventually arrives. Everything is a surprise when I welcome the unknown with open arms.

204.

We are naturally curious, but for the idea that we aren't.

205.

July 22, 3:00 p.m. – Goose Bay, Labrador
The family who'd invited me to the campfire after Daniele and Fabien gave me that first fish (#54) lived in Goose Bay. Darren and Heather had insisted I reach out when I was in town.

Casper and Coddi had waited faithfully at the ferry dock in Goose Bay while I was on the Hebron adventure. Since I'd flown back to Goose Bay, I'd need a ride from the airport to the ferry dock, and there were no taxis.

I messaged Darren and Heather. They were excited to give me a lift! On the fifteen-minute drive, Darren said he'd checked on my rig a few times after seeing my Facebook post about my adventure on the ferry. Wow, that really touched me.

Heather and Darren dropped me off at Coddi, and I invited them to hang out at my campsite over the next few days, even though I had no clue where I'd be. As I was leaving the ferry dock, a man in a green pickup stopped to say hello and welcome me to town. Half an hour later, I was in the tackle-shop parking lot when the same green truck pulled up beside me. Robert asked if I needed help with anything. He was about sixty and had a strong accent that seemed part Scottish or Irish and part something else. I asked him for some local fishing tips, and went on my merry way.

206.

Something shifts deep within when I accept that I live in the unknown. My brain still clings to its ideas of what *should* or *might* happen, but when I lean into the truth that I don't know, the edges of my imagination soften. I walk with more purpose and less force. Expectation gives way to openness, and I meet each moment as it is.

207.

How do you keep yourself safe and do you have a gun?

I've been kept safe. Part of this is street-smarts; the rest is listening to a feeling I find difficult to describe. In seven years, I haven't felt threatened or in danger. No guns now, but for the first two years I kept a handgun and a rifle in Coddi's wardrobe closet, in cases and unloaded. Taking a gun to Canada requires a lot of paperwork, and hauling them around was too much of a hassle.

Street-smart examples—I do little things to camouflage my single-ness. I put two chairs and two pairs of shoes outside to suggest a couple. Occasionally, if I'm somewhere that seems a little iffy, I'll say "we" instead of "I" when talking with people. When I'm out in the bush and there's an

RV nearby with friendly-looking folks, I'll walk up and say hello. I enjoy chatting with people, and most people I meet are caring and we look after each other. When hiking in grizzly territory, I carry bear spray. I keep a wood billy club and a can of hornet spray in Coddi.

Listening to my gut examples—When a place doesn't feel safe, I trust that feeling and leave. Sometimes, halfway down a road, something shifts in my chest—a quiet alarm that says *turn around*.

The first time this happened was in 2018, west of Sedona. I was headed to a desert boondocking spot for a week. As I tootled down the highway, about twenty minutes out, that familiar tightness crept in. Not fear, but a gentle insistence. I kept driving, waiting for clarity. Instead, the feeling grew stronger. I pulled over on the dusty shoulder, engine ticking in the heat, checked the map, and found another spot. I still wonder what might've happened if I'd kept going.

208.

July 22, 6:30 p.m. – Gosling Lake, Labrador
Thanks to iOverlander, I found a perfect lakeside boondocking spot just outside of town. A few hours later, Robert knocked on my door and gave me two huge lake-trout fillets, caught since I last saw him, and a bag of four frozen cod fillets. That's ten fish received in a few weeks from strangers and new friends. I hadn't told Robert where I was staying, so when he was at my door, something inside me whispered, "Not good. Not good." I wasn't scared or threatened, but a man appearing three times in one afternoon felt strange. Granted, the extremely caring and helpful culture in Labrador was different from what I was used to. My heebie-jeebies might have been caused by my conditioned thought process about what's normal. If Robert had been with a woman, I doubt I would have felt any heebie-jeebies. It was the single-man thing. Whether men see it or not, women live on guard in most public places, and some private places too. It's a fact of life in our culture. I hope that changes someday.

Since my Spidey sense was on high alert, I shooed Robert off after a quick conversation. He went happily on his way, which was a good sign. William called while I was talking with Robert. My heart fluttered when I saw his name, but something told me not to answer or call back. There was too much left unsaid, and we were too close in distance for me to admit what my heart wanted me to admit. Instead, I sent a message and wished him a wonderful evening.

This isn't part of my journey. This isn't my journey. This isn't. I can't. My knowing was clear: a romantic relationship with William wasn't right for me, and I knew to trust that inner wisdom. Besides that, the idea of living so far from my family was unimaginable. Plus, fresh vegetables and unprocessed foods were hard to come by on the northern Labrador coast (aside from wild game). That was a deal-breaker. I could go on. Truth is, I just knew.

After Robert left, I messaged Darren and Heather to invite them over on Saturday to enjoy Robert's cod in the form of fish tacos. I ran into Robert at a museum three days later. He was repairing the building. We were surprised to see each other. We shared a bear hug and I thanked him again for the fish.

209.

If I'd have known, I'd have bathed in love, like a daisy bathes in sunshine. With every fiber of my being, I would have bloomed and stretched toward warmth. I'd have loved as a momma bear loves, with tender fierceness. I'd have shown my teeth and roared when needed, snuggled on chilly nights, and frolicked in summer fields of berries. If I'd have known, I would not have hidden my tears and myself for decades. I would not have walked alone. If I'd have known, I'd have quit society long before becoming another cog in the wheel. I'd have taken better care of my body and kept my childlike love of life for all my years. I'd never have stopped loving myself. I would've had no fear. If I'd have known, I'd have hugged, made love, and never judged myself or another.

210.

July 25 – North West River, Labrador

This is where the road ends on the east coast of North America. I followed a gravel path up a small hill with a view of the bay and camped at the northernmost spot you can drive to along the Atlantic coast. Later, I rode my bike around town and ended up at the docks. I sat down, legs hanging over the edge, and a man pulled up in a small boat. He had just caught three salmon and seemed excited to tell me all about it—probably because I was the only one there. I congratulated him and asked how he'd caught them. He leaves a net stretched out, hoping salmon will swim through. His family has fished the same spots for generations.

"Since the water is so warm, I have to check my nets every few hours." He had loaded his boat on a trailer, and I stood beside it.

"When are you headed out next?"

"Oh, about six o'clock."

"Can I come with you?"

He smiled. "Be here at six. I'll bring an extra life jacket."

That's how adventures and new friends happen in this heavenly place. An hour later, I got a text from Jade, William's daughter.

> Look what I just noticed
> [photo of my Columbia button-up sun shirt hanging in Cecelia's bedroom]

> Oh shoot!

With my pale skin, that shirt was a lifesaver.

> Could you mail it to Newfoundland for me?

> Sure!

She sent it to a post office near Gros Morne National Park.

211.

I have an open invitation to close friends to join my coddiwomple. Several have come along for a few days, up to a week, both male and female. Each visit has been its own adventure.

My mom has traveled with me many times. She flew out west for three weeklong visits between 2018 and 2019. Since 2020, she's joined me on at least ten trips in the Southeast for a week or two, and in 2022 we jaunted up to see the fall colors in New England for a month.

The most notable of adventures I've had with anyone was in 2021, when Mom came along on what she thought would be a month or two journey out to Colorado. We left her house in North Florida in late May. We ended up making it to California, back through Idaho, to the Grand Tetons in Wyoming, up to Montana to Yellowstone. She coddiwompled with me for a very special three months. My stepfather had died less than a year before, and Mom's health wasn't great. She needed a respite and a reset. Being out in nature, taking daily walks, and meeting new and interesting people brought so much life back into her life. I loved being with her while she experienced this wandering existence with me in a way no one had before.

212.

Long Walk
Bare feet, pant cuffs soaked with sea foam,
sand unblemished thanks to a long evening storm.
The sun took her sweet time.
She stretched, yawned, and snuggled into her blanket of clouds.
A ray at a time she said, "Good morning, Loves," in a whisper
to the gulls, the family of deer that left their tracks in the sand,
the sandpipers scurrying along the wave-breaks,
the jellyfish, lucky to wash up the moment her sunbeams landed,
before being whisked off to the deep again,
to the crabs scurrying to and fro,
to the waves lapping up and back,
and to me, as I stroll, toes wet and cold, ankles crusted in sand.

213.

July 2021 – National forest south of Steamboat Springs, Colorado
"This is …" Mom said. She inhaled deep as she stared at an ocean of mountains; half a bronze fireball hung behind the furthest peak. Mom seemed lost for words. We sat in camp chairs beside Coddi. Purple lupines, fuchsia fireweed, and yellow wildflowers swayed in a cool breeze. "Now I understand why you live like this."

We were at the top of the highest peak, at over 10,000 feet. We'd been camping there for six nights. The Fourth of July campers had left and we were relaxing into the peacefulness and beauty of this place in solitude.

"I can't believe we get to live here," she said. "This is amazing."

Mom and I had settled into a rhythm of living together in close quarters. We were seven weeks into our three-month journey. This was the first time someone had stayed long enough to fully appreciate this lifestyle. There comes a point when it stops feeling like a vacation, when there's no rush to move on or see the next thing.

214.

When I slow down to the speed of life, soak in the sensuality of nature, fall back into the knowing of who I am, and how infinitely linked everything is—it becomes obvious. The whole point of life is the experience of being alive.

215.

July 26, 7:00 a.m. – North West River, Labrador
A thunderstorm had rolled through the night before and shook the shine right off the walls. This sandy spot at the top of the hill was the turning point. When my wheels rolled today, it would mark the start of a long, long, long meander south. Where I was headed beyond Newfoundland was unclear, but I'd promised Mom I'd be in Florida by Thanksgiving. There would be many winding roads ahead.

Today was the day I would drive the longest stretch of the Trans-Labrador

Highway. After fueling up in Goose Bay, I'd be southbound with the hammer down.

216.

If I need something shipped while I'm traveling, there are several options. If the item is shipped via the postal service (either in the US or Canada), I can have it sent to almost any post office "general delivery." The post office will hold the item for thirty days. This is how the address looks:

Kristy Halvorsen
General Delivery
TOWN NAME, STATE/PROVINCE
ZIP CODE

If the item is shipped via UPS or FedEx, I can ask a local UPS, FedEx, or private postal store if they'll accept delivery for me. They usually do for $5 to $10.

When I'm far from stores and an item is shipped via UPS or FedEx, I reach out to a local person either on Boondockers Welcome or in the Airstream Club. I introduce myself, share the situation, and ask if they'd be up for receiving a package for me. That works too.

217.

July 26 – Trans-Labrador Highway
I drove 260 miles on a narrow two-lane road from Goose Bay to Port Hope Simpson. No towns, gas stations, buildings, cell service, or houses. Trees, lakes, rivers, and rolling verdant hills stretched to forever in all directions. In all my wandering, I'd never been in such pristine nature. My throat tightened as I realized: *This is how the world once was before we carved it up.*

218.

It's a mystery to me
We have a greed, with which we have agreed

219.

The locals had warned me about this stretch. Most vehicles towing trailers strap extra fuel jugs to their roof. Casper's 32-gallon tank would make the journey with at least one hundred miles to spare. For over an hour, I didn't pass another soul.

220.

You think you have to want more than you need
Until you have it all you won't be free

221.

I rolled along in silence, windows down, as waves of pine scent washed over me. After a couple of hours, I played my only downloaded album—the soundtrack to *Into the Wild*. When my favorite road song, "Society," began, something cracked open inside me. I pressed repeat, each verse striking deeper than the last, as if the lyrics had been waiting for this exact moment and place.

222.

Society, you're a crazy breed
I hope you're not lonely without me

223.

Tears streamed down my face, for everything lost, for everything still here but vanishing, for the arrogance of progress, for the beauty that once covered our entire planet. Overwhelmed with emotion, I hoped for a shoulder to pull onto, somewhere to stop and write. But there was no place for pause, just like in the world we've built. All I could do was drive and hope I'd remember all these feelings.

224.

When you want more than you have, you think you need

225.

After almost four hours I rolled up on a dirt pull-off just big enough for my rig. I hit the brakes hard, swung open the door, and pulled down my shorts and panties in one motion. Oh, the relief!

I strolled toward the forest and tilted my head back. Sunlight drenched my face. For a few deep breaths, I marinated in blue sky and evergreen scent. Then I heard it, a river roaring. I bushwhacked through thick shrubs until I caught a peek: chocolate waters tumbling over rapids, massive flat boulders, and smooth, quick-moving water further down. So much for writing. This river begged me to fish.

226.

And when you think more than you want, your thoughts begin to bleed

227.

Mosquitoes were thick and ferocious. I pulled on my head net, grabbed my pole, and cast my line until evergreen shadows stretched further into the river. Out here, darkness belonged to the moose and I needed to be off the road soon. I climbed back up the boulders, pushed through forest to my rig, and set off on the last stretch.

228.

I think I need to find a bigger place
'Cause when you have more than you think, you need more space

229.

For a moment, I felt one with this untouched world. Places like this are disappearing, and once scarred by humans, virgin land can never return to innocence. The thought of going back to society, to noise and concrete and the relentless want of things, left me hollow—like trying to fit back into clothes that no longer belonged to my body. This was freedom: blue skies, white clouds, green hills stretching into forever. I realized I was driving through the colors of the Labrador flag: blue, white, and green. Blue and green have been my favorite colors since I was a kid.

230.

Society, you're a crazy breed
I hope you're not lonely without me

231.

Driving without cell service or radio creates a different kind of presence, just the hypnotic rhythm of a slender blacktop with its yellow line snaking up and down. I thought about the familiar five-hour drive between South and North Florida: cities, towns, barns, pastures, fence lines, stores, billboards, and intersecting highways. Without this experience in untouched wilderness, I couldn't have imagined a place where you could drive for five hours and see no signs of humans. What a gift that a place like this exists.

232.

Society, crazy indeed
I hope you're not lonely without me

233.

The silence became its own music. I felt grateful that the podcasts I'd thought I'd downloaded weren't there after all. Being wrapped in the quiet of this grand expanse felt like an offering—a clearing in the cluttered mind. When I was drawn to hear something other than the wind, only one song would do.

234.

There's those thinking, more or less, less is more
But if less is more, how you keeping score?

235.

Most of the world sleepwalks through profound confusion, believing that having is the path to being. Somehow I was lucky enough to fall out of that collective hypnosis. To see the cage for what it was; to find the door standing open.

236.

Means for every point you make, your level drops
Kinda like you're starting from the top
You can't do that

237.

If only everyone could step outside the bubble of normal and marinate in pure nature, just once.

238.

Society, you're a crazy breed
I hope you're not lonely without me
Society, crazy indeed
I hope you're not lonely without me

239.

If only everyone could see with fresh, untainted eyes how ridiculous "modern life" is, and how insane our economy of consumption is. I'm not immune; I'm tainted too. Part of me still longs to leave all technology behind, to shed every trace of greed and lack, to let go of every ounce of selfishness.

240.

Society, have mercy on me
I hope you're not angry if I disagree
Society, crazy indeed
I hope you're not lonely …

Without me[8]

241.

With each person I meet and each unspoiled scene I soak in, my vision clears a little more.

242.

I'm staring at empty lines on a page. Ideas have run dry. I wait for the pen to move. Each word a surprise. My mind is empty. Hang around and see. Patience. Something will come.

Until the ink runs dry, and I write with my blood.

243.

I let my clothes tell me when it's time to change things up: I wear them until they stink or have stains. My closet is about two feet wide, but I can go a month or more before laundry time. Panties are my limiter. I have thirty pairs of knickers. Undies for each day of the month. True freedom is a drawer full of drawers.

Sometimes it's hard to find a laundromat in the bush. When I run out of panties, I pull out two red buckets and a toilet plunger that has never graced a toilet. Boil water, add soap, plunge the panties, rinse, hang dry. Good to go for another few weeks. Simple.

244.

July 27 – Mary's Harbour, Labrador
As I hung my laundry on a makeshift line outside Coddi, I caught myself imagining what it would be like to stay in Nain. Not just to have William's washing machine at my disposal, but to have his smile greet me in the morning, to explore the northern wilds together. And yet, something deeper than attraction or compatibility was at stake—freedom, and the journey I wasn't finished traveling. The simplicity of washing clothes in red buckets somehow felt safer.

Over the past seven years, I'd liked a few guys and enjoyed their company, but I hadn't fallen for someone in this way. William checked on me via Facebook Messenger. He asked how I was, where I was, shared what he was up to. William never expressed his feelings, yet his texts were playful and loving, and there were heart emojis.

245.

Time zones in Newfoundland and Labrador are straight up nutty. Quebec runs on Eastern Time, most of Labrador uses Atlantic Time (Eastern +1 hour), but Newfoundland has its own weird half-hour zone (Eastern +1.5 hours).

To add a lil twist, the southeast coast of Labrador follows Newfoundland Time, while the ferry terminal from Labrador to Newfoundland sits just inside Eastern Time. This is where most people start scratching their head, making the sign of the cross, and praying somehow they won't miss the ferry.

246.

I adore you and appreciate your love and care, the unique ways you show it, how you gently hold space, and allow me to experience all of This, all of you, and all of myself.

247.

July 28 – Mary's Harbour, Labrador
A typical day (if there is such a thing) goes something like this.

I woke up in Mary's Harbour and continued south to Red Bay National Historic Site to tour the Basque whale hunter museum. After strolling through the museum, I took a boat ride to Saddle Island. There was a little old man at the front of the boat who invited me to sit with him. His thin frame took up half the slick white fiberglass bench seat in the crook of the boat's bow, which left just enough room for me to squeeze in next to him.

"I'll sit next to you," I said. "But only if we can cuddle." From the get-go, his smile had a hint of mischief. I sat next to him.

"I worked here for thirty years," he said. "Retired yesterday."

Turns out, he was born and raised on the little island we were motoring to. His family ran the lighthouse until the 1970s and continued to live there. In the 1990s, he started working for the national historic site. He had to retire because his eightieth birthday was the day before.

After strolling around the island, I saw the man waiting for the boat at the dock. He held a plastic bag. We sat together in the bow again.

"What's in your bag?" We were cruising across the bay, toward the museum.

"Rhubarb." He opened it to show me bunches of crimson stalks topped with large crisp green leaves. "I had a garden at the lighthouse. My family tended it for many decades. It's part of the park now, but I still tend to it and reap the benefits."

That sweet fella was the living history of Red Bay National Historical Site.

Back in Coddi, I had a client meeting on Zoom, then drove to the Tracy Hill and Boney Shore trailhead, where I wrote an article for the Airstream Club magazine. At the trailhead, I met Matt, who was loading a long kayak on his car. He'd spotted my rig several times on the Trans-Labrador Highway over the past couple of weeks. Apparently Coddi and I were becoming local celebrities on that remote stretch of road. After my hike, I parked for the night at Point Amour Lighthouse. The next day brought more work and trip research for Newfoundland.

At 9:20 a.m., Matt knocked on my door. What a surprise. We toured the lighthouse together, and then I walked some seaside trails on my own. As I reached the parking lot, Matt was about to leave. He was going to the end of the road in Quebec, while I had a reserved spot on the 3:30 p.m. ferry to Newfoundland. We said our goodbyes again.

248.

In 2022, I began writing for a print magazine called *Blue Beret*, which is sent to over 20,000 members of Airstream Club International. I've been blogging on my website since 2016, and had a few articles published in a variety of places, but until working with *Blue Beret*, I'd never had a monthly deadline and editors. It's been an experience that has helped me broaden my horizons in writing, get real-time feedback from readers, and hone the craft of offering engaging articles that both entertain and educate.

249.

July 29, 1:45 p.m. – L'Anse au Clair, Labrador

Casper's "low fuel" warning had been flashing for fifteen miles when I parked at the Northern Lights Inn to return the satellite phone. It hadn't occurred to me that several towns in Southern Labrador wouldn't have diesel. "Where is the next diesel station on the way to the ferry?" I asked the receptionist. We stood in a lobby with that same sickly sweet, musty scent of old buildings as the hotel where I'd picked up the phone.

"You're gonna need to drive back north to find diesel," she said, without looking up, as she thumbed through a stack of paperwork. "There's none between here and the ferry." Behind her were racks filled with souvenir sweatshirts, jackets, and T-shirts. "Here it is. You'll need to sign and date here."

She took the yellow phone case to a back room and disappeared.

I had to check in at the ferry dock in thirty-five minutes or I'd lose my spot. The dock was ten minutes away. I looked up gas stations in Blanc-Sablon, the town where the ferry was, and called each. One had diesel.

250.

Some think my life of coddiwompling is one big risk. I live in the forest where anyone could find me and have their way. I hike and bike in treacherous areas, without cell service, and no one knows. I become friends with strangers, and they invite me into their homes. Funny thing is, I don't find my life risky at all. In seven years, I haven't been afraid of physical harm. Sure, things have startled me occasionally. But being scared? Genuine fear? Not one bit. If my mind isn't filled with desires, there's not much to be afraid of. I live. If in living, my body dies, well, that happens to all of us. What will be will be, and the more at peace and in love I am, the more people will feel love for themselves and everyone else.

251.

July 29, 2:15 p.m. – Blanc-Sablon, Quebec
I made it to the gas station on fumes. The diesel in Quebec was half again as much as it was in Labrador. I got three liters, enough to roll the dice on a better price in Newfoundland.

252.

I risk everything, I risk nothing, all at the same time.

253.

July 29, 3:00 p.m. – Blanc-Sablon, Quebec
Rap! Rap! Rap!

I jumped. Someone had banged on my passenger window while I was waiting in line to board the ferry. I rolled down the window.

"Hey there!" a man said. "I changed my mind and got a ticket for the ferry late tonight." Buckets of rain were pummeling him and I couldn't tell who he was. He was in a gray rain parka. "Maybe I'll see you in Newfoundland."

Oh, it was Matt, the kayak guy. Clearly he wanted to get in the truck and chat, but my passenger seat was full of bags and jackets, and everything was now soaked.

"Great, I'll see you there!"

With that, he disappeared into the downpour and I sopped up water with a hoodie I found lying in the back seat.

254.

The more time I spend in nature, far away from the distractions of modern life, the more I sink into the way we once lived—one with the mother, one with God, one with everything.

255.

I am beyond grateful for, and in wonder with, you.

256.

The rugged trek from Baie-Comeau, Quebec, up QC-389, through the entire Trans-Labrador Highway, to the ferry to Newfoundland isn't for the faint of heart. Your rig must be fully self-contained. You must be mechanically sound. You'll likely need repairs, and if it's broke, you fix it. If you need a part, good luck. Come prepared and be prepared to think like MacGyver. Many times I was thankful I had collected so many tools and supplies over the years. They came in handy!

257.

When I met the little old man with his rhubarb, that was wild-eyed love. The wave of love arrived in an innocent joke that instantly bonded our hearts and grew into friendship. I was in awe of a life story so simple, and amazing. Eighty years tending to an island, and he still had a love and care that ran deeper than most can dream. I'll never see him again, but he's changed my life forever, and maybe, given how our hearts cuddled on those two boat rides, maybe that changed him too. We need more love like this, in us and among us. Not butterfly and unicorn twitterpated love, or forced love. We need more genuine love. Tenacious, impartial, daring, wild-eyed, everyday, soul-freeing love.

258.

Yes. I'll have a bottomless helping of that, please.

Maybe love between a man and an island can transform all of us. Maybe he's proof.

259.

Even though I am often alone, I don't feel lonely at all.

For most of my first year on the road, I drowned in a pit of loneliness and regret. Then Life lured me far away from humans: into forests, mountains, and remote deserts. In these serene spaces I found clarity about our true nature (that is, who we are at our spiritual core) and recognized the interconnectedness of everything.

A significant insight struck me on February 28, 2019. I've nicknamed it "the Poof." I was sitting in bed replying to an email from a client when I typed something I didn't know was true:

"Marinate in wisdom all you can. Be gentle with yourself when you think you haven't. And wonder if it's possible that life is playing out the only way it can."

As if the keyboard were hot, I jerked my hands away.

The last sentence was what grabbed me.

My whole world flipped on its head. *What appears to be choice is the whole universe expressing itself.*

Every thought, action, sensation, feeling, perception, and "decision" flows from all that is: the energy of everything. Thinking that I—as in, a separate individual—am in control is an illusion. I get to have the experience of making choices, and at the same time I can just live, without judgment or blame. Everything is unfolding just as it is. In this understanding, I am completely free to live.

This is also a sacred invitation to feel compassion for everything and everyone, including myself. Even my struggles are a flawless experience, an expression of Life itself. Before this moment, I had often judged myself and others, putting labels on feelings and experiences. When everything revealed itself as divine creation, I realized I can't get life wrong. I can follow the tickles of my soul in all ways.

For years, I'd been encouraged to believe that there were two voices within me: deep knowing (my intuition, or "tickles of my soul"), which I'd labeled as "good" divine nudges; and wild thoughts full of "shoulds" and stress, which I'd labeled as "bad" personal thinking. The Poof expanded my understanding beyond this belief. All of it is divine. Whether I follow what feels like messier thinking or deeper knowing, it's all part of the great unraveling.

When the Poof happened, loneliness, fear, worry, and regret vanished. If everything is a universal unfolding, worry makes no sense. What will be will be, regardless of my imagined futures. The same goes for the past. It's just what happened. So, no reason to regret. All urges to seek something better or different vanished.

Thinking quieted and life became remarkably clear. *There is one energy that is us: people, animals, nature ... the whole universe.* Loneliness became impossible because separation itself was just a belief.

Another interesting twist was I no longer felt angry. It became ridiculous to blame anything or anyone. "They know not what they do" took on a whole new depth. How can I be angry with someone for being lived by Life? I might feel sad for humanity or heartbroken for people's pain. I can even experience anger bubble up. But whenever I am mad at someone, in short order I remember truth and the anger dissolves. What most call "forgiveness" happens naturally, without needing to try.

"You fell into a pool of nonduality," a friend said, after I tried to explain what I'd experienced. "Without searching or trying, you fell in."

I Googled "nonduality." *We are not two.* Yeah, that put words to it.

At first, when people asked if I was lonely on the road, I was hesitant to tell them I would never feel lonely again. It felt too good to be true. But this was my direct experience. I've come to know direct experience is my greatest, and only, teacher. After all these years with zero loneliness, I know it's true.

260.

July 29 – Gulf of St. Lawrence
During the final half hour on the ferry crossing, I spoke to Charles. He'd lived in Labrador his whole life, and in Goose Bay for several decades.

"Have you been to Hebron?" I asked. We stood on the deck at the front of the ferry. Charles was Inuit or Innu, but I was too self-conscious to ask which. A gold condom wrapper lay on the deck next to his right foot. *What's with ferries, condoms, and me?* The waves were so tall we held on to the railing to keep our balance. Honking from car alarms blasted out from the floor below.

"No," he said. "I keep meaning to get up to Hebron. I haven't made it yet." We both flinched as sea spray splashed us. He was dressed as if he were meeting someone for a nice dinner, shiny black leather shoes and all, but he didn't seem to mind getting wet.

I felt privileged and spoiled that I'd been in Labrador for a few weeks and had already made the journey. He appeared old enough to have been born in Hebron. Charles was curious about what I'd seen and how I'd gotten there. He seemed open and able to go. Maybe our chat turned the tides for him.

261.

Rarely do we see our own backyards through the eyes of wonder. Either those special places lose their luster because we can visit them anytime we wish, or we keep saying we'll go and never take action. Humans have a knack for "somedaying" our lives away: Someday I'll take my kid fishing; Someday I'll visit that park/museum/scenic vista/trail/great restaurant/historic site. Someday I'll take that class; I'll leave space to create something special; I'll visit my parents. Someday I'll let myself fall in love. Then life slips away, leaving an empty space in memories where life's golden geese could have landed, had they been given space and a chance.

262.

Compared to the person who took that Quebec-Labrador border photo, I felt freer, wilder, and more connected to the land and its people. I'd experienced tenderness—in William's care, in the warmth of strangers who became family. My heart overflowed with love for this journey and for the man who had kindled a passionate fire within. I had gone north hoping for an adventure and left with a heart broken wide open.

Part Three:
Navigating Survival in
Newfoundland

Newfoundland would test me in ways I hadn't anticipated. What began as exploration became survival. The island's ancient rock, weathered by centuries of Atlantic storms, mirrored something essential in me—a strength born not from resisting life's challenges but from moving with them, becoming both stronger and more malleable.

263.

I guessed a month would be plenty of time to explore Newfoundland. The island's land area is 42,031 square miles: slightly larger than the state of Tennessee. Newfoundland is packed full of history, rugged beauty, tiny coves, unique landscapes, thousands of smaller islands, and over 120,000 moose. Same as in Labrador, the rule is this: be off the road by dark. Death by moose accident is all too common in Newfoundland.

264.

July 29, 5:15 p.m. – St. Barbe, Newfoundland
I hauled my home on wheels off the ferry and onto the island of Newfoundland, which locals endearingly call "the Rock." A gas station selling diesel was a third of a mile from the dock. Here, it was over a dollar per gallon cheaper than in Quebec. My gamble saved me at least $40.

"How's fuel prices back to Lab City?" a semitruck driver asked. With his hand still on the trigger filling his rig, he craned around the side of the pump. He wore a stained and faded navy-blue jumpsuit with yellow reflective bands on the ankles and sleeves.

"You better squeeze in every drop you can here."

"They right high?" He had that same accent as Robert, which I found difficult to understand. Storm clouds muted the evening sun.

"Goose Bay is a bit more expensive," I said. "It's been a long while since I was in Lab City."

As I got in my truck, I saw the satellite-phone return form on my dashboard. July 12 was the pickup date. It had been seventeen days since I crossed into Labrador and drove through Lab City. It seemed like a lifetime ago.

I pushed through the rain toward the northern peninsula. I'd been searching for fresh vegetables for over three weeks, and hoped Newfoundland would deliver. At the one store along the way, the produce looked like casualties of war: wilted, bruised, defeated. I strolled out with a mercy purchase: one block of goat cheese.

I found a tiny isthmus between Burnt Cape Ecological Reserve and Raleigh. Coddi sat perfectly positioned: sea behind me, bay in front, and my bedroom and office windows overlooked a weathered graveyard. Before bed, I snapped a photo of the view and texted Mom: "I'm snuggled up with a bunch of buried old skin suits." I thought about her every day and missed her dearly. The wind howled and rocked Coddi all night.

265.

1989 – Tallahassee, Florida

It was my eleventh birthday. Mom had planned a little celebration, and she'd made a cake and bought some of my favorite treats. I loved football, especially Florida State. That morning, someone gave my best friend's dad killer tickets to the big game—the last of the season, and it was against our archrivals. They invited me. We were poor. Never in my wildest dreams. *Go? To THIS game? What?? Best birthday gift ever.*

I didn't go. "We can have cake when you get back," Mom said. I was in tears. No one understood. It wasn't the cake I loved with every part of me. I didn't want to miss a moment with Mom, much less an entire special afternoon. Love. True love. The greatest love story of my life started in the womb.

266.

July 30, 7:30 a.m. – Raleigh, Newfoundland
The weather cleared before daybreak. I rode my bicycle to the ecological reserve, pedaling up a muddy gravel drive past quaint and colorful seaside homes, piles of fishing nets, bright purple and yellow wildflowers, and old wooden boats in the bay. The road swung left and wound up, up, up. Potholes the size of MINI Coopers riddled the road. At the top, the land was flat rocks and gravel carpeted with patches of pint-sized plants and dwarf evergreens. I locked my bike to a stunted, scraggly, fragrant spruce and set off, overwhelmed by the beauty that flooded my senses. Tears welled up.

I sat on a cliff's edge and typed this into my phone.

But a Dream
This jungle of miniature plants,
a plush carpet of greens and golds under my bum,
and little violet bells that jiggle with each puff of wind.
Does everything grasp bedrock?
Or are their roots in a dreamy Neverland?
Waves thunder and crash, roll up and over rocks,
and gather in crystal pools that kiss the cliff's edge.
Sea air, cold and damp, blows against my right cheek.
A gull glides with grace, held by breezes that caress the back of my
     hands.
My palms on my knees, which rest over my feet,
which press against the same jungle of tiny plants, inches from the
     edge.

A cliff drops to a rock face that is caressed by turquoise waves,
that crash and tumble white as snow,
then melt back into the sea of love that warms my soul.
This world of mist and dreams holds more truth than reality.
If I am alive in flesh and form, if salt air tickles my cheeks,
if beauty as rich as this does exist ...
I'll breathe it in, and breathe again,
until my waves of breath return to the sea of all that is.
This sea that I am.

267.

July 30, 11:00 a.m. – Raleigh, Newfoundland

After the reserve, I zoomed back to Coddi, scarfed down lunch, and then rode to Treena's Trail in Cape Onion. On the way, a restaurant advertising a $20 "pick your own lobster from the bay" dinner caught my eye. I stopped to inquire. The shoebox of a building was a restaurant, convenience store, gas station, hotel office, and post office. A guy inside said the restaurant shut down a couple weeks back because the cook quit. No lobster dinner.

"If you head toward L'Anse aux Meadows, my dad makes a killing selling moose burgers and cod plates." He sat at a disheveled desk squeezed into what looked like a closet. Someone had to have built the desk inside that room. He leaned back in his chair and looked up at me.

"I'm headed that way tomorrow. Where is it?"

"It's called the Viking Inn. You can't miss it. Dad owns the inn and restaurant."

I continued riding to Treena's Trail and saw a speed limit sign on a long two-lane paved road that read MAXIMUM 60. Below it, a wooden plank was nailed to the post. On it, IF U DARE was scrawled in thick black paint. *Note: 60 kilometers per hour equals 37 miles per hour.* I laughed out loud. I'd been in Newfoundland for less than one tooth-jarring day and already knew this sign said everything that needs to be said about Newfoundland's roads.

268.

Leaving normal life required tough choices about what to bring. Two bicycles and my kayak made the cut; all three live in Casper. I ride my bikes often, at least twice a week. My recumbent road bike usually gets double the action of the mountain bike, but I never used it once in Quebec or Newfoundland and Labrador. Ice heaves, potholes, cracks, and rough chip-seal meant my mountain bike was the only choice.

269.

Finding clean food on the road means balancing fresh with practical. I prefer local markets, regenerative farms, and stores with organics, though they're scarce in remote areas. I go to Costco too, since they have organics, wild fish, and grass-fed meats. Coddi's fridge is large enough to go three weeks between restocking. When organics aren't available, I rely on the Environmental Working Group's Clean Fifteen list and avoid their Dirty Dozen. In very remote spots, I resort to my backup pantry: beans, rice, quinoa, flour, yeast, dried coconut, oatmeal, dried fruits, and nuts. There's even a bag of emergency MREs (military-style ready-to-eat meals) I've thankfully not touched in seven years.

Québec City was the last place I found quality organics for months. Eventually I found two places in Newfoundland and Labrador that had some.

270.

July 30, 11:45 a.m. – Raleigh, Newfoundland
After the sign, I rolled up on two people weeding a garden on the side of the road. I stopped to say hi. They invited me to take a look.

"Do you sell any of your veggies?" The garden was at least fifty feet across and twice as long. It held neat rows of onions, potatoes, greens, carrots, turnips, herbs, and more. I stood inside the fence. She was bent over weeding, he stood facing me, holding a gas-powered whipper snipper.

"No, we eat 'em and share with family and friends," he said. "This is one of five gardens."

Five of these? Hand-weeding this one garden alone seemed like an all-day job.

One thing I miss about my house is my vegetable gardens.

271.

Locals call this island "the Rock" for a reason. Most of Newfoundland is solid rock with shallow soil, except for the bogland. Flat land is rare and most of the forests are too thick to walk through. I don't recall seeing a single field of crops. Small family gardens fifteen feet from the road are the norm. Rumor has it the reason the gardens are beside the road is that the dirt imported to make the roadbeds is the best for gardening. I was living off rice, beans, oatmeal, and my last few frozen veggies, and hoped to find nice veggies soon. Luckily, I had a freezer full of fish.

272.

July 30, 12:30 p.m. – Cape Onion, Newfoundland
I mostly walked my bike up Treena's Trail to craggy cliffs towering over the Atlantic. Cobalt-blue water stretched to the horizon, speckled with tiny rock islands. The climbs were steep, and some had several flights of stairs. The downhill rides were an adrenaline rush. I kept getting walloped in the face by tall white flowers the size of dinner plates. On my ride back to Coddi, a big, black, shiny truck pulled up next to me.

"Excuse me, can you tell me where the Viking Inn is?" asked the driver. There was a man in the passenger seat and a woman in the back seat.

I stopped in the middle of the road, straddled my bike, and looked up into his window. He had a beard like Santa Claus. The empty blacktop snaked through the forest as far as I could see in either direction.

"No, but I can look it up on my phone." I reached for my pocket.

"That's OK. We have it on GPS." He pointed to the dash. "It's not right. We've been driving in circles for a while."

"I met a man at a convenience store up the road whose dad owns the Viking Inn."

"Can you give me his phone number?"

"I don't know his number, but if you go back to the end of the road and take a right, the store can't be more than a mile away."

He looked back. "Well, all right. We'll do that. Thank you!"

I rode my bike in awe of the seamless synchronicity of everyday events.

When I was back at Coddi, William came to mind. He'd turned on something in me that had been dormant for years: desire. Even though I couldn't stay in Nain, and being with William wasn't a part of my journey, my soul longed to tell him. *But is telling him fair?*

When I'm drawn to do something from the quiet space within, I can trust these desires. They aren't driven by self-interest and carry no expectation. These desires take the entire universe into consideration.

7:52 p.m. – (Text to William):

> Hey you! I have been looking at the photos and videos from our trip this evening … I SO enjoyed being with you, Jade and Cece. And you are quite special … I kinda fell in love with you over those couple days. I mean, not that I want to marry you :) more like as a super amazing kind human with a huge heart … who is a whole lot of fun.

273.

If no one were watching, I'd live differently. I'd do less and rest more, live in the wild and not come out for a long while. I'd let all the frivolous stuff die on the vine and forget the "shoulds." I wouldn't ride my bike as far or as fast, and would live instead of making a living. I might put on some pounds and I'd shave my peanut head. My hair can be a pain. Twice I've chopped off my long auburn curls, given them to Locks of Love, and felt the delight of soft stubble, cool breezes, and unclogged drains. If no one were watching …

274.

July 31 – L'Anse aux Meadows, Newfoundland

I found a quiet spot to park, in a lot used to store wood and other odds and ends. It had an ocean view. I checked my email before leaving Coddi and venturing off to the historic site. My German friends from the ferry to Nain, Heike and Eckhi, had emailed. They asked if I was in L'Anse aux Meadows. *How the heck? What timing!* And suggested I go to the Norseman Restaurant to meet the owner, Gina, their close friend.

L'Anse aux Meadows is an archaeological site that, in the 1970s, was partially reburied to protect the remains. My tour guide was the great-grandson of the man who owned this land before anyone knew it was such an international treasure. I enjoyed seeing, touching, experiencing, and hearing about the history. On the tour, I saw the big white flowery plants I'd been riding through and getting walloped in the face by on my bike ride. I asked the guide what they were.

"It's giant hogweed," he said. "The sap is poison. It'll cause second-degree blister burns, and it'll blind you if it gets in your eyes." We stood next to one of the huge white flowers, which was as tall as I was.

"Wait. How? I got smacked in the face by these things all afternoon on a bike ride yesterday."

"You better be glad it was an overcast day. The sap is harmless until the sun hits it. It's UV-activated. You'd be all blistered up, or worse, if it was sunny."

Sheesh, I could be blind right now.

Afterward, I drove to the Norseman Restaurant and had a $16 bowl of seafood chowder. Although delicious, I could have eaten three bowls. Gina and I chatted at my table and then again on my way out. To my surprise, she'd written three beautiful children's books—self-published, self-distributed—and had sold over 30,000 copies. She gave me hope, and her printer's and illustrator's info. I've had an idea for a children's book series since 2018, and I haven't known where to start. Another instance of *how did this happen today?*

275.

I'm falling deeper into This with you. Into love and play, and all the possibilities we haven't fathomed. Deeper and higher, deeper and wider, like surfing a never-ending wave.

276.

If you could take anyone with you on your next adventure, who would it be?
My mom.

277.

After my confession text, William checked in with me more often. He asked for photos and my location, curious about what I was doing.

> Just get to Goose Bay, I'll fly you to Nain

> Come back

> I'll take you on better adventures

278.

August 2, 6:30 p.m. – Flowers Cove, Newfoundland
While boondocking at a small-town wharf, I was ready to hit the hay early. In my pajamas, I went outside, planted my grounding rod, and watched the waves crash. A couple of guys came up to chat. Other than what looked like a large shrimp boat, the place was deserted.

"Is that your boat?" I asked.

"Yes, ma'am," the younger one said. "We came to invite you over for scallops and beer."

What a pickup line!

My real-time trust in my inner knowing is absolute, happens behind the scenes, and takes no deliberation on my part. Nothing felt fishy. I changed clothes, walked to the dock, barraged them with questions about scalloping, then asked if I could check out their boat. I hopped aboard and got the royal tour. They had caught 500 pounds of scallops (cleaned weight). Since I politely declined their beer, they gave me extra scallops and refused to let me pay. Nice fellas—a little smelly, but I guess that goes with the territory.

While on their boat, the younger scalloper hit on me. Fifteen minutes into his flirting, the older fella mentioned the younger one was getting married in September. The younger guy's look could have killed. What motivates blatant cheating? I can't imagine cheating, especially with a stranger from a parking lot. Although, I can somewhat sympathize with organically falling in love with another. This smelly fella would have screwed me in my trailer if I'd invited him. For what? A quick orgasm? Maybe it's a guy thing. I can't wrap my head around it.

279.

Plant a grounding rod? Yup! In 2013, while researching natural performance-boosters for cycling, I discovered "grounding," or "earthing." It's a practice pro cyclists use; you sleep on special silver-threaded conductive sheets connected to the earth via a small rod. Humans used to exchange electrons with the earth by sleeping on the ground. We've lost this connection. This simple practice improves sleep, blood flow, wound healing, cellular repair, and stress levels and helps ward off health issues. Walking barefoot has the same benefits.

280.

Deep down, I'm still a little girl who wants to belong. When I was in elementary school, I'd sit in my bedroom and cry because I didn't have friends. What an empty flower, what a lost little soul, what a quirky, unique kid who wanted some lovin'. After my usual private weeping, I'd wait for the puffiness to clear from my crybaby eyes and go hang around Mom. One particular afternoon, I remember bothering her in the kitchen.

"I'm not put on this earth to entertain you," Mom said. She continued to scrub an old pot, neck craned down toward the sink. Her brown ponytail stuck up and out from the back of her head. As if attached to a real pony, it jiggled in rhythm with each harsh scrub. Sunlight made a perfect trapezoid on the floor. We had been learning about those in school. A crumpled yellow sticky note lay on the wrinkled linoleum between Mom's bare feet.

"Ten laps right now, go!" Mom said. She motioned toward the back door as if she were flicking a bug. A pile of foamy soap suds landed on the floor.

281.

The faces of my friends have changed since 2017. I have more close friends now than ever. I once ranked friendships by longevity, believing depth of connection depended on time. My early loneliness stemmed from this. Now when I meet a beautiful human, I'm meeting myself again. No hopes or desires. Pure being. Relationships have flourished, though some have faded. The freedom to be with family more often has been a godsend too.

282.

Remember the kayak guy, Matt? I realized days later that we hadn't exchanged info. He'd knocked on my window in the rain to tell me he'd changed his mind and would be on the next ferry to Newfoundland. Newfoundland is a huge place with many roads. He must have wanted to stay in touch. I'd whisked him away. We never saw each other again.

283.

August 3 – Port au Choix, Newfoundland
I backed up my home to a flat, rocky beach dead center of a U-shaped bay. The next morning, I sat on a red porch swing that hung on a homemade A-frame a few feet from the sea. At 4:30 a.m., the water and predawn sky blended into a pristine pastel masterpiece, the air still and cool.

"G'd mornin'." I jumped when the deep voice shattered the silence. A man with a scruffy beard and a thick Newfoundland drawl was out for a stroll. He walked through waist-high muted-sage seagrass, heading at an angle toward the water and away from me. "Where ya from?"

"Right here at the moment."

He stopped and scrunched his eyebrows at that.

"That's home." I nodded toward Coddi. "I've been traveling for seven years."

With a slack-jawed smile, he waded toward me through the seagrass. Above the grass tips, he held a clear drinking glass between his thumb and forefinger. The glass was filled almost to the brim with something a bit more gold than apple juice.

He sat on a boulder between the sea and me. We chatted while he drank in quarter-teaspoon sips. He was more introspective than he looked, and younger than I'd have guessed. I was four months his elder.

We were deep in conversation until dawn and walked along the wharf at sunrise. He owned a commercial fishing boat (think *Deadliest Catch*, except fish instead of crabs) and invited me on a three-day fishing trip. He'd leave in a couple of hours. I'm embarrassed to admit that because of his accent, clothes, and career, I had judged him as "not deep." That'll teach me. Our conversations about life and spirituality surprised, stretched, and intrigued me. We walked to his mom's house for a steak-and-egg breakfast. Her house was outside of town. The further from civilization we got, the more my Spidey sense kicked in.

"Just a heads-up, I know karate," I said. "And I'll bloody you up if need be." I was joking, but leery, yet held a firm presence.

"I dies at dat," Nate said, with a rise in the pitch of his voice. "Yous a hard ticket." His face and neck flushed as he created a bit of space between us.

He seemed to get the point, and I thought it best if I let him believe. We strolled on.

The more I got to know him, the more obvious it was: the karate lie was for naught.

284.

Without stories about who I am and what I can and can't do, I float with no strings attached. A marionette with head held high, arms slow-dancing as if conducting a soulful song. Without stories, I can be anything. I float back down to solid ground to walk through fields, streets, and forests. I see Life through simple eyes, for the first time, again and again. Curiosity wipes windows clean, revealing a spotless view of all that is. I see in. I see love. I see myself in all the possibility I was born with.

August 4 – Port au Choix, Newfoundland

My goodness, the steak took up almost the whole plate and dwarfed two fried eggs. All three sat in a puddle of shimmery crimson juice. My first bite was orgasmic, so tender, chewing was optional. After breakfast, Darlene (Nate's mom), Nate, and I chatted about the offer to join Nate for three days of fishing.

"Just to confirm," I said. "No funny business on the boat, right?" We were lounging in the living room. Their huge Newfoundland dog was sprawled across the floor between us. He looked like a brown-and-white rug, over six feet long.

Darlene doubled over, roaring with laughter. Nate and I both flinched. Nate ran his hand through his hair while pursing his lips and looked back and forth between his mom and me.

He still looked like a deer in headlights, and his mom, after seeing the perplexed look on his face, laughed even louder. She could barely breathe.

"There is no time or space for sex on that boat!" Darlene said, between laughs.

Nate looked sheepish and confirmed he wasn't planning anything of the sort. Nate's mom was a hoot. They were all such good, wholesome people.

We talked for nearly an hour as they shared their heritage: generations devoted to commercial fishing, with Darlene breaking ground as the first full-time female fisher in the area. They recounted the cod industry's collapse and how their community persevered through hardship. Darlene described fierce storms and big catches, and I wondered what it'd be like to be at sea.

I accepted Nate's offer to join him for three days of fishing. I felt comfortable with them in a way that usually takes weeks to develop. There was something about Newfoundlanders that cut straight through the usual small talk and connected heart to heart. I walked back to the beach, readied Coddi, and moved her to Darlene's yard. Darlene drove us to Nate's fishing boat, two hours away.

286.

When life is approached with ease and openness, fear has no place. There's nothing to lose, nothing to protect, and no expectations to meet. Worry and suffering fade, and peace and contentment flood in.

287.

From the get-go, being in Darlene's house felt like home.

"Home" is everywhere. Once upon a time I stepped off a plane and planted my foot on the concrete tarmac in Prague, Czech Republic, for the second time. It was March 2019. I felt completely at home. I'd traveled to many countries and was familiar with the feel of stepping onto a tarmac, but this was different. I hadn't felt this way when I was in Prague six months earlier.

This was the same feeling I'd had as a youngster when I returned to my family's cozy little red-brick home after a long visit with my grandparents. I couldn't remember having this "home" feeling since my mom moved my brother and me out of our childhood house when I was thirteen. After Prague I traveled to Bratislava, Slovakia. That felt like home. Next stop, the High Tatras. Home too. Then to Wrocław, Poland. Home. Los Angeles. Yup, same. This continued, so much so that I rarely think about it anymore. Home is not a place; home is a space within. I am eternally home.

288.

August 5 – Docked at the wharf in Quirpon, Newfoundland
Nate, Darlene, a crew member, and I loaded the boat with supplies. We said goodbye to Darlene and were ready to go. Two fishermen from another boat boarded the captain's deck.

"How'd ya meet?" Clint, the captain of a neighboring boat, asked Nate, gesturing to me.

"Found her at d' beach."

Nate and Clint had strong Newfoundland accents, and I didn't recognize half of what they said.

"So she's a mermaid!" Clint said, tipping his drink in my direction.

Everyone erupted in laughter. So did I. I didn't understand the rest, but I suspect that was for the best. It felt like a firehouse, except we were floating at the edge of the world.

From then on, my deck name was Mermaid.

We had an hour before we'd set off, so I hiked with my laptop and phone to the top of a hill, hoping to find cell service, and sent one of my monthly newsletters. If my subscribers only knew the behind-the-scenes adventures that went into sending those newsletters!

289.

When I tell you "I love you," it's so infinite. I can't quantify it, nor do I want to. Just relish its completeness.

290.

August 6, 7:00 p.m. – Offshore Quirpon, Newfoundland

The fishing boat expedition was interesting, but not enjoyable. Dinner was mashed potatoes mixed with Spam, and the plates and silverware tasted like soap. My bunk was next to a snoring guy and, thanks to a broken water pump, there were no working toilets or showers.

August 7

4:30 a.m. – I had to poop off the side of the boat. Luckily everyone was asleep.

I had to let go of the idea that I'd rather be somewhere else or that I'd wasted time on this dumpster fire of a fishing expedition. I was in the midst of an adventure of a lifetime that most never dream of having. *I will take it all in. I will write a book about this one day.*

6:00 p.m. – Daniele and Fabien texted me, as they often did. We exchanged photos and stories and wondered about future rendezvous points. We hoped to meet up and tour Newfoundland together. They were at least a week ahead of me heading east. I was on the fishing boat, docked at Quirpon again, and seriously considering hitchhiking back to Coddi. She was a two-hour drive south. I felt like a fish out of water.

291.

No magic happens when I'm sitting on my hands.

292.

Every moment is a gift under the Christmas tree of life, wrapped since the infinite beginning. Whatever is inside the next unwrapped box remains a mystery until the moment arrives, though it is a gift, whatever it may be.

293.

August 7 – Docked at the wharf in Quirpon, Newfoundland

9:00 a.m. – There was a kerfuffle with the crew. We were short two guys and couldn't go out. Nate asked if I wanted to stay on as a greenhorn, an official crew member, and continue until we reached our limit. It would mean three straight days and nights at sea, but I would get a fair share of the profits, around $3,500 or more. When I heard the amount of money, I felt my head jerk back. I went for a walk to settle into what felt best. *This could fund the rest of my summer.* I checked in with my heart. *Do I want to do this? Or is money the only reason?* The answer was clear.

I don't want to be on this boat. The tickle of my soul asked me to reunite with Coddi and explore this beautiful land.

3:00 p.m. – Darlene picked us up from the dock and drove us back to her house.

294.

I don't have dark thoughts. Sometimes, I feel as if I've made a mistake. It could be damage to Casper or Coddi, saying something I wish I hadn't, knowing I could have done better, or getting on a commercial fishing boat. I might feel frustrated or embarrassed, but eventually, my mind quiets. I remember Life is living me. What happened, happened. There are no mistakes, no worries. I am not in control and I am free. I am open to learning from everything. Then I move on, without dwelling on it too much. Life is clean and simple when I allow without judgment.

295.

I sit on the precipice of what's next without a worry or regret. I lie at the feet of nothingness until my soul is tickled to move. Time is not wasted, nor do I make the most of it. I live in a dream that fills my sails with wonder and awe.

296.

August 8 – Port au Choix, Newfoundland
Once back at Darlene's house, she and Nate sent me on a wild goose chase to a secret berry patch. I drove a long way up a rutted-up dirt road and then bushwhacked to a GPS point through thick forest and soupy bog. After over an hour of searching, I found two scraggly berry bushes. Muddy and tired, I gave up.

I passed one driveway on the way back: "Uncle Jasper's place." Before I left on my berry hunt, my new friends had suggested I stop to see Uncle Jasper (Darlene's brother) because he knew where to find berries. But who drives up to off-grid cabins way out in the middle of nowhere, uninvited? Desperate times call for desperate measures!

I whipped Casper onto two tire tracks that disappeared into the forest and crossed a homemade one-lane wooden bridge over a large creek. The bridge popped and snapped so loud I thought Casper and I were goners. As I rolled up the hill toward the Taj Mahal of cabins, a lean fella in a white T-shirt and blue jeans walked out with an inquisitive look. *I sure hope this is Uncle Jasper.*

"Hi, I'm Kristy," I said. "Darlene and Nate told me to drop by and ask you where to find berries."

297.

"To love is to accept risk and pain." A friend wrote that.

This doesn't ring true for me anymore. Risk ... Is love dangerous? This comes from a calculated mindset: "I want guarantees. I don't want a journey; I want to go from point A to point Z." Yeah, with this mentality, the unknown might seem risky and painful. People hop into relationships in this space and then wonder why they don't feel anything after the honeymoon stage. Trying to stay within the known leaves no room for wonder, magic, wander, exploration, or transformation. If I begin any relationship with the belief it could be risky and cause pain, then we're screwed from the get-go.

If love seems like a risk, I don't know Life at all.

298.

August 8 – East of Hawke's Bay, Newfoundland
Thankfully, the guy was Uncle Jasper. He was as friendly as everyone else and invited me for a drive. After ten minutes of bumbling down an even more rustic two-tire-track "road," Uncle Jasper laughed right out of the blue.

"Hard to believe you're riding in my truck to pick berries, and fifteen minutes ago I didn't know ya," he said in his lyrical Newfoundland drawl. My seat belt was fastened behind me, not around me. Jasper said if I wore it, it would try to strangle me on our bumpy drive. We were bouncing through the forest, past a pristine lake, in his old maroon pickup. "When a nice lady shows up at the cabin looking for berries, well." He chuckled. "You take her to find berries!"

I belly-laughed in recognition of this truth. There we were, two friends rolling through a forest in joyous laughter. His statement was the epitome of Newfoundland niceness.

Boy, did Uncle Jasper deliver! After a couple of hours on a steep hill covered in wild raspberries, we headed back with our bounty. He invited me in for tea. His solar-powered cabin was luxurious. He'd built his masterpiece thirty-five years ago. He pumped all his water from the creek and had two veggie gardens and a view to die for. Jasper served up two double slices of homemade bakeapple cheesecake, tried to give me fresh jam, and succeeded in sending me home with another sack of Newfoundland's most prized berry: the bakeapple (also known as a cloudberry). Uncle Jasper said the long, rough road leading to his property is a blessing, "'Cause it keeps people from comin' out here."

Well, almost everyone. That day, Uncle Jasper was my blessing.

299.

Summer 2018 – Los Angeles, California

Love is a curious thing. I once was infatuated with a self-absorbed guy. I had known him for years but was blind to the self-absorbed thing. He began as my business mentor, and I became friends with him and his wife. Their marriage got rocky, and they got divorced. He got friendlier, and then I thought I was falling for him. He flew cross-country to visit me as I meandered in Southern California. We had sex three times on the first night we were intimate. The next day, he told me I was "needy" and hopped a Greyhound bus from Los Angeles back to North Carolina. No joke. A friggin' bus.

What a wander.

My body went into "abandonment" reaction. This was the third time someone I'd loved had left me in dramatic fashion. My body had perfected the dry-mouth, wobbly-legs, racing-heart-thumping-in-my-ears, utter-panic response.

Needy, my ass. I was expressing love. I needed no one. The self-absorbed guy, I can only guess, was too scared to love or was in the mood for a fuck-and-run.

Brokenhearted, I cried alone. I texted and called to check on him as he changed buses in shady places all the way across the continent. Underneath my grief and programmed reactions, I knew I was OK, and this too was for the best. Granted, I secretly wished he'd have a change of heart. With the help of wise friends, I noticed that he only reached out when he needed something. All the more reason to let go, and that I did. And I am better for it. Maybe he is too.

My coddiwompling heart wanders. No risk. All love.

300.

Wild berries are soft, and delicate; they must be handled with care. The act of receiving berries from their plants is a lesson in patience. Only ripe berries want to be picked. I was stubborn and tugged too hard on a few. The whole berry and stem broke away with a snap. The plant bobbed back with a rustle of leaves, as if saying "Ouch!" I felt responsible for its pain and ate its berry to avoid wasting it. The meat was crunchy and tart, not the experience I was keen to have.

The wild berry patch taught me to ask if it was ready. Not with my words, with a gentle touch. If the berry was ready, it gave itself. A ripe bite aroused my taste buds; my mouth tingled. Nature is my teacher.

301.

I have experiences, and sometimes I label them. There are no mistakes.

302.

All love is a wander. Intellectually, I know there is no risk in love. Although, I wonder if in a dark corner of my body's reaction center, the abandonment mode is still curled up asleep, waiting for its chance to shine again. If so, that is proof I still think there is risk in love. If I'm protecting myself, I'm not all-in. I'm not fully allowing and receiving love. I am not wandering.

I love to wander. No risk there. Dammit, I wish I could drop the silly idea there is risk in love.

303.

August 9 – Northwest of Rocky Harbour, Newfoundland
Since 2017, I'd parked Coddi in many spots, public and private, and had never gotten the dreaded knock on the door telling me I was parked illegally. If there were signs saying No Overnight Parking, I wouldn't park. If I was at a private business, I would either call ahead or ask inside.

My streak was over.

I was parked in a paved pull-off on a quiet two-lane road by the coast. I found the spot by chance, without any apps, and it seemed safe and legal. The boundary for Gros Morne National Park was somewhere up the road toward the Lobster Cove Head Lighthouse, which I planned to visit in the morning.

I knew Parks Canada was strict about people sleeping in national parks outside designated campsites. I follow rules. At 9:45 p.m. on a rainy night, while I was in bed about to doze off, I heard an engine rumble and saw headlights through the rear window. It was a Parks Canada car decked out with lights like a police vehicle. It parked behind Coddi. Two gun-toting, bulletproof-vest-wearing people got out and walked toward my front door. *This ain't good.*

304.

Where do you pee when you're living in your Airstream?

The freedom, simplicity, and quickness of a pee outside is something I enjoy no matter where I am. Once done, I put my flat right hand on the inside of my thigh and give it a shake to get rid of lingering drops. Then up with the panties and off I go. If I'm camped in a place where I can't pop a squat, I pee in the toilet inside Coddi. Casper has huge step rails that run below the doors. Standing on them is even better than squatting in the dirt: no splash back on my shoes and ankles. I create my own private Porta Potty: I stand with my feet on the rail, one hand on the grab bar, the other hand on the seat back, and pee to my heart's content. Hanging off the side of Casper is my all-time favorite place to pee.

305.

August 9 – Northwest of Rocky Harbour, Newfoundland

"Good evening, ma'am," the warden said, looking up at me from the foot of Coddi's steps. His flashlight lit a bright circle on the wet blacktop. Raindrops glistened on his dark uniform. A pale Stetson hid his face. Beside him stood a smaller, thinner person in the same uniform.

"Hi." My heart beat double time. I was exhausted and wanted to sleep. I was gonna have to pack up and leave.

"Do you know it's illegal to camp or sleep in your vehicle overnight in a national park, unless in a designated campsite?"

"Yes, sir." *That's why I parked here, not in the national park.*

"Do you know you're in Gros Morne National Park?"

"Umm, no sir. I made sure to park outside the park, and I checked to be sure there weren't any No Overnight Parking signs, too."

"Ma'am, you are in the park. The boundary is right about there." He shined his light toward his car and lit a stand of trees fifty feet away. "There aren't any signs, but this is the national park and you are gonna have to move." A stronger rain pitter-pattered on Coddi's roof and on the warden's uniform.

I apologized. "Is there anywhere I can go nearby? It's dangerous to drive after dark with the moose and all."

"Yeah, it's late to be on the road." He looked back toward his car and took a deep breath. "There's a campground in town, but it might be full." His hands were still on his belt and pelting rain was splashing off his hat. "Head east on 430. Ten kilometers up, there's a gravel road on the left that leads to a clearing with an RV and a logging truck. You'll be fine there for the night."

Moving Coddi isn't just hopping in the truck and turning the key. Secure doors, cabinets, equipment, awnings; put away all items on counters and tables; stow the steps and hitch the truck (if unhitched); lift the jack; and close any open windows. It took some searching, but I found the clearing with the logging truck.

306.

The more we unwind This, the more I see you, know you, feel you, and understand you, and the more I understand myself and realize how much more I have to experience and understand.

307.

Hope
I watched a man with hope die a painful death.
He battled like a prizefighter to avoid that place called hell,
until a couple minutes before the end.

His brow softened, fists let go of choke holds on bedsheets,
frantic gasps slowed to tenderness.
The fight was over, his work done.

He gave up the god-awful belief
that he wasn't good enough to get in.

Sixty-nine years of putting up a fight.
For lies boiled in expectation.
For hope.
For wasted prayers.
For Pete's sake, if I am begging to the man upstairs,
I am rooting against God.

The old fella smartened up in the end.

Hope.
What an awful thing to teach the masses.
What a waste of time, faith, and lives.
What a mess, the shitty lie of original sin.

At least he got it, that old man.
Sayonara to want.
Hello livin'.

Yeah, there's hope for all of us.
Even the slowest get it,
just before the end.

308.

Putting pen to paper is a whole different game than flipping off societal norms. When I avoid writing, it means I'm too scared to bare my soul. In doing that, I'm flipping off myself and anyone who might see themselves in my words. I shut the door on all the wild possibilities that keep me on my toes. I know to write. When I don't act on what I know, it's a big "eff you" to all that could be.

309.

Pooping in nature? I prefer not. I'm out here to be with Life, not to crouch over a hole and wonder if a squirrel is judging me.

In Coddi, I use my composting toilet. It looks normal, but it has a solid bowl and a trapdoor. Inside the front are two small holes where female pee naturally drains into a 1.5-gallon jug (males must sit and aim). A lever opens the trapdoor for poo, which drops into a sealed box filled with coconut coir (shredded husk). After deposits, I close the trapdoor and twist another lever to mix everything. The poo composts, becoming dark, rich soil. After about six weeks, I dig a hole and bury the compost, then refill with fresh coconut coir. No water wasted, no smell, no black water dumping. Some guests fear my toilet initially, though most enjoy it once acquainted.

310.

August 10 – Trout River Campground, Gros Morne National Park, Newfoundland

I joined a fireside sharing-circle led by a local Indigenous elder. Twenty-five kind people, all from Canada, introduced themselves. The lady leading the circle and I were the only ones not on vacation. While I may've had an inkling that most people I meet in the wild are escaping "real" life, it struck me as if for the first time. Crisp air, blue skies, shimmering green leaves, streams, and seaside cliffs—this grand beauty isn't home for most. It's just something to visit for a week or two.

311.

Ed, a man I've never met, writes me notes. He's seventy-eight and reads my newsletters. At 11:57 a.m. on a Sunday he sent: "Thanks for all the peacefulness you send to others."

Blue ocean waves crashed against cliffs, sea spray dotted my windows, and I was sad. Sad about not writing, sad about procrastinating while stuck in the jumble of my head. I expect too much of myself, especially with writing. Outside, sheep trotted through tiny yellow flowers wiggling in the wind. With gratitude for Ed's nudge, I went to my computer and pressed fingers on the keyboard.

An encouraging word—the honey of life. Nourishment sent and

received. A flicker of hope that all is OK, that I'm not a slacker. Thanks to Ed for his thanks, and the encouragement to be unabashedly me.

312.

For many people, vacation is another form of conquest. Context: I met Vancouverites yesterday hiking the Tablelands in Gros Morne. They're visiting Newfoundland for one week, drove seven hours from St. John's for that hike, and are cramming Gros Morne in today. My goodness gracious, it would take at least two weeks to see all of Gros Morne. Tomorrow they'll drive to another part of Newfoundland, then race back to St. John's for their flight.

Good for the Vancouver couple for making it happen. And, have they sat still in the woods? Or noticed how the sea breeze tickles the peach fuzz on their feet and forearms? Or watched the shadow of the sun climb down from treetops while a wild rabbit with coffee-colored eyes nibbles soft grass beside them?

A little brown rabbit is munching on grass a couple feet away as I write this. I want to reach out and touch her silky coat. Maybe she will let me …

313.

August 11 – Stanleyville Trail, Gros Morne National Park, Newfoundland

A thin trail snaked through tall grass up a gradual hill. A hiker walked down. If I rode my bike up, he'd need to get off the trail for me. I circled the trailhead until he neared halfway, then waited with one foot on a bench.

"How kind," he said. "I watched you wait for me. Thank you." He had a curly white ponytail, a large backpack, and hiking poles.

"You're welcome. I'm in no hurry."

Keith and I chatted for fifteen minutes. He told me about a writers' festival in nearby Woody Point the next week, and shared his number and Newfoundland must-sees.

314.

People often ask what my sweet spot is for how long I stay in one place. As with everything in life, I'm open. Some places, days. Some places ask me to stay a month or more. I might arrive with a plan, or not. Even when I think I know, that often shifts. The pull comes from Life itself, not usually people or the land. When I love being somewhere, I stay as long as possible.

315.

August 11 – Stanleyville Trail, Gros Morne National Park, Newfoundland

After Keith and I said our farewells, I rode up the trail. A small brown bird hopped along in front of me. I rode slower. It kept hopping. I thought it'd fly off as I got closer, but it stopped. I slammed on my brakes, my gut smacked the handlebars, a groan escaped my lungs, and I almost toppled over. The bird continued hopping merrily, unaware it had come within inches of a painful death.

I got off and walked. As it hopped in front of my toes, I tried to pass, but it wouldn't give way. Tall golden grass lined the narrow dirt path, which made it impossible to go around. It stopped. While squatting down, I reached out my hand. My fingers were within a beak of its feathers before it hopped up the trail some more. At a wider spot, I scooted beside and passed. My arm reached back to my bike, which was still behind the bird. It had no fear. I tried to pull my bike by, but it kept hopping within inches of the tires. I stopped. It hopped by and led the way again.

I heaved my bike onto my shoulder then scurried by, holding the bike in the air with all my attention on the little creature. Once in front, I stopped and turned back to face it. It stopped. I squatted and reached out again, slow, almost touching. For the first time, it took one hop back down the trail. I stood, smiled, and wished it well on its walk. I hopped on my bike and continued up the trail, and so did it.

316.

I feel most alive in untouched places. Nature is no longer a conquest. Instead, I receive what's offered: the startling blue of a hidden lake, the scent of pine after rain, the silence that teaches my heart to slow. Nature expects nothing and is never disappointed. Nature just lives.

317.

The more I soak in this wildness, the more in wonder I become. If this is a dream, I don't want to ever wake up.

318.

I love the thrill of mountain biking. There's no room for my mind to drift: full presence and flow, the body shifts and moves without thought, the senses take care of decisions. I am one with the forest. I think, I crash. Riding is a workout for the body and a meditation for the mind.

If I never take risks, I condemn myself to the certainty of missing out.

319.

August 14 – Cape Blow Me Down, Newfoundland
We rarely experience nature in its natural state. Backyard gardens, park trails, and a picnic on mowed grass are nice, but raw nature has a different feel, an aliveness. It smells earthy and wild. The forest is untamed. The night sky is ablaze with millions of stars. Pretty much everyone thinks they've seen a starry sky. I did too! Get one hundred miles away from city lights, look up, be astonished, and wish for more. Nature communicates with experience and does not discriminate.

320.

I used to move fast so I could see more; now I linger longer, and see more.

321.

August 17 – Writers at Woody Point Literary Festival, Woody Point, Newfoundland

9:15 a.m. – "Are these seats taken?" a tall gentleman asked. I sat in the second row, ready for my first book reading.

"They're taken by you."

With a gentle hand on the shoulder of a smiling woman, he guided her to sit next to me. Once she was settled, he sat. They introduced themselves as Karen and Stephen from Antigonish, Nova Scotia. Stephen owned a bakery, and Karen had retired from journalism. We crossed paths again and again in the days ahead, unaware of what the future might bring.

12:00 p.m. – After the reading and a stroll around town, I went to an old schoolhouse for a meet and greet. A man in jeans and a black blazer over a white T-shirt stood at the door, arm around his young daughter's shoulder. He grinned, nodding slightly while surveying the mingling crowd. I stood beside him, curious but hesitant to interrupt.

"This room is a melting pot of best-selling and award-winning authors," he said, as if reading my mind. Tables covered with a rainbow of books lined one side of the room; tables with coffee and snacks lined another. Tall windows lit everything with all the natural light the early-afternoon clouds let in.

"Really?" They looked like regular people. I'd assumed these were attendees.

He rattled off names that meant nothing to me, eyes sparkling as he told me about the special ones. I enjoyed seeing everyone as regular ol' folks. For three days, these people, their stories, songs, and open hearts became my buffet, and I became theirs. And we all became part of each other's stories.

322.

Teach me, I am listening.

323.

There was a time when the tender affection, adoration, passion, and all-encompassing devotion that I am experiencing now would have sent me running for the hills. Too much pressure, too much expectation, too much risk. Better to run than stick around and feel, or worse yet, lose the love of my life; have my heart ripped out and stomped on again; silent cry into my pillow; suffer alone, while praying to be held by the one who isn't there. Better to never begin than risk all that. Or so I thought. This is beyond expectation or any made-up risk. This is beyond love.

324.

Back in 2011, my boyfriend, Jack, and I thought it'd be fun to ride bicycles in the mountains. We rented a cabin in North Georgia and set out to give our flatlander legs their first taste of climbing.

"Smell the roses!" Jack yelled. We were on a two-lane road fifty-five miles into a century ride. Patches of high-noon sunlight found their way through the canopy and flashed by on the asphalt. I looked over my left shoulder. Sweat dripped from Jack's grimaced face and darkened his lime-green jersey.

"There aren't any roses," I said, between gasps, as I pounded away at the pedals. My eyes were glued to the crest of the road, where the blacktop met the sky. The top came and went. Wind howled in my ears and the forest blurred into waves of green and brown. The faster I flew downhill, the wider my grin. There was a point when one wrong move meant face-planting on a tree at over fifty miles per hour. Living at the edge of dying, that's where I felt most alive.

325.

August 17, 4:00 p.m. – Birchy Head post office, Newfoundland
On my way back to camp from the writers' festival, I stopped by the post office to pick up my Columbia sun shirt that Jade had shipped from Nain. It had been over three weeks, so it'd be waiting for me.

It wasn't there. The postal clerk found the mailing label in the system, but the scan showed it had never left the Nain post office.

326.

August 18, 10:00 a.m. – Writers at Woody Point Literary Festival, Woody Point, Newfoundland

"All you have to do is put yourself in the way of beauty, put yourself into the incredible swing of it." As Elizabeth Hay spoke these words from the small wooden stage, something shifted in me. I sat in the back row of folding chairs, mesmerized not just by her words but by her presence—the way she inhabited them completely.

What I experienced in that seaside town over a handful of days was the beautiful, spunky, and hilarious humanness of writers of great books and music. Since I didn't know anyone, I spoke to "famous" people while assuming they were attendees. I am thankful for this innocence. Before receiving this gift, somewhere deep down, I assumed books materialized spontaneously from the ether. I met the creators and I was touched by their craft.

These writers were as quirky as the rest of us. They doubted themselves. They struggled with the same human messiness. Yet they'd found the courage to put their truth on the page, to be vulnerable in ways I was only beginning to understand. After hearing great writing from the lips of those who wrote it, and getting to know what made them tick, I wanted to read more. I wanted to write more. I wanted to stop hiding.

While listening to, and being in intimate conversation with, an Indigenous author and an Indigenous songwriter, my heart ached for all of humanity, especially Indigenous peoples. I took a stroll, saw a bench overlooking the sea, sat, and wrote this.

Some awful thing happened to the white man thousands of years ago.
Wars, slavery, greed, bigotry, alienation of nature, and sexism.
The worst of us has spoiled my blood.
A sprout from one tainted seed grew into a tangled forest of lust and greed.
A cancer ate away at our hearts and consumed our goodness.
I didn't feel love, so I hated.

My father was given it by his father and his father before that, and his
father, and his father's father.

A rotting sore festers, grows.

Modern culture smells like a hog farm that curls nose hairs, gags
throats, and induces dry heaves.

A stench has filled our nostrils so long the cesspool doesn't register.

Ownership is normal—lines drawn in the sand, the haves and
have-nots.

I propagate the infection and act as if I am the victim.

As a tiny tot, my first words reflected the shame I was born into.

Mine. Mine. Mine. More More. Mine More Mine. More!

I haven't grown out of it, though I've tried.

Sophisticated words gloss over the "mines" and "mores,"

tricking me into believing I am kind and different.

Behind the gentle smile of my eyes, I see skin color.

Behind closed doors, I keep the best for myself.

Behind hugs and encouraging words, I judge.

Behind the backs of the wicked, I am a selfish, hypocritical bitch.

327.

When traveling, what touches me most is people. Everyone around the
world is doing their best to love and live.

Me too. I'm not perfect. Earlier in life, I had ideas about different
cultures, countries, and ethnicities. When I lived in southeast Florida in
my twenties, several people with Spanish accents and tan skin treated
me unkindly. Even though I had many wonderful experiences too, this
led me to have preconceived ideas about people with similar accents and
skin tones.

When I began my adventure, I thought I was free from racism and
bigotry. Before a trip to Germany in 2019, I assumed people there would
be stoic and unfriendly. To my surprise, they were kind and happy. Even
though I want to let go of bias, I sometimes fall into the trap of judgment.
I miss being a kid, back when prejudice wasn't even on my radar.

The more places I call home and the more people I meet from across our little planet, the clearer it becomes: we're all the same.

328.

"That thing the nature of which is totally unknown to you is usually what you need to find, and finding it is a matter of getting lost."[9]

— Rebecca Solnit

329.

My greatest adventure is a love story, a shocking one, a wild dream I hadn't dreamed because this story is wilder than my subconscious could imagine. I received a gift I didn't know to ask for.

330.

August 18 – Stuckless Pond Trail, Gros Morne National Park, Newfoundland

After the morning sessions at the writers' festival, I drove into the national park for a bike ride.

I was bombing downhill on a straight stretch of trail at twenty-five miles per hour when an awkward jolt sent shivers up my spine. Time stretched as my body drifted further off-center. *In the stillness of free fall, milliseconds last hours.* A gray boulder with sparkly speckles was on a collision course with my face. I floated between "I can save it" and the impending yard sale of impact.

BAM! Body parts spun, thrashed, and smacked in a triple-speed flail. No up or down, a limp ballet. I was a blueberry in a blender.

THWACK! My helmet whacked a rock and my neck cracked as if I'd had a chiropractic adjustment. No fear, no time to hope, a body being battered in an absence of feeling, in ways a body is not meant to be battered.

STILL. I lay on my back in scraggly shrubs, legs pointed down a steep drop, bike sprawled across my chest. The front wheel still spun. My ears rang, vision dimmed to a tunnel. I lay dizzy, fighting unconsciousness, waiting for the world to return. Iron filled my mouth, darkness like a coffin, heart banging like a speedy metronome while my face and cheeks prickled in waves. I hovered so close to blacking out that I might have. I am nowhere, with no one. Will I be a news headline: *Biker found dead after she went missing for a week?*

331.

To mark areas and paths, and to keep from getting lost, Inuit stack stones in the shape of a human pointing. These statues are called inuksuk, and they helped the Inuit survive.

332.

Since the Poof (#259) I walk on clouds, Life lives me, and I see my body kinda like it's a robot. Injuries and pain are separate from who I am. My body is a miraculous machine that sometimes has hiccups.

333.

August 18, 3:00 p.m. – Stuckless Pond Trail, Gros Morne National Park, Newfoundland
My sight and hearing returned. Birdsong continued as if, to the forest, the crash hadn't meant a thing. I stayed on my back in the shrubs and checked my robot. Arms and legs worked. No pain. Everything seemed OK. A freaking miracle! When I pushed myself upright, I noticed the blood on my shirt and the S-shaped bend in my gloved right pinky finger.

I stumbled onto the trail, walked my bike toward the trailhead, then flagged down two hikers about thirty minutes later.

"Do either of you have medical training?"

The man winced at the sight of my hand. "Geez. I'm military, but I can't help with that."

We stood in a circle, staring down at my hand as if it were a wounded bird. "I doubt the clinic can handle that either," he said. "And the closest hospital is a few hours away. Where is your partner? Or your friends?"

"I'm traveling alone."

"You don't have anyone to help?" He rubbed his forehead, his expression a mixture of concern and disbelief.

334.

The writing festival changed me. I opened up to possibility more than ever. I felt the difference between the aliveness of creating from the energy of everything, and the staleness of writing for a reason from the bureaucracy of my brain. I made friendships and connections and realized superb writers were regular people with an unquenchable thirst to share their truth, and that superb writing, fiction or not, is our truth.

People at the festival asked what I was up to, and I told them about writing a children's book series based on my journeys. I'd tell one person and then a small group would form with people listening in. This happened several times. They wanted to read my books. I wanted to write them for kids of all ages. I had no idea my life was about to be turned upside down. My journey would be slower. I would not write in the ways I'd imagined. I would spend months recuperating, healing, and being. This festival was a turning point for many things.

335.

Summer 1994 – Tallahassee, Florida
The front door slammed shut.

I was fifteen, and sat on crumpled sheets at the edge of my bed, hands on my knees. Unruly strands of frayed jean shorts touched the heels of my palms. Piles of disheveled clothes, a shoe on its side with laces tied, and crinkled school papers littered the floor. The house was still except for a *drip drip drip* of the faucet in the bathtub. My family, if you could call them that, was going on a two-week vacation to the Great Lakes. Next to my bare right foot was a black chess piece. A pawn. Dim morning light filtered in through haphazard and half-broken vertical blinds.

The engine of my stepdad's RV turned over with a screech like a wounded bird. It sputtered for a bit and then hummed a dark rainbow. The RV, with my mom, stepdad, and stepsisters inside, had stopped by Dad's place to pick up my brother. The engine growled and gravel crunched. A roar trailed off until there was nothing left but a *drip drip drip.*

I flopped back and stared up at a popcorn ceiling. I was a problem. I was not welcome. This was the story of my life. Left behind. Not enough. Unwanted. Unloved.

336.

August 18, 4:00 p.m. – Stuckless Pond Trail, Gros Morne National Park, Newfoundland

An hour after the bike crash, I'd made it to my truck and loaded gear one-handed. The military man's words echoed: *You don't have anyone to help?* No. I didn't.

My gut twisted. My aloneness was my penance for building invisible barriers to protect myself from love, life, and loss. I'd thought I'd let that all go, but maybe I was still hiding. After all these years of wandering, and decades of noxious independence before that, I stared at my bent twig of a finger. For the first time in a long time, being on my own felt heavy. I was surrounded by trees, sky, wind—no voices, no one who knew where I was, no cell service. No one waiting for me to check in.

This solitude wasn't the poetic kind I'd written about. It was blood on my shirt, a mangled finger, and the ache of having to handle this alone. I'd chosen independence, even celebrated it, but I didn't feel brave. I was the forgotten kid again, left to fend for myself. The forest knew my secret.

I heard bird wings flap and glanced up. A white blur. I felt it land behind me. I turned slow and looked up into the eyes of a white-and-gray bird on the top corner of Casper's open passenger door. The bird's black claws wrapped around white metal. No wants, no thoughts. Its beak and my nose were as close as the length of a water bottle. Wind tussled feathers on top of its head. A guttural wail bellowed up and out of my throat. My shoulders heaved. My eyes did not leave the bird's; its eyes did not leave mine. A river of tears flowed. The bird sat, unmoving, watching, being. More unashamed wails, eyes fixed on the bird's quiet gaze. It cocked its head curiously, gave one caw, and flew back to the forest.

Something washed through me, clear and certain. This bird had come to comfort me; a messenger. Perhaps my stepsister Ellan, who'd passed in May. She was a doctor and healer. I felt her tender presence, reminding me my body was already mending itself. Or Dad, gone two years. We weren't as close as he'd wished, though he loved me. I felt him hugging my heart and telling me I'd be OK. Or Don, my stepdad who died in 2020, a man of few words but loving, nonetheless.

I was silent as tears gushed. I felt endless love and presence.

I'd thought needing help meant weakness, that freedom meant self-sufficiency. But the universe taught otherwise, first through the loving care of strangers in Labrador and now this accident. True strength wasn't independence. It was asking for help, and accepting help when offered.

I drove to the campground. There was no phone service there either, but there were people.

337.

I may seem brave or crazy, but life feels pretty relaxed. I'm not afraid. In the best of ways, I have no responsibility. If fifteen years ago someone had suggested I'd live like I do now, I would have been three parts thrilled and ten parts freaking out.

338.

August 18, 4:30 p.m. – Lomond Campground, Gross Morne National Park, Newfoundland

I went straight to the rangers' station. Two rangers inspected my finger and contacted the medical clinic (which was an hour's drive away). The receptionist seemed more concerned that I had no insurance than the fact that my finger looked as though it belonged to a Mr. Potato Head doll that had been put together wrong. "You'll need to prepay for X-rays, a preexam, and the doctor's exam, and we'll need a credit card on file. Depending on the severity, the doctor may or may not need to transfer your care."

Thousands of dollars for a clinic doctor? Yeah, no thanks.

Back at my primitive campsite, a long hot shower called to me. I headed toward the bathhouse, the one place with running water. On the way to the bathhouse, I happened upon Keith, the guy with the curly white ponytail I'd met on the trail the week before. We'd become great friends.

"Hey there, I've got a favor to ask."

"Sure, my dear, what can I do fer ya?" Keith was sporting his backpack and hiking poles, and was drenched in sweat.

"I've mangled my finger, and I'm hoping you can help snap it back into place."

Keith's eyes bugged out when he saw it. "Eww, how'd ya do that?"

I told him, and begged him to yank on it. It wasn't too swollen and hadn't changed color, so I was pretty sure it wasn't broken. Keith tentatively placed his burly thumb and forefinger on my sideways pinky.

"Sorry, I can't," he said, as he jerked his fingers away. He looked certifiably woozy. "That's just. It's too." He winced, sighed, and shook his head. "I can't." He placed his hand over his heart. "My dear, yous need a doctor. Let's go to the hospital."

I thanked him, told him I was going to hold off for now, and continued to the showers. This felt like a big deal, and a big decision. I wasn't scared, but I was frustrated and very aware of how alone I was. I wanted to call someone who'd know the answer. Moments like these are when I wished I lived in a place with a community of friends, and had a doctor I trusted nearby. I needed help. This wasn't going to fix itself. During my shower, I realized the next best step was to try to find someone, anyone who could help. Worst case, I'd go to the hospital after that.

After an hour of my asking every camper I could find, one lady mentioned she'd just met a physiotherapist on a trail. She dashed off into the forest and returned ten minutes later with said hiker.

"Wow! You did a number on that." The physiotherapist was fit and sweaty, and she wore an aqua backpack that towered over her. "This needs to be reduced," she said, as she looked up at me. "Do you mind if I touch it?"

"Go right ahead. Do anything you want."

She cradled my hand and moved my finger in the slightest of easy circles. *Pop!* The lady who'd found the physiotherapist jerked her head away as if she smelled something awful. The physiotherapist's forehead furrowed as she held tension on my finger and wrist. *Pop!* My finger no longer had an S curve, but it was still pointing to the side.

"OK, this is going to be a big one," she said, without looking up. "Are you ready?"

She gently pulled and twisted.

SNAP!

"That's it, you're fixed." She looked up at me with an ear-to-ear smile.

"Whoa, I can't thank you enough." I inspected my almost-normal-looking finger. "You're a godsend."

"You're welcome. You'll need to splint that." She was already walking away. "Even if you just brush it against something, it could dislocate. Tape a stick or something to it and the finger next to it." She was heading toward the forest.

I waved to her with my left hand, but her back was already turned. "I will. Thank you." The aqua backpack with tiny tanned legs disappeared into the forest.

The heavy boulder in my gut vanished. No hospitals or wasted time and money. The irony hit me: I'd gotten exactly what I'd wished for in the shower, a community of friends ready to help. It just didn't look like I'd expected. Almost everywhere I wander, there are caring people waiting to become friends.

While splinting my finger back at Coddi, the left side of my ribs throbbed, and it hurt to take a deep breath. When I sat down, my hip ached.

339.

How do you date on the road? Do you date? Sex?

I've never enjoyed dating. Both of my boyfriends bloomed from friendships, so we skipped the dating part. Prior to my Poof experience in 2019, I wanted a partner. Since then, I haven't wished for romance. I'm in love with nature and God, utterly content. If a guy were to come along, he'd have to be super special, and we'd have to meld into a unique way of living together. Returning to societal norms is a hard no. I'm open to being less nomadic, but someone needing endless material things, city living, or enslavement to the clock and their boss? No thank you. I haven't had sex since 2018. I'm intimate with Life and feel whole and complete. It seems strange, even to me, but I'm not interested. This is why the feelings for William were unexpected. Suddenly there was desire.

Yeah, back when I answered that question, I had a lot more to feel about feeling in love.

340.

August 18, 7:00 p.m. – Lomond Campground, Gros Morne National Park, Newfoundland

The week before, Keith had asked if I wanted to join him for a traditional Newfoundland concert during the writing festival. I didn't want to miss it. He picked me up from my campsite as if I were his date, opened the truck door and all. *I love me some chivalry.*

We walked up to the two-story schoolhouse. A line of people spilled out the opened solid-wood double doors. Sunset painted the sky pink, garnet, and gold.

"Listen, I know yous a firefighter," Keith said. Peppy Scottish-sounding fiddle music and laughter rang from the building. Keith bounced from foot to foot with the beat of the drum. "There's gon be heaps of people. Too many, some migh' say, but tis fine, my dear." He smiled so big his eyes turned to slits. "Fire marshal looks the other way." He pinched my cheek. "And you will too!"

He held my left hand and led me up the stairs. I held my right arm tight across my chest, right hand on my left shoulder. That finger throbbed like the dickens.

A soft-spoken, humble, young Indigenous man quieted the loud, over-packed schoolhouse with the thundering soulfulness of his singing voice. Goosebumps pricked my arms and legs. Listening, I settled, lifted, and felt permission to break open, too. Many others sung and got all the notes right. This wasn't that. Sharing from the divine and tooting some pretty notes are two different worlds. I felt it. The same with written words; the difference is palpable: a special author allows, welcomes, and comes from that space the Indigenous man sang from. Words appear. Words that grab hold and don't let go

341.

I am in bed in Coddi with the back window open, lulled by the sound of the breeze, birds, lapping of the water on rocks, and the sight of the shape-shifting clouds, and slow meander of light, from bright, to pastels, to dark, to stars and your moon, and then back to light again. This piece of art is alive. Each night I sit, look out, read, and think of you. Each morning, I open the window and let the cool fragrance of dawn seep in, and think of you. I wish your warmth was a felt sense on my skin, and still I know you are here, a part of this masterpiece I get the pleasure of calling Life.

342.

August 19, 1:00 a.m. – Lomond Campground, Gros Morne National Park, Newfoundland

By the time Keith and I rolled into the campground after the concert, I felt as if I'd been hit by a semitruck. He let me out at Coddi's door.

"Ya sure you gon to be OK?" Keith asked, as I inched out of his vehicle. "I believe yous hurtin' more than you'd like to let on."

I couldn't sleep. When I lay on my back or on either side, my rib clicked with each breath. The sound made my skin crawl. I had to either lie on my stomach or sit propped up. My right hand was as useless as a club. A purple-and-green bruise covered my upper arm, right where I suspected my broken rib was. Maybe my arm was cracked too. It probably hit the boulder I thought was going to smack my face. My hip was also purple and green, with an abrasion that oozed yellow plasma.

343.

Ponderings: My Composting Toilet
I have to take a shit.
But my shitter is full. I must empty it today.
I don't want to add more poop to the pile.
I sit with a bulging sphincter full of yesterday's indulgence.
I shouldn't have eaten the second helping of black-bean-and-corn chili.

344.

August 21 – Pilley's Island, Newfoundland
It had been three miserably painful days since the bike crash. I'd driven a couple of hours from the national park and was boondocking in Northern Newfoundland.

2:00 p.m. – Cliffs, ocean with islands in the distance. What a view. Rough seas outside and inside, too. I am exhausted. Dull and stabbing pain. Small shallow breaths are like a sword in my side. Fatigue out of this world. Headache. Both hamstrings ache like they've been shot. I have a fever.

August 22
8:00 a.m. – Fever spiked. Too weak to eat or sit up. Get throat tickles or feel a sneeze coming on and hug the rib with both hands. Then nothing. It's like my body is saying, *No! I'll die if I cough.* I had a thirty-second moment of self-pity. I wanted to be taken care of. I wanted my mommy. This struck me: nature doesn't feel sorry for itself. It does what it must with what it has. I am nature. This is what is happening. I will figure it out.

10:45 a.m. – Fucking COVID. Years of being a COVID virgin. It got me. Forgot it existed. So beat. So done. So spent. Can't stay here. RV park with power two hours away. Must get power. Can't deal with cold, rain, and solar. No one is coming.

4:30 p.m. – At RV park. No trees, no privacy. No nature. Backed in, unhooked, collapsed. Didn't register or pay.

6:45 p.m. – So hungry. Beyond exhausted. An Airstream two sites over with windows open. Older couple eat and chat inside. I'm crying and writing, watching them. If I were OK, I'd visit, we'd talk and laugh. I want to go outside, stand in the empty site between us, ask if they'd feed a leper.

8:00 p.m. – I cooked. All that work, couldn't eat. Food repulsive. Exhausted. Dizzy. Awful pain. Can't sleep.

345.

During the dislocated finger incident, the locals told me the medical system in Newfoundland was horrible, and expensive for an American. I Googled the closest hospital in Maine: twenty-three-hour drive and a six-hour ferry ride. Couldn't do it. I lay in bed, in too much pain to sleep, and too exhausted to do anything other than think. I missed Mom, my best friend. I missed her hugs and her voice, and felt so grateful for how close we've been for the last twenty years. I remembered in vivid detail the two days my whole life changed. The first was when I was thirteen and thought I'd lost her. The next was in 2014 when I thought I was going to lose her again.

346.

1992 – Tallahassee, Florida

I was thirteen. After school, Mom loaded my little brother, Ben, and me in the car with all our things and drove us to my dad's small one-bedroom apartment. Mom and Ben cried the whole way. I sat stone-faced in the back seat and swallowed my pain and grief, never dropping a tear.

At 5:15 p.m. I stood on the curb of Dad's apartment like a little soldier in cutoff jean shorts and a dirty blue T-shirt. I couldn't stand my dad.

"Mommy, no," Ben said, in blubbers between wails. "Please, Mommy, don't go."

He stood on my left. Two little suitcases sat to my right, one red, one blue. Two black leaf bags bulging with our clothes lay on the cracked and faded asphalt between the curb and the open hatchback of Mom's car. Mom's shoulders heaved as she shut each door of her empty white Volkswagen Golf. Mom plopped down in the driver's seat with a flump, her left foot planted on the asphalt. There was a pause. I hoped she was changing her mind. Then the foot lifted, the door pulled shut. I watched the hatchback turn the corner and disappear.

347.

I'm proud of Mom for choosing herself. Mom sent Ben and me to live with Dad because she was in love. Dad wanted custody, and I didn't want to live with Mom's boyfriend. It was what was best for her. This was best for me too, for everyone. Mom married her boyfriend and they were the loves of each other's lives. He passed away just after their twenty-seventh anniversary. My stepdad and I gave each other the silent treatment for ten years, until we patched things up in my mid-twenties. We had a friendly, fun-loving relationship. Understanding and perspective changes everything. I'm glad my childhood happened the way it did, and I'm grateful Mom had the guts to follow her heart.

348.

August 23 – Fallsview Campground, Bishop's Falls, Newfoundland

10:00 a.m. – "I figured ya'd check in before ya left," the RV-park manager says, when I call him.

1:00 p.m. – I sit on my front steps and take a deep breath, then my first cough. Then a coughing fit. The pain is like being stabbed and jerked by a gutting knife. Coughing up greenish yellow phlegm. My lungs are full. I had no clue. *Better get that out before it turns into pneumonia.* I press both hands on the rib and cough it all out.

August 24

11:30 a.m. – Sickness much worse.

2:00 p.m. – This is Bad. I don't have the strength to get out of bed. I hug my rib and cough to get more junk out. It's as thick as aged rubber cement. My pulse races, thready. If I sit up, I am faint. A chill runs deep through me, even though I am bundled in blankets in the middle of summer. I'm a paramedic and know the signs.

I have COVID and pneumonia. I might die here.

I grieve for Mom and wish I could pre-erase her pain when she's told I died alone. A wave of panic rolls in. It lasts less than a minute. I remember my true nature. My robot is sick. I am as well and unbroken as ever. I am the energy of everything and cannot be harmed. *This is what's happening. This is the perfect unfolding.*

I fall into complete peace with my body dying. Cool air showers down from an open window above onto my clammy forehead. With eyes closed, in absolute stillness, without fear, regrets, or loneliness, I listen to birds sing a symphony of beautiful melodies and feel as light as their songs. I am curious, eager even, to have the experience of crossing into what comes next. Bathing in birdsong, I drift off.

349.

No one is coming.

This is a gut check. Life and death are at odds. Giving up is an option; so is giving in. When I give in and allow, I discover capabilities beyond my imagination. The sickness is the second time I've known: "My body might die soon." Both times, peace flooded in. Without resistance or fear, I take one step, then another, with no expectations.

To accept mortality so completely, feels like freedom. The fever coursing through my body is neither enemy nor friend. Just what is happening. My job: witness with curiosity. All the nights alone in the wilderness have shown me my place—just another creature living and returning according to ancient rhythms beyond my control.

350.

2014 – Tallahassee, Florida

"My mom does not have a stopwatch on her forehead," I said to Mom's oncologist, in a shuddering voice through clenched teeth. We were in the staff area next to a printer with half a pistachio shell on its LCD screen.

Two nurses sat behind him, pretending to focus on their computers. "Don't you *ever* tell her when she will die."

He stood in his long white coat, leaning a smidge away from me, his elbow resting on a chest-height counter. I was thirty-five, full of spit and vinegar, and my heart had just been ripped in two. Once my whole family was nestled in the elevator, I bolted out to find this pompous idiot. He gazed at me with an *Oh shit!* look.

"So help me God, I swear to you, this little incident will seem like child's play if you ever so much as hint at how long she might have left," I said. "You *do not* know."

I'll give it to Mom's oncologist. He listened. He'd told Mom she had six months to live, maybe two years, max, if the treatment worked. He never mentioned that again, and became Mom's trusted adviser. She loves him, and he lets her do pretty much whatever she wants as far as treatments go. He still gets that *Oh shit!* look when he opens the door and finds me sitting next to Mom at a checkup. It's been over a decade since the little incident. Maybe I'll thank him next time. Call a truce, even.

351.

August 24 – Fallsview Campground, Bishop's Falls, Newfoundland
I wake up in a puddle of sticky sheets and soaked clothes. It's pitch black and I can't see my hand in front of my face. My watch shows 2:30 a.m. I slept over twelve hours. It feels like an instant.

I want to rip off the sheets, undress, and get cool. That small task feels monumental, but I'm not faint. My pulse is slower and stronger. I lie in bed with a cheesy grin in the dead of night, alone in a province thousands of miles from what I once called home. A thought bubbles up with unexpected delight.

I will live!

352.

All my layers of toughness, burned off in the fever. I am tender, raw, new, like a snake that molted its skin. Silly memes, books, and regular emails bring me to tears, good tears. I feel an overwhelming sense of love for and with everything. I've never felt so one with God, the energy of Life, the love that is who we are.

Because I didn't want anyone to worry, I hadn't told a soul I was sick (except the campground manager). I feel ready to share, though not the seriousness of it.

353.

August 27 – Sleepy Cove, Newfoundland

Three days after my fever broke, I drove two hours to Sleepy Cove. Packing up, driving, and setting up took every ounce of energy I had. But I needed the ocean. I stayed for five days, windows open to the salty breeze, parked near the edge of a cliff. My large rear bedroom window faced due west. I lay in bed gazing out, watching the sun soften the sea. Cobalt blues melted into burnt orange, then crimson, then deep violet, each color rippling across the water's surface until sky and sea became indistinguishable.

I slept, long and deep. Eleven to thirteen hours daily, the most I've ever slept as an adult. Other than a ten-minute walk the last day, and daily sits in the sunshine, I never left Coddi. The rhythmic sound of waves against the cliffs below became my lullaby, the changing light my clock. I would have stayed longer, but it was supposed to rain for three days straight and the road was steep with huge ruts. Packing up was exhausting, but my body was healing.

354.

The nearness of death made me more aware of Life.

355.

People sometimes ask where my resilience comes from. I don't think of myself as tough or brave. I just do what needs to be done. Resilience isn't never falling; it's getting up.

Life's challenges have shown me I'm stronger and more adaptable than I thought and that being "in control" is an illusion. Independence, I realized, is often unrecognized interdependence. Life isn't something we have to live through—it's a space to live into with full presence, gratitude, and wonder.

I don't need to learn to survive alone. Even in my most isolated moments, the kindness of strangers supported me, the beauty of nature nourished my soul, and a presence that I struggled to name but felt with increasing clarity comforted me. I mean, how does a physiotherapist who can reduce a mangled finger just show up in the middle of nowhere?

356.

August 31 – Cape Bonavista, Newfoundland
Oh my! This was the most gorgeous place I'd ever lived. Pastureland on cliffs, jagged pristine shoreline in all directions. Waves crashed day and night. Herds of dirty cotton balls grazed all around. Horses and cows munched on grass and a few licked the salt spray off Coddi.

I stood leaning on Casper's front fender, watching a herd of horses, when a Clydesdale with cream feathers on his ankles cantered right at me. A feeling of unease crept up. He was huge. I hoped he was friendly because if he didn't want me here, I was a goner.

My heart raced as his huge nostrils came right at my face. I was trapped between his massive body and my truck. His warm, grassy breath hit my eyes, and I closed them. There I was in the dark, waves crashing, the sound of his billowy sniffing as loud as thunder. Casper's cold metal on one side, his body heat on the other. His musky sweetness filled my nose. He sniffed my hair for a while, long enough for my heart rate to slow and for me to fall into a lovely peace. He was just curious, a gentle giant. A glorious gift.

Two days later I went for my first post-COVID bike ride: got lost in a bog and my robot fatigued quickly. It was a deep hollowness in energy. An exhaustion I'd never experienced.

357.

Boy do I live. That's a quote I'll take on my tombstone. I'm not done yet.

358.

September 4 – Port Rexton, Newfoundland
Two months ago, Perry Dyson suggested I hike the Skerwink Trail. Today was the day. A few minutes in, I noticed two people on a far hillside with white buckets. I guessed they were berry-picking. I looked as I walked, and there they were, tucked in and waiting: wild blueberries.

With all the berry-snacking, it took me an hour to hike the first mile. As I walked further away from houses and people, I slipped into a serene buffet for the senses. Everything slowed. The sounds, sensations, and views invited my stillness. Breeze through the trees, seabirds calling, the scent of pine sap, light filtering in through branches, the feel of long, green grass and scruffy tree bark, the wisp of gentle waves rolling up on beaches below, and an occasional thunder and rumble of a wave ending its journey in a sea cave.

This was one of the most serene and spectacular walks of my life. I wish I could have bottled all the sounds and sensations, not to mention the loveliness of nibbling on wild berries. Thank you, Perry. This was well worth the wait.

After the hike, I called the Birchy Head post office. My Columbia sun shirt had finally arrived. I won't be back there again. The clerk said she'd mail it somewhere else, if I wired her cash. I have no clue where to send it.

359.

The ride is a wild one. The unimaginable paints a masterpiece of happenstance. I can't say when, or how, or why—but I go. Not the easy way, no. This miraculous journey has swept me off my feet and dropped me to my knees. I am not a player in a game. I am the bride and the whore, all tangled into one. I'm a virgin in a white dress and a seductress who licks the cream off my lips to prepare for what's next. A merciful missionary and a beast in a spiked collar dripping with desire. I am strummed by divine fingertips. I am played by the game.

360.

Meeting so many people means there are countless new friends who want to stay connected and enjoy checking up on me. This gets overwhelming. I'm a notorious minimalist when it comes to texting. I crave quiet time and sometimes forget to respond to a text or email for months. I lose track and can't keep up. The friends who don't mind radio silence and can fall into where we left off (even if that was years ago) are the ones I feel closest to.

361.

The daisies outside my window dance and bob as they stretch toward a stormy sky. They are free but for their roots, the same roots that hold them in the patch of dirt that gives them life. The daisy is uninhibited in being a daisy. I may feel restricted by the laws of society, but I am unbridled in living. I don't choose what to do next, but welcome both the unconventional and the mundane with a warm rush in my gut that knows the two are the same. My body breathes without input or decision. The moment my last breath becomes air, the primal drum in my chest takes its first and final rest, and I am released from my roots into the infinite wander ...

In that moment I will remember: I lived to watch the daisy wiggle in the breeze and stretch for the sun that shines in the clear-blue pane, just beyond this rainy Saturday.

362.

September 5 – Port Rexton, Newfoundland
Blueberries galore! The sun hasn't risen yet, and microscopic dew beads dust each berry. Blueberries in Newfoundland are ground cover. Picking is hard on the back and the berries are tiny. Each is a unique explosion of intense sweet and slightly tangy flavor, with a hint of earthiness. Until now, I'd thought store-bought wild blueberries were legit. Nope, they're faded photocopies with merely a hint of the original. Life seems the same way. It's all Technicolor now. I had no clue I was living a black-and-white life.

363.

Fabien and Daniele texted me. They were home and cleaning their boat. Fabien asked me to come visit them in Québec City. I thanked him and said I would head south toward Florida once off the island, but would love to visit, maybe next year.

"Don't wait until I'm dead and buried," he replied.

364.

September 6 – Come By Chance, Newfoundland
Woohoo! First farm-fresh veggies in two months! A roadside angel with an enormous garden was selling veggies out of his truck. I told him I'd been looking for him for months. And how about the serendipitous name of this town? Come By Chance. Best town name ever. I wish I were from here. *Oh wait, today I am.*

I parked at an abandoned campground on the water in Come By Chance: picturesque nature, privacy, a picnic table, fire ring, beautiful hiking trails right from camp. I'd thought I'd stay a while but had to leave to get my computer fixed the next morning. I was bummed. Then I remembered: "You are on this journey to learn to say goodbye."

A raven told me this in 2018. I thought it meant with people, Mom in particular. Years later, the scope of the message keeps expanding—places, people, spaces, sickness, pain, hope, expectations, hurt, worry, resentment, ideas, beliefs, my body, life itself. When I allow and let go of everything with gentleness, this is a gift. There is so much freedom in release. Each time I see a raven or even a crow I am reminded: *You are on this journey to learn to say goodbye.*

When nothing is left, I'll know I'm there.

365.

So, about the little town called Dildo. For the last two months I've seen the T-shirts, stickers, and coffee mugs, and I swore I'd never set foot in that tourist trap of a place. Life has a sense of humor.

My computer had a major hiccup. No fret! I carry a backup computer.

I hadn't logged into it in four years and forgot the access password. Not good. My livelihood depends on Zoom calls and writing. There aren't stores to buy computers here, and ordering anything takes a month or more. I spent an entire day on YouTube trying to fix it myself. Nope. I called all over Newfoundland. Repair guys said the soonest the part would arrive was October 20. BUT this one guy said there was hope. He could definitely hack the password issue and was fairly certain that my laptop fan needed to be cleaned and lubed, no new parts needed. It was an hour's drive. Guess where? DILDO!

366.

Now that my soul has been touched like this, and my lips have experienced kisses as delicate, sensual, and slow as caressing a butterfly, I am again changed. More alive, allowing, and aware of a silent knowing. Life glistens. I am more awake to carnal sensations, where a single glance of the lips might linger for many moments, a pause of revelation, a sipping in of this timeless time, a remembering of everything.

367.

September 7 – Dildo, Newfoundland
I went to Dildo to meet the computer magician, Randy. Yes, Randy lives in Dildo. I can't make this up. Randy was kind, helpful, and the best computer tech I've ever met. He took apart all the little bits of my internal laptop fan, cleaned and lubed everything, put it back together, and it purrs like a kitten! He also wiped the software clean. I don't think my laptop ran this well when brand-new. The cherry on top is I had a beach-side rustic boondocking site for three nights, one of the most stunning and secluded seaside spots yet. I kinda fell in love with the small town, but I wasn't buying a T-shirt.

To sum things up: I left Come By Chance to meet Randy in Dildo. Randy cleaned all my parts, lubed everything up, and now I'm happy as a clam. I'm blushing.

And yeah, as with everything else, this really did happen.

368.

Free at Last

A man in a seaside town wears rubber boots,
a stained orange vest, and the stench of dead fish.
He slogs along and hauls carcasses off boats under a swarm of
seagulls.

Twenty-somethings drone on like robots behind a gas station counter.
A man drops two toddlers at daycare and works the whole day to pay
their way.
Outside a barbershop, women hold cigarettes
between rusty brown fingernails and prune lips.
A lady in a suit at her desk after dark is a slave to her house and car.

A wrinkled old man, swallowed by heather gray sweats and frizzy
white hair,
sits in a wheelchair on a cliff beside an empty wooden bench.
He gazes over a cove of crashing waves.
Alone with the wind; salt spray dots his glasses. He watches familiar
seagulls swarm.
He breathes and sits and breathes and breathes.

Eyes steady, focused on the deep blue, he reaches down and releases
the brake.
He digs the heels of threadbare brown slippers into grass dotted with
gold flowers.
He leans forward and pulls his heels back. The chair moves forward a
smidge.
He breathes and sits and breathes and breathes, eyes still and full of
wild sea.
He digs his heels in again, leans forward, and pulls back.

As free as a seagull … one last time.

369.

September 9 – Dildo, Newfoundland

A big hurricane was coming. At 4:30 a.m., I bit the bullet and booked the Argentia ferry to Nova Scotia for the 14th, in five days. My rig is fifty-two feet long, and spots that big had been sold out for weeks. Talk about lucky!

Tears filled my eyes as I booked the ticket. I'd fallen in love with the people and this land. The kindness of Newfoundlanders was like something out of a fairy tale. I hoped the hurricane would leave my friends alone.

I felt greedy. These months had been an amazing gift, yet I wanted more. That thought dried my eyes.

I will step from this land onto a metal beast that will take Coddi out to sea. This heaven on earth is forever etched into my soul. The summer had been a coming home, as if I belonged in Newfoundland and Labrador, and it had found me again. Something deep within recognized itself here.

I prepped Coddi for a trip to the big city of St. John's to restock with propane, food, and essentials.

370.

I'm tired of fending for myself and fed the hell up with bad roads. These roads must have been paved by a one-legged hooker while she was trying to get laid. My back's knotted; zaps of pain take me to the floor. My rib, snapped almost a month ago, still clicks when I breathe. What a friggin' mess.

Coddi and I are both broken-down old broads. I'm ready to sit in one place for a month. Let weeds grow round my tires, wake up without wracking my morning brain to remember where I am—a forest, a new friend's driveway, or a hardware store parking lot. I'm ready to walk into that hardware store and rent the man who can fix it all, then leave him at the curb, tool in hand.

371.

September 10 – Signal Hill, St. John's, Newfoundland
While hiking rocky cliffs, I spotted a cruise ship out at sea. Twenty minutes later, I sat on a steep slope munching blueberries as it passed below. Hundreds of people crowded its balconies. Their flashing cameras seemed zeroed in on me. Exhaust hung in a blue haze filling St. John's bay. I judged them as spoiled sheeple paying to pollute, wasting food, and buying up needless trinkets that would soon fill a landfill. I knew none of that to be true.

372.

September 12 – Cape Broyle, Newfoundland
Yesterday, I parked on a tiny peninsula on public property in Cape Broyle, Newfoundland (population 450). A lady was walking her dog, and I asked if I could stay there a couple of nights. An hour later she surprised me with fresh molasses raisin bread. When I asked about the fish market, she said, "Come, darlin. My neighbor's got fresh cod." As we walked, afternoon sun shone on her face, the skin beside her eyes etched with deep laugh lines.

This morning, I went kayaking along the rocky shore, exploring sea caves and tiny coves. I heard and saw my first waterfall from a kayak. *How can I leave this place?* Tears welled while I floated next to a twenty-foot waterfall. On my left, a bald eagle perched on a submerged boulder ripped apart a fish. It was time to leave, and Fabien was right. I didn't want to wait till he died to visit. I messaged that I'd be in Québec City in a couple of weeks, and had the post office ship my shirt to them.

373.

When a crystal-clear body of water fills to overfull, one small storm can be the tipping point. The dam bursts. Everything pours out in a deluge. All the dirt and debris settled at the bottom gets stirred in the rushing water until it all becomes churning chocolate milk. These floodwaters ravage the landscape and take no prisoners. I was about to experience this firsthand.

September 13 - Colinet, Newfoundland

Before leaving Newfoundland, I wanted to visit a bird sanctuary. I was twenty miles from a boondocking spot on the beach. My plan was to drive there, sleep, and go to the sanctuary at dawn before boarding the ferry.

The two-lane paved highway turned to dirt. After another mile, it was a washboard with potholes as big as Volkswagens. I thought it was just a rough patch, so I crept along. An hour later, my blood was boiling. I'd gone six miles. Nowhere to turn around, no phone service to check for alternate routes. It was sunset, moose-hazard time. I hadn't eaten since breakfast.

I stopped to check Coddi. Spices fell. There was turmeric powder all over the counter. Both sliding doors fell off the cabinets. Food was strewn everywhere. This road was killing Coddi.

I kept driving.

"FUUUUUCK!" I screamed so loud my throat was raspy. It was dark, and I was at least ten miles from my sleeping spot.

"What the FUCK? Fucking road. All for a fucking bird! Motherfucking road. Fucking tearing up Coddi."

Coddi couldn't take much more.

"Motherfuckerrrrrrrr!"

"Fuck this fucking road!" Alligator tears fell.

"For a fucking bird!" I hunched forward, my forehead almost on the steering wheel.

"Motherfucking rooahooahoooooad!" I full-on wailed while Casper crawled down the road from hell.

"Fucking destroying my Coddi."

Looking back, this frustration was the culmination of everything. I'd skated the knife's edge of suffering for far too long. I needed, no … it was more than a need. Somewhere deep inside, I *was ready* to fall over the edge, and bonk. I dreamed a secret wish—to collapse into a heap, spent, and for someone to scoop me up, tend to my wounds, and whisper in my ear that everything would be OK. I was sick and tired of fending for myself, by myself. I was fucking done with being strong.

"FUUUUUUUUUUUUUCK!" I shouted between gasps and guttural moans.

I wailed with snot dripping down my face until utter exhaustion kicked in.

"I'm fucking hungry," I said, in a soft, melancholy tone.

"I'm fucking tired."

375.

One velvet movement, guided by all that is. A touch so gentle, a flutter of energy, intense yet tender, when two exhale as one, and the corners of mouths both curl up in almost imperceptible smiles. A recognition of a playfulness at the heart of all of This. The next touch of the vermilion zone and a closing around each other, a soul hug, in the most serene of ways. Then the gradual opening, a dance that continues indefinitely.

376.

September 14 – Argentia, Newfoundland

Rather than staying at the beach, I boondocked at an abandoned US military base five minutes from the ferry. I skipped the bird sanctuary, slept in, and fixed a few things on Coddi. In the middle of washing dishes at 1:20 p.m. (1320 hours), it struck me that the ferry left at 1500 hours, not 5:00 p.m. I had to check in two hours before departure or I'd lose my ticket. *SHIT!* I readied Coddi in a whirlwind and called the ferry-ticket line while driving Casper and Coddi like a bat out of hell. "I'm three minutes out. Can you keep my reservation, please??"

"You haven't missed the ferry," the lady on the phone said. "The ferry leaves at 5:00 p.m. and you have until 3:00 p.m. to board." All the tension melted away. I exhaled and eased off the gas. *I gotta get a grip.*

Because of high winds and seas, the approximate sailing time to Nova Scotia was seventeen hours. Since I'd bought a last-minute ticket, I didn't get a bed on the ferry. Passengers couldn't go on the vehicle decks once the ferry left. Staying in your RV wasn't allowed.

I parked on the ferry, hopped in Coddi, shut the door, and pulled down all the blinds. I was a stowaway in my own home and slept all night in my comfy bed.

377.

Even good girls have unruly streaks.

Part Four: Beliefs Unbound Migrating South

As I left Newfoundland, I carried with me not just memories of stunning landscapes and unexpected connections, but also a deeper recognition: the bike crash, COVID, the broken rib, and the horrible roads weren't interruptions in my adventure. They were the adventure itself, each challenge revealing how everything that arises in life is here to help us discover our infinite and eternal true nature.

I continued south, carrying Newfoundland and Labrador's lessons with me: resilience in the face of injury and illness, gratitude for the kindness of strangers, and growing reminders that true coddiwompling isn't just about traveling, and I don't have to do it alone.

378.

September 16 – Cape Breton Island, Nova Scotia
Reporting live from Nova Scotia, in the outer bands of a hurricane! Last night I hunkered down on the Gulf of St. Lawrence with a large hill to the east and south to block the wind.

My close friends from Iowa, Jim and Rhonda, saw my Facebook post about leaving Newfoundland on the ferry. As it ended up, we were all on the Cabot Loop. They were on a bus tour and it seemed as though we wouldn't be in the same area. I rounded a bend and saw a tour bus parked in a small cove. There was a man who looked like Jim walking a hundred yards up the road. Then the man's arms shot up in the air, and it looked as if he were doing a little victory dance. As I drove up, the look on his face was priceless: shock, awe, and pure joy. We hugged and laughed and hugged. What were the chances? We hadn't seen each other in two years!

379.

September 18th – Antigonish, Nova Scotia

New Friends in Nova Scotia

Apple trees shade my house on wheels.
Raindrops drum on my aluminum roof.
The old sky-blue home I'm parked next to is cute and tidy.
Perky flower beds and gardens ring all sides.
Wind chimes jingle and clang.

The little house is crawling with spiders,
big ones with bulging abdomens.
Webs stretch under cabinets and across bookshelves.
Fruit flies, houseflies, and mosquitoes have free rein.
No one seems to mind.

I minded—until I realized no one else did.
While sipping tea, I found a snail in the bowl of blueberries,
pea-sized, wet, and translucent tan.
I set it on the table beside my plate.
No one seemed to mind.

We had a candlelit dinner in the middle of a hurricane.
An orange moth fluttered from atop a pile of green beans,
to my hand, to the lip of my glass, back to my fork.
We watched and giggled, in awe of our guest.

I'd met the fascinating couple who lived in the blue house, Karen and Stephen, at the writing festival in Newfoundland. Weeks later, they invited me to visit. It was a special time of slowing down, understanding, and sharing. After four days of conversations, walks, and meals, it was clear that Karen and I would make a great team. Since then, she's been editing my blogs and magazine articles.

380.

Having an Airstream is like joining a massive circle of kindred spirits. Just about every Airstream owner feels like a friend. In the past few years, I've made many connections through Airstream Club International. There are rallies and caravans for club members throughout the year. I go to one or two rallies a year. Each is a few days or up to a week long. Some rallies have ten or fewer Airstreams, others have over a thousand. We look out for each other and have fun together.

381.

September 19, 8:00 a.m. – Antigonish, Nova Scotia
Coddi is broken. She's cracked her aluminum skin above the door. I drove her too hard over those god-awful roads. Or maybe it happened when the wind from the hurricane slammed her door shut a couple of days ago. Or maybe both. Now my beautiful girl needs a patch. I have to find an Airstream specialist. I'm not ready to go back. Back to where? I guess the US. I've got no "back" to get back to.

382.

People wonder about my wandering. Some think I wander to find something.

383.

Road life: all fun and games, huh? Let me tell ya, right now it's a bitch. In the last three days, I lived through a hurricane, threw out my back, bent Coddi's rear end driving through a gully in the storm, and found a horrible crack in the aluminum above my door. Now I have to drive to Maine to get the crack repaired ASAP, by a guy who's never seen a crack like that, which gives me a heap of faith.

384.

Since setting off on this journey, the questions I get asked the most are: *Have you found someone yet? Do you have a special guy in your life? What's your dating life like on the road?*

385.

September 21 – Prince Edward Island, Canada
I'm exploring the island while listening to *Anne of Green Gables*, an entirely new discovery as of yesterday. My next stop is at the house with the green gables, a national historic site. My parents didn't read for fun, there were no shelves of books in the house, and I don't recall reading a book except for schoolwork. When I was a kid, I felt (and looked) just like this orphan girl, Anne. I wish she'd been my friend when I was growing up, even if only between the pages.

386.

Flash-forward to November—I wander to Virginia to visit a friend. I meet someone else. This meeting isn't normal from the get-go. On the front porch of a cottage, on a crisp afternoon, with the vibrant colors of fall surrounding us, I get caught in the tractor beam of a pair of cerulean-blue eyes. I gasp as my head snaps to the right, a full-on look-away. A surge of electricity runs from my scalp to my toes. Looking into these eyes feels like staring into the sun, but they aren't too bright. They are too something else. Too knowing, perhaps? Too seeing? Too strong, maybe? Yes, too strong, an uncomfortable strong that seems to read parts of me I've kept hidden even from myself. Yet I keep wanting to look.

387.

What looks like wandering is Life exploring its own infinite nature. I look, but I am not looking for anything. The thrill isn't in the unknown—it's in the recognition that what I was seeking (to know myself) was what was looking (awareness).

388.

Can a woman not enjoy her life, solo? No, I don't date. For Pete's sake, I am in love with God.

389.

September 22 – Blooming Point, Prince Edward Island

Man in the Storm
Bang Bang Bang
A grumpy old man pounded on my trailer.
Bang Bang Bang Bang
I opened my door. Wind howled, rain pissed.
His wrinkled jowls sagged into the collar of a burnt-orange winter
    slicker.
He spit words laced with greed, jealousy, and bitter rage
at the person he imagined me to be.
His forehead as rutted as a prune, fists balled.
I stepped out in thin cotton pajamas and shut the door.
He stepped back.
He was pissed I'd parked on the beach near his house.
As mad as he tried to be, he couldn't hurt a fly,
which had to piss him off worse.
Once he knew I was all he'd get, he laid it on thicker.
"You're being a bit aggressive," I said.
"I am not!" he spat back, with fire in his eyes.
I held back a giggle while he pummeled me; round two.
Waves of rage rose up in my throat like a rabid badger.
I swallowed that shallow bugger.
Grump asked what I did for work. I told him.
"Well, maybe you can straighten me out," he said,
with a genuine laugh and a split-second smile.
"That's quite possible." We stood as friends.
His old-bastard Broadway act swooped back in.

Beach sand crusted up between my clean toes,
my pajamas wet, my hair a tangled, drowned rat.
"I'm going back inside," I said, and opened the door.
He half-turned away, then stopped to spit back more.
"I'm Kristy, by the way."
He looked me in the eye.
His mouth moved one syllable with no sound.
His rain jacket fluttered like a bird wing against his cheek.
His eyes dropped to the ground as he turned into the storm.
He hated me yet didn't know me.
The storm rumbled most of the night.
Squalls jostled my trailer.

I don't know myself.
I am him.

390.

I'm in the real world again. This ain't no Newfoundland fairy tale.

The people of Newfoundland are an invitation for me to drop my belief in separation, to give without reason, to care, to love, to see the good in everyone. Newfoundlanders don't think they're being nice. They're simply living. I want to be like them. More than anything, I want to know there is no such thing as "them."

391.

I may not continue this way. People infer I'm running from something or seeking a lost piece of my soul. *Is that true?* My heart says no. Yet there are moments I question myself and this lifestyle.

These moments are like when the sea's surface stills. Looking into the depths, I see I've been running from shadows, from a love I didn't realize I was missing. I've found everything else. Nowhere new I need to go, no one else to meet, nothing more to be. It's all right here, crystal clear. Then wind blows, the sea's surface ripples. I forget and wander to the next place, the next experience.

392.

September 25, 2:00 a.m.

I woke up with an eerie feeling that I hadn't locked Casper. My brain reached and reached into the abyss. *Where am I?* Even the country I was in was a mystery. I sat up in bed. Blank, black, unknown. *I could be anywhere.* My head was dizzy with vertigo. I planted my feet on a cold hardwood floor and stood. My left shoulder crashed against the closet door like a middle linebacker going in for a tackle. I bounced to the right and stumbled. My gut smacked a cold slick countertop and my palm caught the back of a kitchen sink. It felt as if I were on a boat in rough seas. I shuffled to the door, blinded by a moonless night. My hand found a slim metal handle, cold as ice. I had no idea what was on the other side. I lifted the handle, a click, then a slow, whiny screech. *I need to oil that in the morning.*

393.

November – Virginia

The first day we meet, I never want to look into another pair of eyes more. A cerulean tapestry; the right eye has a speck of brown at the nine o'clock position, and three smaller specks ring the underside. Those specks in a sea of blue painted with textures and lines of love and youth. Looking feels like admiring a fine painting by peeping through a neighbor's window, and simultaneously like awareness recognizing itself—too intimate, too immediate, like seeing my own face in an unexpected mirror.

We hike and I am invited to lunch at M's cottage. We cook together and talk for hours. I overstay my welcome for a first hang-out with someone I've never met. I invite M to the national forest to see Coddi the next day. Invite accepted without hesitation. We hug on the porch, share a second hug at the door of my truck.

I get to Coddi and I can't stop thinking about those eyes, about the way time seems to stretch and contract in M's presence. I find myself replaying that first moment of connection, wondering what has happened. Why has this affected me so strongly? I haven't felt this kind of immediate connection since ... well, maybe ever. The wanderer in me recognizes something kindred, something that both excites and terrifies me. It's as if one of the last walls around my heart cracks, just a whisper of an opening, but enough to let a ray of light in.

394.

If being in awe is a flavor of love, then yes. I wander for the sake of love.

395.

September 25, 2:00 a.m.

I peeked out the door through a six-inch gap, one cheek pressed against the cold door jamb, the other tight against the door. Frosty salt air met my nose. Could this be how a baby sees? Shapes and shades without names, without reason or meaning. I saw without seeing, a kaleidoscope of blackness and grays. Then a million-piece jigsaw puzzle fell into place. Dark silhouettes turned into trees, an empty camp chair on flat gravel, the faint lull of ocean waves; past some bushes, a fire ring and picnic table. *I'm in a campground.* Billions of stars and the Milky Way, its misty swath stretched vertical across an onyx sky, pointing to a ribbon of ocean between a gap in the trees.

My breath hung in frigid air, and my entire world rushed back into resolute knowing. *Fundy National Park. I'm in New Brunswick!* It was my second night here. My neighbors were Ted and Mary. I'd locked Casper before my campfire burned out. *All is perfect.* I closed the door to my capsule and slipped back into bed. I missed that soupy muddle of blissful drunken cluelessness. What a beautiful mess.

396.

The dark is an interesting space. It's the unknown. It's where I came from and where I will go. Sometimes the dark is scary, but only when my thoughts run wild.

397.

What if I labeled nothing? What if no one labeled me? What if I had no beliefs? What if there were no judgments and all expectations fell away?

398.

Speaking of labels, I am a coddiwompler. I'll take that one.

399.

When I don't know what to do I ask myself one question and I know my next step: *What would I do if I couldn't get this wrong?* Life is oh so clean in this decisionless space.

400.

September 27 – Augusta, Maine
I slept in a Walmart parking lot. When I woke up, I bought three gallons of oil, gathered my tools, changed Casper's oil and filter, checked all the fluids, and tightened Coddi's lug nuts. After showering and recycling the used oil, I was on my way to the Airstream doctor by 10:00 a.m. He patched the crack in Coddi's aluminum and took care of a few other issues in three hours. The service was superb. I'd planned to head to Québec City to visit Daniele and Fabien for a few days, but Daniele's mom was unwell and Fabien was struggling with a new treatment. I continued south.

401.

November – Virginia
Here's the deal: I'd have looked into those blue eyes more if I'd known I couldn't get it wrong. Even I forget sometimes.

402.

I'm Back
The window is open and sounds of the highway blast in.
I miss the simple way.
I miss quiet mornings with birds chirping.

I miss kindness and care and Newfoundland accents thick as mud.
I miss slowness and chilly mornings.

Back in the US.
Good hearts get crammed into busy boxes.
We learn to perform instead of just being.
To-do lists crowd out wonder.
I've forgotten too.

People gave me dolls and tiny ponies.
My brother got G.I. Joes—we learned our roles.
School trained the creativity out of me;
my job was to follow orders.
Homework taught me productivity outranks peace,
and my work is never done.

My mother's story is the same, her mother too.
The whole lot of us, poisoned.
Sadness fills my windows and cages my wild heart
like a tiger behind bars.
Being back is like waking up in an arena,
packed with a sellout crowd.
So many are walking around with the flu.
I can stay, or …

403.

September 28 – Freeport, Maine

I stopped in Freeport, an outlet store mecca, to pick up a "real coat" from the Patagonia outlet. I don't like shopping, so I beelined it right to Patagonia and straight back to Coddi. On the walk back, William called. In July, when I'd texted him about my feelings, I'd played it safe. If he'd known the depth of what I'd truly felt, he might have moved mountains. I sat on a bench just off the sidewalk, in the hustle and bustle of outlet stores, phone to my ear.

"All you have to do is get to Goose Bay," William said. "I'll fly you here. I'll take you everywhere. We can hunt and fish."

People walked by with bulging bags of clothes and trinkets. The further I got from William, in time and distance, the less the pull. I still wanted to go back, not to live, but to see more.

"When the ice comes, I'll take you on skiddoos anywhere you want, further than Hebron. We can go to Killiniq, all the way north."

I stared at SALE and DISCOUNT signs hanging from store windows. "You're such a special man, so sweet and kind, and I'd love to see Labrador with you." People beside me ate candied peanuts out of paper cones, and perfectly good peanuts littered the sidewalk. My feral instincts wanted to gather them up, waste like that made my stomach turn. "I'm so far away now. I need to keep going south. I'd love to come back someday."

Truth was, I'd rather be in the wilds of Labrador than in this blight of materialism. But, as much as I think I'm feral, I am more this than that.

404.

"Love says, come hover near my window, abandon your home, forsake being the candle, instead learn how to savor being the moth."[10] – Rumi

Fire has always captivated me. My parents built a backyard campfire ring when I was five to keep me from burning down the neighborhood. Often I'd sneak out before walking to the school bus. Using leaves and twigs, I'd restart a fire from hot coals from the night before. A "no-match fire." My moth was drawn for no reason.

Then I grew up and learned to ignore that pull. Society teaches us to be smart, and to drown the flame of our passions in a flood of sound decisions. Many of us go to school (where creativity is taught out of us), get a job, search for the right partner, buy the big house, adopt the pet, have 2.5 kids, and work the rest of our lives to pay for our sins.

Thank God my moth survived deep inside, and clawed its way back into my awareness.

405.

2006 – North Port, Florida

At 2:00 a.m., I walked into the firehouse after a medical call. Everyone was asleep except me and Randy, my EMT on the ambulance. I sat down at the computer. Most EMTs go to bed and let the paramedic type up the report on their own, but Randy insisted on keeping me company.

"I love souls," Randy said, with a soft resolve. He sat a couple of feet to my right, reclined in an office chair, palms resting on his navy-blue uniform pants.

I paused and looked at him. He gazed back, emotionless. I wondered if lack of sleep was getting to him and what he was talking about.

"I love souls," he said again. "It doesn't matter what body they're in."

It took me a moment to get what he was saying. Randy was married and had a three-year-old son.

Fast-forward twelve years. The scene: It was a crisp mid-October evening in 2018. Close to 300 eyes were welling with tears, beautiful love-filled tears. We were mesmerized by the most gorgeous and touching wedding ceremony.

Randy was standing to the left struggling to read his vows through overflowing emotions; Kaiden, Randy's son and best man (who was fifteen years old), had tears of love streaming down his face; and across from Randy was Jon, a kind, handsome young man Randy had met seven years earlier.

Kaiden has two fathers and a rich family atmosphere that is helping him grow into one of the finest young men I have ever met. Jon is the father and husband he dreamed of being. Randy not only has a loving, strong, and kind partner, he has the huge, loving family he wished for. The foundation of all this is love. A love of souls.

406.

October 1 – Dover, New Hampshire

There is a fly on the ceiling above my head. It hasn't moved a muscle all night. Warm morning light drips in around the window shades. I duck low and sneak out of bed to brew green tea. Opening the oven door little by little, to ward off loud creaks, I reach in and pull out my pot with extra care and set it on the stove without a sound.

Who is this courteous so as not to disturb a sleeping fly?

I slip back into bed, crawl low and slow, and hope he is still there. He is.

407.

November – Virginia – Day Two

M is due to arrive at Coddi at 11:00 a.m.

I wake before dawn, my mind racing. Those eyes haunted me through the night, not in a scary way, but in the way a song stays with you long after the music has stopped. I plan the day with care, straightening up Coddi, choosing the mug I'll offer for tea, even changing my shirt twice. This attention to detail is so not me.

At 10:15 a.m. I drive to find firewood and pass a sign on the road: "Firewood for sale." A lanky ol' fella in a beat-up pickup, Gary, greets me. I follow him further into the farm, where split wood lies in piles.

"The views!" I say. "What a place." We stand at the crest of a hill and look out over a picturesque scene: two red barns, three silos, and rolling fields sporting the last fall colors.

Gary tells me about his seventy-year passion for milking cows. He tells me about cancer, relationships, and love.

My eyes well with tears. I tell him about my mom's long cancer journey and my wandering journey. Gary softens even more. We hug. More tears, more sharing. This is the most love I've ever felt with a complete stranger. Gary and I fill the back of Casper with enough wood for several fires, and he refuses to let me pay.

"I hope to see you again," I say. "You are a special man, Gary."

Tears well up a couple more times on my way back to Coddi. I imagine introducing Gary and M, and sharing the views together. For the first time in a long time, I'm not just having experiences. I'm gathering things to share.

408.

October 4 – Green Mountain Wilderness, Vermont
My friend Randy (the Randy in the wedding ceremony) stayed with me in Coddi for two days. We understand each other, share endless laughter, and fart all the livelong day together. We love each other somethin' fierce.

"So, one thing," I said. I stood in the kitchen, and Randy sat on Coddi's front bed, next to his overnight bag. "I've got a roommate."

"A roommate?" Randy tilted his head to the side and squinted.

"Yes, it's a housefly." I busted into laughter. Randy cackled, bent over at the waist, shaking his head as if wondering what the punch line was.

"I know that must sound crazy, but he's been traveling with me for over a week and he's very courteous. He sleeps on the ceiling above my bed."

Randy pressed his lips together in a smirk, trying not to laugh, and his eyes shot from side to side with a twinkle of inner mischief.

"He won't run off or anything, and he's free to go if he wants. I just don't want you to smash him."

"OK, no smashing the fly," Randy said, through laughter, with raised wiggly eyebrows.

409.

The more I come to know who I am, the essence of our true nature, the less there is to fear … until fear itself fades into an illusion that grabs hold only when I forget.

410.

Enough
I give everything away.
My time, my attention, the fruits of my labor, life's greatest
    wonderments.
To devices, to life, to people I meet and have known for forever.
My income is half of what it was, but I do just fine.
Once upon a time, I sold my house and bought a guy for a year.
I paid to be an apprentice to master the art of coaching.

It felt like buying a pack of gum.
Life set me free.

It was worth every bit of 75,000 bucks.
I got it all—freedom in every form.
Now, I give it away.
I get paid to point out the obvious.
This is a fairy-tale dream.

A doctor hired me to coach him.
"I've paid coaches three times that! And my life is still a mess,"
he said, as we sat fireside surrounded by vibrant autumn wilderness.

I love the forest and yet,
I'm here because it's free livin'.
The doctor has two cars and a mansion, and he wants what I've got.
My fee is a drop in his bucket;
for me, it's more than enough.

411.

October 9 – Green Mountain Wilderness, Vermont
On my last day in Vermont, there were two flies in Coddi. One was not
courteous. It flew at my face, buzzed my ears, and walked across my skin.
I tried to shoo the annoying one out. I closed the door and sat down on
my bed. A fly buzzed my face. The wrong one left. That was the end of
being roomies with a fly. I missed falling asleep knowing my little buddy
would be there when I woke up.

412.

November – Virginia – Day Two
I drive to camp with Gary's firewood. M arrived early and is waiting.
Standing behind Casper, we hug, chat, and I tear up sharing about Gary and
his insights on life and love. As if doing a triceps press, I push myself up
on Casper's tailgate. I sit, weep, and blabber about gratitude while looking

into those cerulean-blue eyes. "Then I get back and you're here," I say to M. As soon as the words leave my mouth, I wonder what I meant, and I wonder what M heard in that.

M puts both palms on my knees and leans toward me. I stiffen and do not respond.

413.

October 12 – Martha's Vineyard, Massachusetts

I left the forest in Vermont, dropped Coddi at Randy's house near Boston, and drove Casper to visit a friend in Martha's Vineyard for a few days.

"You wanna go swimming?" my friend Sharon asked. We wore jackets and layers, with pants rolled up to our shins, bare feet crusted in sand. Jagged pewter cliffs towered to my right, and the Atlantic churned to my left. It was 2:00 p.m., and a few small dark figures peppered the alabaster sand as far as I could see.

"Aww, I didn't bring a suit," I said.

Sharon's lips stretched up in a smile. Waves crashed and white foam rolled up the sand behind her. Wind blew wispy gray hair across her face.

She cocked her head and looked up at me as if I were a tall, innocent kid. "Nudeness is accepted here," she said. "And no pressure if you're uncomfortable."

Reasons not to undress flew through my mind like stock-exchange ticker tape.

It's too cold.

There are people.

It's daylight; skinny-dipping is for the dead of night.

We don't have towels.

We'd be naked on a public beach.

It's way too cold.

I haven't shaved down there in a month.

I'll get sand in my clothes.

Sharon's boyfriend will see my tits.

Nudeness is fine, but not with people around.

It's cold.
It's cold.
It's freezing cold.

Sharon held my eyes with that sweet, no-strings invitation. She and the sea waited for my answer.

"OK," I said, soft and unsure. I unzipped my jacket.

She unzipped hers. Our hands moved faster as we took off each layer, leaving a lumpy pile of clothes on the sand.

Frigid wind, wet sand, tits and pubic hair. I didn't mean to look, but it surprised me that Sharon's was jet-black when her hair was silver. She turned toward the sea. Her ass cheeks jiggled and seawater splashed as she scampered into the surf. And there I went too. My feet slapped water and frosty needles stung from my shins up to my chest.

The icy sea grabbed the soft skin of my belly; it stole my breath. A wave rolled in. My body went rigid and I rocketed up on my tiptoes to get more of me out of the bitter cold. There'd be relief once my head went under.

I took a deep breath, gritted my teeth, and dove in.

414.

October 17 – Guilford, Connecticut

As I drove south from Boston, I carried that wild freedom from Martha's Vineyard with me. I thought about how my beloved misfit collection is a jumbo human crayon box: various sizes, ages, nationalities, social statuses, races, sexual preferences, religions, and more. In three days, I'd slept in three different beds, eaten meals at five different homes, cheered on South Africa's Springboks at a rugby World Cup party, enjoyed a colossal bouquet of hugs, and shared stories full of laughter and learning with everyone. I am an expression of all of us. Now, I sit in the solitude of my little sanctuary on wheels, typing as the sun rises over the Atlantic. As that last sentence appeared on the screen, someone knocked on my door, inviting me for a walk.

415.

November – Virginia – Day Two

I hop off Casper's tailgate and give M a tour of Coddi. Next, M and I coddi-womple up a mountain with no trail. We bushwhack toward the peak to take in the view. Halfway up, I fall into awe. To be in the presence of one who loves to wander in conversation and in life, and is not afraid ... What a day of exhales. Halfway up the mountain and the whole way back, I fight and fight and fight against the unrelenting urge to reach for, and hold, M's hand.

416.

October 18 – Guilford, Connecticut, visiting Lorna and Edi

Edi mentioned he had a profound experience involving flies many decades ago. In the middle of sharing, Edi's face stretched and wrinkled with emotions, and tears streamed. He wasn't able to speak. He looked at Lorna and cried. She gazed back, silent and full of love. Witnessing them together flamed a fire inside. This depth of connection was what I desired.

Once Edi's waves of emotion settled, he shared how the feeling of flies walking on his skin saved him. They brought him back to the now, back from the dark place he'd been living in, back from the need to end his life.

Later, I shared about my fly roommate and said, "I imagined that fly could have been my dad."

"What do you mean by that?" Edi asked.

"If you can hear me, Dad, I'm sorry for this," I said. "What he said and how he lived his life didn't match. He loved to preach at me, and behind closed doors, he judged and did things that didn't seem right and fair. I didn't feel comfortable being around him when I was young, or as an adult. That fly? Maybe Dad just wanted to share space with me in silence—no agenda, no need to save my soul or try to change me."

Edi's profound respect for flies became even more obvious. He described how special flies are, the uniqueness of their eyes, how they walk on glass windows and defy physics because of suction cups on their feet. Edi loved flies, and he was here today thanks to them.

"So I take it you don't swat or kill them?" I said.

"No," he said, then giggled. "But I don't have the same reverence for mosquitoes."

417.

November – Virginia – Day Two
I'm enjoying looking into those cerulean eyes when M's head snaps to the right. M's whole body follows—it's the head-turn, sharp-inhale, too-strong look-away. Just like my experience yesterday; a dose of the same medicine. I smile on the inside. On the outside, I just sit there looking.

418.

While visiting Lorna and Edi in Connecticut, I was on Zoom for an online writing class when a close friend, Antra, shared that her cancer was back and the diagnosis was serious. I looked up flights. There were direct flights from Newark and New York to Portland. A friend, Garret, in New Jersey, popped to mind as a possible place to store Coddi. I called him. He said to come on over. An hour after hearing about Antra's health, I'd booked tickets.

419.

October 23 – New Vernon, New Jersey
Three zinnias traveled with me for over three weeks. Cut flowers in a jar of water, bumbling and bouncing down the road across five states. These beauties came from a friend's garden in New Hampshire. They traveled to Vermont for a week, then Boston for another week (where they spent three days in Randy's kitchen while I was in Martha's Vinyard). After that we traveled to the Connecticut coast for six days, then down to New Jersey. What a bouquet of miracles. I was hopping on a plane, so I left them on Casper's roof, parked in Garret's backyard.

420.

"*Miracle*, a noun meaning 'amazing or wonderful occurrence,' comes from the Latin *miraculum* 'object of wonder.' Dig way back and the word derives from *smeiros*, meaning 'to smile,' which is exactly what you do when a miracle happens" (Vocabulary.com).[11]

421.

November – Virginia – Day Two

The second day with M, I am clumsier than a June bug.

I trip and fall going up the stairs into Coddi. Like fall to my knees in the dirt and act as though it happens all the time. My body seems to be operating under different laws of physics whenever M is near. Inside Coddi, I drop limes, which scatter like marbles on a bowling alley, and a couple roll out the door. I scamper to grab them and trip again.

M arrives before 11:00 a.m. and stays till after dark. We sit by the fire and talk for hours about everything and nothing: childhood memories, philosophy, the way stars look different depending on where you view them from. The conversation flows in waves, sometimes rushing forward, sometimes receding into comfortable silence.

"I love souls," M says, into the pitch-black forest, as if making an announcement to the universe. Both of our faces and fronts flicker in an orange glow. The words land like rocks in still water, causing ripples. My heart catches. This feels important, significant, a confession wrapped in philosophy, a door left ajar. I toss a log onto the fire. Sparks fly and scatter, high up into leafless trees. Another twenty minutes of stillness interspersed with chatting.

"I don't want to go," M says, while leaning forward, toward the fire, elbows on knees, eyes straight ahead. Another announcement to the universe. My throat tightens. I want to say *I don't want you to leave either.* The silence stretches between us like taffy, sweet and tense. Another tongue-tied me who has lost all comprehension of how to communicate with words. An owl hoots in the distance, and some small critter burrows in dry leaves to our right. We watch the fire for another five minutes, the flames whispering secrets neither of us is ready to speak aloud. M stands up, thanks me, hugs me, and leaves. The hug lingers just a breath longer than usual, our bodies having the conversation our voices cannot.

422.

October 23 – Lake Oswego, Oregon
Less than a week after hearing Antra was not well, I was in Oregon lying on Antra's son's bed. He was at college, otherwise that would be strange.

Antra and I went on rainy walks each day. Wednesday we hiked to seven waterfalls—moss-draped trees, yellow leaves, ferns, and friendship. I'd never have guessed Antra's cancer was back and so serious. She was full of energy and life; strong, happy, funny. One night she was all perky. She took a bath and came out somber and sad. I woke up at 4:00 a.m. and heard her crying and Mike, her husband, consoling her. She cried for a long while.

We've talked a lot about her kids over the years. She's worried about them and how they'll cope without a mom. She's such a loving, fun, good-hearted human. I hope she knows what an amazing mom she is and how well she has prepared her kids for life. I've watched both of them grow into incredible, authentic, wildly intelligent, fun-loving young adults. I hope she knows she will always be with them in every sunrise, holiday, and big life event, and in the small moments when a scent, sight, or sound reminds them of her. She will always be alive and well in who they both are.

After writing that, I feel how the same applies to my mom. She will always be alive in me, my brother, and my nieces.

423.

October 26 – Lake Oswego, Oregon
On long walks with Antra, I shared about William. I'd had time to sit with everything and put what I was feeling into words. My knowing was crystal clear: I hope to go back one day. I no longer dream of William in a romantic way. I dream of those Arctic adventures with him.

424.

November – Virginia – Day Two
I'm showered and in bed after day two with M, one of the best days I can remember. Here I am for the second time in four months, falling for

someone. This feels different, deeper, and more significant. This isn't part of my journey, either. I am in love with God and nature.

I was dying to tell M how I felt, but the time wasn't right. Or I wasn't ready. Or ... Who am I kidding? I was tongue-tied!

There is some kind of cosmic connection, and we both agree we want to be in each other's lives forever. This is too important to ruin with some kind of fling.

There's a tug-of-war within me. One minute I'm happy this isn't a good match, with M being eighteen years older and such. The next moment, I'm sad. If everything was "perfect" I'd have no excuse to shy away from whatever this is.

I told Gary I loved him after knowing the man for five minutes, but I can't say the same thing to M. It might mean something. One fact I can't deny: My loins are *very* alive for the first time in years. I am in my midforties and had assumed things dried up at this age. Not so. My body sure seems to think M is pretty darn perfect.

425.

October 27 – Lake Oswego, Oregon

A bird landed on a branch right outside Antra's son's second-story window. The branch bobbed slowly up and down, up and down, as if the tree were nodding. I'm thankful to see this at eye level. I love to be alongside the living. Childhood is often when humans are most alive. It's fascinating how those nearing death have the most profound awareness of Life.

426.

Homefree

I share fires with people who live
in sleeping bags under pinyon pines.
Freedom and love ooze from their being.

427.

October 31 – Lake Oswego, Oregon

"It's Samhain," Antra said. "The veil between the living and the dead is at its thinnest today." She sat at the kitchen bar. Strips of paper and colored markers lay scattered on the granite countertop. I stood at the stove, facing her. Kale, leeks, and garlic sizzled in a pan. Between us sat a cookie sheet covered in squash with caramelized edges. "Come on, Blondie, don't be a bah-humbug. Write down what you'd like to see disappear in your life and burn that shit with me." (She and I have one pet name we call each other: Blondie). Antra wanted to do a burn letter ceremony. Her husband even made a list. I didn't see the point and bowed out. After dinner, I folded. Supporting her was more important than sticking to my guns.

On one sheet, I wrote my throwaways: *Carrying the weight of everything alone. Choosing strength over softness. Swallowing the words my heart wants to speak.*

On another, I wrote my wish: *Peace and freedom for Antra, without the need to find answers. May she feel her perfection, her kids' strength, and the grace entwined in everything.*

I was grateful to sit around a fire on a starry night talking with these two special humans. Antra and Mike are a wonderful gift. I am thankful to have happened along the path that led me to them.

428.

November 1, 2:00 a.m. – Flight from Portland to Newark

As I looked down from 35,000 feet—seeing Minnesota's lights in one moment, Michigan's the next—I felt how much I cherished the slowness of life on the road. Land-travel breeds connection, understanding, and appreciation for beauty. *Everyone on this plane has no idea what they're missing. I have no idea what I'm missing.* I want to move slower and soak in all of Life. The ultimate slow is still.

429.

When I judge, I'm judging things, people, places, and ideas before I know them. If I really knew them, I wouldn't judge.

430.

On November 1, at 6:30 a.m., I landed in Newark, New Jersey, Ubered to Coddi, got her ready to roll, hiked, and had dinner with Garret and his wife.

On November 2, I drove from New Jersey to Virginia. November 4 is when I met M.

431.

November 7 – Virginia

Back to the M debacle: The thing is, with William, I wanted to get far away before I admitted my feelings. With M, I want to tell all, in person. I wish I'd had the guts to do it at the campfire. I made up an excuse to go by M's cottage before I left town. I thought I was ready to share, but it didn't feel right to spill my beans over a quick lunch break. With our work schedules and my commitments in Florida, there was no time.

Since my stepfather died in the summer of 2020, I've traveled to North Florida every November. From Thanksgiving through New Year's I've spent time with Mom and my brother's family. In all my years of traveling, this is the closest I've had to a home base. This year, my niece's tenth birthday party is on November 11, and it feels important to be there. I ruminated over staying in Virginia to share my feelings with M, though my heart knew this family time was more important. On November 8, I meandered south.

432.

Earlier this summer, I spent four days boondocking on a farm in Canada. I helped Joe, the farmer, stack fence posts.

"'Never' and 'always' are four-letter words," Joe said. We stood between four silos and a prairie full of grunting bison. Joe's brown cowboy-style bandanna fluttered in the breeze; his eyes were locked on mine. I held a fence post, rough-cut from a limb. We both wore jeans with dirt smudges down the front, and threadbare leather work gloves. Sage wisdom had been pouring out of Joe all morning. Half a dog-eared ace of spades stuck up through dried mud beside the tire of a rusted red tractor. "The wise scratch them from their vocabulary." Cotton-ball clouds tinged Pepto-Bismol pink hung over the prairie. "'Never' and 'always' rarely pass the test of time."

He heaved a half-rotted post toward the tractor. It landed with a thud.

433.

November 9 – Columbia, South Carolina

The Wait
A woman on the corner holds a wrinkled cardboard sign.
A cart holds everything she has.
Cars hold humans idling in a line.
They wait to pay seven bucks for flavored poisoned water in a plastic
    cup.
The cup will outlive the great oak that shades the woman.
Cars creep past as their humans sip fancy water.
Most don't give a thought about the woman or the oak.
They don't give a thing.

434.

The highway miles between Virginia and Florida allowed space for things to settle. Each state line I crossed felt like turning a page in a story I hadn't planned to write. I'd set out years ago to find freedom in solitude, to wander without attachment. Now here I was, driving south with a constant ache in my chest, a yearning for someone not beside me.

I tried to sort through my feelings as if I were organizing a junk drawer: separating physical attraction from emotional connection, curiosity from genuine affection. But they refused to stay neat. By the time I reached Georgia, I'd stopped fighting it. Whatever This was, it didn't fit in any box. It would require new language, new feelings, new ways of understanding myself. I would have to coddiwomple through these unknown emotional landscapes the same way I coddiwompled through the physical ones—one step at a time, following the tickles of my soul.

Maybe it was the ache, or the chaos of feeling so much at once, but something had shifted. This experience with M was the final nudge. I knew I had to write a book. Friends and family had been urging me for at least six years, asking for stories about my wandering. I hadn't known where to start or what exactly the book would be about. With Hebron, the commercial fishing boat, Uncle Jasper and the berries, the bike accident, COVID, and visiting Antra, I was pretty sure there were some worthy stories. But after falling in love twice in just a few months, I knew this was the year. I didn't know when the year began or ended, how I'd write the book, or what else it might include. All I knew was to keep journaling. The book would eventually show me the way.

435.

November 10, 6:58 a.m. – Balls Ferry boat ramp, Georgia
A flock of birds, tiny and soundless, fly overhead. Seeing the ebb and flow of their silent cloud brings my awareness to the cacophony of songs of their brethren: tiny ratcheting chirps, long melodic calls, the *tap-tap-tap* of a woodpecker. Only when I became conscious of it did the magnificence of the soundscape reveal itself.

Part Five: Pushing Boundaries in Florida and Mexico

Florida was supposed to be familiar ground, a soft landing after months in the wild, but some journeys crack me open in ways I never see coming. After my transformative experiences in Newfoundland and Labrador, the Canadian Maritimes, and the eastern US, I was drawn south, back toward family. Yet I carried with me a heart newly tender and ready to explore depths I'd never anticipated. Florida would become not just a waypoint on my journey, but the starting place of an adventure beyond my wildest dreams. One that would challenge my understanding of love, identity, and connection in ways no wilderness expedition ever had.

436.

November 18 – Havana, Florida

M has ignited a unique desire in my body I've never felt before. My nipples are hard, nonstop. They are sore and chafed. Nothing softens them. I am perpetually moist. I want to share how I feel and experience the sensations of being skin to skin with someone I am smitten with.

Confessing my feelings is my job. M and I spoke in depth about being in each other's lives forever, in a friendly way, to explore our philosophical and spiritual understandings and to collaborate in our work. Then there's the age thing, and lifestyle differences. That night at the campfire in Virginia, M opened the door to a conversation about being more than friends. I didn't take the bait. Do I confess or move on? It's been two weeks since I was in Virginia, and I need to soothe my nipples. They are rubbed raw. *What would I do if I couldn't get it wrong?*

437.

While my body has seemingly made its decision about M, my mind is still catching up. I find myself simultaneously pulled toward this new possibility and paralyzed by it. Some days the uncertainty has me retreating from the world entirely.

Bed rotting. I feel empty. I hide. I miss out. I lie in a haze and waste all I've been given. Another day, another chance to taste something fresh, another breeze that doesn't tussle my hair, another cloud alone in my cocoon, another moment that's whisked away into the deep, a perfect shell stolen by the tide. I sink lower inside and gaze out the window. How simple it would be to get out and soak in the sun.

I roll over. Bright light from Coddi's skylight beats down on a hot spot where my hand landed, in the jumbled mess of violet sheets. It must be almost eleven. My eye mask holds tight to the crown of my skull like a 1980s hairband. My hair is a royal, tangled, frizzy mess. The bottom half of a yellow plastic Easter egg sits tilted beside my pillow. I'm still in my cotton Christmas-tree pajamas, which I put on two days ago. I roll back, away from the day, into my comforter's warm womb.

438.

November 21 – Havana, Florida
After three drafts deleted, two walks to clear my head, and one ridiculous moment of nearly throwing my laptop into the nearest river, I'm finally writing this email. My hands shake slightly on the keyboard—not from fear exactly, but from the weight of what feels so important to express.

Subject: A Breath of Gratitude
From: K
To: M

... So here goes the guts of this note: For weeks I've been called to share something I haven't had the words for, but now I trust they will arrive as they are typed. The infinite loop connection experience ... the "There you are, love, so good to see you again" ... the getting lost with you ... all that and a sense of being drawn in, like a tractor beam.

Many times on this journey, I've experienced the illusionary veil of separation being lifted, and falling in love—with people, places, and all of nature. But I don't recall experiencing anything similar to the connection with you. Listening, sharing, sitting fireside, the feeling of being. That Sunday evening, I did not want you to go and I would have sat by the fire till after the sun came up.

I've been drawn to share this with you, and it hasn't felt like a choice. I could make up reasons why, but the only true truth I know is this: It's as if I've been holding my breath, and at the same time life has been nudging me to exhale into itself a breath of light, of love, of appreciation for all that is, and of gratitude for the allness that arrived in the form of a couple of wanderers whose paths joined for a moment on the great meander.

In the realm of emotions and such, I'm still getting a feel for diving in and playing in the infinite pool of my humanness. Sometimes I feel like I'm decades behind. Then always, eventually, I remember the divine perfection of the unfolding of life. Pure awe floods in.

There is nothing I'm asking for or expecting from you. No underlying need for you to write back or anything of the sort. This note is a dove being set free, a true thanksgiving.

I am beyond grateful for, and in wonder with, You.

I pause before hitting Send, reading the words for the umpteenth time. They feel both too much and not enough. *What if I'm misreading everything? What if this connection is just friendship through M's eyes?* The cursor hovers over Send as doubt creeps in. Then I remember the campfire, the declaration, the lingering goodbye. The coddiwompler in me whispers: *Take the step. The path will appear. What would you do if you knew you couldn't get it wrong?*

439.

Have you encountered any legal or logistical hurdles while traveling?

No legal hurdles (knock on wood). Logistical hurdles? I jump over those things like an Olympic gold medalist. Living a nomadic life is hurdle after hurdle. Even the biggest figure themselves out. In March 2020 I was in Los Angeles for work. I flew there and left Coddi at a shop in Orlando, Florida, for repairs. I was at a restaurant when Los Angeles was shut down due to COVID. My flights to Florida kept getting canceled. When I got to Florida everything was closed and quarantined.

I had nowhere to live. The repair shop let me stay in their parking lot for one night, but I had to be gone by 7:00 a.m. Talk about getting creative. People were scared because COVID was so new. Family and friends wouldn't let me park in their pastures or backyards because I had been in LA, a "hotspot."

I scoured Boondockers Welcome for anyone who might be able to help. I found someone with the handle Airstreaming Gypsy ninety minutes away. They weren't open for guests. I sent a message asking for one or two nights to figure out where to go next, explained my situation, and promised not to come anywhere near the house. I received a reply right away: "You are me 15 years ago. Get your butt over here."

Ends up the lady, Hunter, was in her seventies. She'd lived full-time by herself in her Airstream for over a decade in the 1990s. I stayed with her for three weeks, and she wanted me to stay longer. We've been friends ever since.

Hurdles are gifts, like everything else.

440.

November 21 – Havana, Florida
My email must have been too ambiguous. M's response was enthusiastic, caring and loving, but M didn't get that I was professing my feelings of romantic love (or was playing it safe).

That email was strike one: a foul ball that skirted the first base line. So,

I step into the batter's box, my heart in my throat, ready to take another swing: I ask M to have a phone call.

We talk for more than an hour. I bleat on and on like a goat stuck in a fence, terrified, with its horns and head stuck baaaa-baa-baaaaaing endlessly. My throat constricts each time I try to steer the conversation toward what I really want to say. I say nothing about my feelings for M. I ask nothing about M's feelings for me. I tell stories about my travels, about silly encounters at gas stations, about anything and everything except the truth hammering against my ribs. I blabber on about the weather in Florida, about plans for the holidays.

"SHIT!" I shout. I sit in Coddi, shirt soaked, sweating like a hog in heat. *I'm forty-five years old, not fourteen! Get a grip!* Strike two.

I see my reflection in Coddi's window—an explorer who can face down hurricanes and navigate strange lands but can't seem to form three simple words: *I like you.* No, that's not even right. What I want to say is far more dangerous than that. This is a ripping apart of my ego, limb by limb.

441.

A fence of judgment and predictions is no fence at all.

442.

November 25, 8:23 a.m. – Havana, Florida
I am lost around love, around unsuitable suitors and unquenchable yearnings. And Life, you big bully, you knowing mother. What a bossy big sister of a thing to do. Life insists I make a fool of myself and crawl back to ask for another chance at confessing my curiosity and doubts.

Life sent me a poem. I opened my computer. The desktop, a patchwork of random photos and documents, stared back at me. One small beige tile caught my eye. A photo with the filename "Not Anyone Who Says.jpg."

I clicked. It opened.

Not Anyone Who Says
Not anyone who says, "I'm going to be
careful and smart in matters of love,"
who says, "I'm going to choose slowly,"
but only those lovers who didn't choose at all
but were, as it were, chosen
by something invisible and powerful and uncontrollable
and beautiful and possibly even
unsuitable —
only those know what I'm talking about
in this talking about love.[12]

443.

In the world's terms, I haven't been getting much done. Books beg to be written, emails nag, research waits, bills must be paid. Oh well. When I overthink it, my belly flips and chest aches. Then a walk with Mom or a bike ride in the forest reminds me how perfect everything is. I follow tickles and do what tugs on my heartstrings.

Back in Newfoundland, turning down $3,500 for three days of fishing was simple. No regrets or worry. It's all simple, even when it's not easy. I live true to myself. Even if I'm chained in a dark cell tomorrow, I will have lived richer than I bargained for. So, oh well to half-done projects. This crazy, original, messy, beautiful coddiwomple life is plenty enough.

444.

November 25
I Google "Not Anyone Who Says."

Mary Oliver. *Of course!* Mary and Life teamed up. I giggle at the image of them in the other realm, snickering like giddy schoolgirls, watching me read Mary's poem and finally get it. The date on the file is February 15, 2021. Several years earlier, I'd snapped a photo of a page in a book and hid it in plain sight, ready for this day.

I need to ask M for one more go at a conversation. Maybe nothing will come of it. If I never see M again, things have already come of it.

A big part of me doesn't want to get tangled up in the slipperiness of Life. But I'm still here, still typing, and still wishing to be cuddled up in a cozy cottage on a hillside with a mirror of all that is and all that isn't. All the while, the apprehension about what a journey in that direction might bring gnaws on a spot right below my rib cage. I am stuck in a fence of imagined judgment—from myself, from my little family, from the world, and from the beliefs I secretly hold true.

445.

If I couldn't get it wrong, I'd share love, be love, and make love. These words feel strange as they form in my mind, unfamiliar and risky. For decades, I'd guarded my heart, convinced that safety meant self-protection. I've kayaked through threatening waters, survived bike crashes, and slept alone in wild places, yet the idea of fully opening myself to another person makes my throat tighten and my palms sweat. How strange that this, of all things, is what truly terrifies me.

446.

November 25 – Havana, Florida
Most of the time, I don't know what I want. In this moment, in my green cotton pajamas with the keyboard on my lap being lit by one bright sunbeam through the window slats, my biggest wish is to walk in wonder with a fellow wanderer. To see more about Life and living than I could ever glimpse on a path dusted by a single pair of footprints.

Ultimate freedom is being completely untethered in all ways, especially regarding my beliefs and made-up rules about love and connection. This isn't just about M. It's about the girl who promised at thirteen never to love so deeply it would hurt if they left. It's about letting go of the last bits of barriers I thought protected me from loss. It's about stepping into the biggest unknown I've ever faced: the unmapped territory of a heart fully opened. I'd followed countless tickles of my soul across continents, and now that same quiet knowing was leading me toward vulnerability I'd spent a lifetime avoiding. I did what any coddiwompler would do. I said fuck it. Fuck all that made-up shit. I asked to talk again.

447.

"We are so conditioned in our conditioning that we don't know any other way until we know another way." – Marlene Mier

448.

Just as the sun makes love with forests, rivers, and fields, so can I with all things.

449.

December 2 – Havana, Florida, phone call with M, take two
Small talk leads to "I'm writing a book about this year."

"Why is this year so special?" M asks. My phone sits face up on my desk in Coddi, and the screen glows in the Saturday-evening twilight. Coddi is in Mom's driveway. I sleep in Mom's guest room but sneak out to Coddi so she can't overhear anything.

"It's been one of the biggest adventures of my life." I take a deep breath. "And I fell in love twice."

"Really? Are you up for sharing about that?"

I share about William and end with "I knew it wasn't part of my journey, so I left without telling him." My heart pounds, my stomach turns. "I told him when I was far enough away that he couldn't get to me, and that I wouldn't go back." Sweat drips down my flanks and under my breasts. My thighs stick to the stool. I have no clue what to say next.

"What about the second time?"

My goat is running toward the fence. I feel faint. *This is the moment of truth. Say it or don't.* I take a long, deep breath.

"I did the same thing," I say, a smidge louder than a whisper. "I left before admitting the truth." *Thump! Thump! Thump! Thump! Thump! Thump!* My heart races as if I'm in the final sprint of the Tour de France.

I take another long, shaky breath and exhale half of it while I watch the seconds climb on the call timer on my phone. "This time ..." My closed left fist rests against my lower lip. A warm exhale slips past my fingers. "I wrote an ambiguously loving email."

Thump! Thump! Thump! Thump! Thump! Thump!

The silence that follows feels eternal. I hear my heartbeat in my ears, the soft static of the connection, perhaps even M's breath catching. When M finally speaks, the words come as a quiet revelation, like something long known but only now acknowledged.

"I've been falling for you too," M says. "I didn't know if you felt the same."

The relief that floods through me is physical. My shoulders drop. The conversation that follows feels both ordinary and extraordinary, two people mapping the contours of feelings they've been carrying separately; two people suddenly sharing the weight.

450.

I wrote this while looking at a photo of six-year-old me lounging in a tree.

My Baby Blues
These eyes have watched life bud and bloom, live and die, sleep
    and sprout.
Through these eyes I reached for wiggly new toes, peered into a
    Dixie cup filled with raisins, watched my parents as they did
    their best, watched my world leave me behind, and tended to
    my wounds.
Through these eyes, I watched oceans and friends come and go,
    learned lessons, saw the sun rise and set, sowed gardens, and
    witnessed life be born into my blood-soaked hands.
These eyes have seen love and hate, and tracked fly balls with
    precision.
These eyes surveyed dire scenes of death and destruction,
    examined wounds, squinted against raging fires, and strained
    to see through moonless nights under starlit skies.

These eyes have seen how locals live and love, in kitchens and
backyards all over the world.
These eyes have witnessed the best and worst of me.
This little body grew, was hurt and healed, burned and fed,
starved and loved, picked at and pruned.
I look at this sweet little soul, and those same eyes well with tears
of love and gratitude.

451.

December 3 – The morning after the confession
M and I exchange love notes via text, not realizing the other had
written too.

Thus began a long-distance writing romance (akin to old-fashioned
letters).

Some of our notes have been sprinkled throughout the first four
parts of this book.

452.

I will not let worry stop me from doing what I am drawn to do. Worry,
some call it fear, is the biggest misuse of imagination known to human-
kind. Emotions are meant to be felt completely. I am the experience.
Waves of life tingle my fingers and prickle my skin. Sometimes I don't live
the guts out of life. I am ready to be freer than that, to feel everything, to
truly live.

453.

December 11 – Cape San Blas, Florida
I'm camping with family on the beach: Mom and I in Coddi; my brother,
sister-in-law, and nieces in the camper next door. We're celebrating my
brother and sister-in-law's anniversary and my birthday with shared sun-
rises, meals, laughter, games, and campfires.

From the outside, it looks as if everything is whole. In the quiet spaces
between the joy, there's another thread running through me, something

tender and unnamed. Texting M secretly, talking only on solo walks. This connection is unfolding, delicate. Raw. Unformed. Neither of us knows what it is, or what it wants to be. I've told just one friend. M has reservations too. What if we're misreading this? What if it's not meant for romance? Worse, what if following my heart unravels something rare and precious? I don't want to lose this, even though I'm not sure what I've found.

Last night, sleepless, my mind circled in what-ifs. I cried, silently for Mom's sake. I'm surrounded by love—sunshine, ocean, family—yet carrying this beautiful ache. The hope of something new. The fear of losing it. The longing for clarity in the middle of not knowing.

454.

Struggle
A woman sits crumpled
in a straitjacket
of sorrow.
While asleep
she tied the straps
herself.

455.

December 14

M and I are in an online writers' group. We don't like labels, so we call whatever's happening between us "This." When M shares the title, something soft breaks open in me. It feels like a serenade, the first I've ever received.

This
We exchange tender prose in a splendid dance of wonder.
Each sentence a glimpse into all that keeps us hidden.
The words slowly undress to bare and share
all the secret and delicate parts.
To explore and play in such this way
that even at my wise age, feels like many firsts.

I blush. I'm bold.
I'm quite good at this, I'm told
to share myself in this way,
with another so open and willing
to give and receive in so many ways
I couldn't even see I needed.
This dance, intoxicating and sweet.
I buzz with cellular knowing.
Who knows how high we'll go
in this alchemy unfolding.

          – M

456.

We can never just be friends.

457.

December 17, 6:15 a.m. – Text to M

> Good morning. As the first soft trickles of light
> sneak over the hill outside your bedroom window,
> I nibble your earlobe and whisper this:
>
>
> All That Is Left
> Without resistance, beliefs, and judgments, all that is left is This.
> Living freely in the divine might seem courageous, though it isn't.
> This is effortless and simple.
> This is an expression of peace, love, and joy.
> In This, there is no teacher or student,
> no concessions or compromises, no responsibility.
> In This, there is infinite freedom.
> You, my love, are the gift and the giver.
> This is where you and I disappear.
> The more we know This,
> the more we sink into pure peace, love, and joy.
> In This, all that is left is simply living.

8:00 a.m. – Journal entry
A blanket of desire has wrapped itself around me, stretched tight, and swaddled me in moist breath. My arms and legs pressed tight under the weight of a divine womb of love and recognition. My heart flutters with the simplest words or thoughts. My nether regions stay wet. So many firsts, surprises, expressions of joy, love, and freedom. Yet I am helpless in the swaddling. For the first time I have fallen in love and been met there, a divine recognition.

458.

As a joint Christmas gift, M rented us a beach house in St. Augustine, Florida. The plan is to meet for three days beginning December 26. The gesture touched me—not just the thoughtfulness, but the boldness of it. M was creating a physical space for us to explore this connection. It felt like both an invitation and a declaration.

I have some lingering concerns. *Will I be physically attracted to M?* In Virginia, the cold weather had us all bundled up, and I didn't check M out. *What if I want to run for the hills?* M and I talk about this, and I admit my reservations.

"Well, I checked you out, and I have no reservations," M says. "That first day we met, I thought, 'Oh my, Goddess Athena is standing on my porch!'"

This tingles something deep inside; maybe we'll be just fine. M rented a place with two bedrooms. We will feel our way through with ease and grace.

459.

The scariest thing that's happened on my journey took place in the fall of 2020. I was on a two-lane road southwest of Moosehead Lake, Maine.

I had a client Zoom call coming up, and needed a place to park. I spotted a wide, solid-looking shoulder and pulled off. Something didn't feel right. I stopped. Casper was on the shoulder while Coddi was still on the road. I eased on the gas. The tires slipped. I threw Casper into four-wheel drive and tried again. The rear of my truck slid right, toward a ravine; it hadn't moved forward at all.

I got out to investigate. Coddi sat in the right-hand lane of the highway, just past the crest of a hill (worst place ever), and Casper was stuck. Bad stuck. The rear tires had sunk into the soft shoulder and drifted downhill. My hands were shaking. If Casper went, he would take Coddi and everything I owned, too. I got myself into a massive kerfuffle.

A few minutes later, a semi with a flatbed approached and slowed to a stop. "I'd pull you out, but can't with the company truck," the driver said. He rubbed his chin and looked up the road. "I'm due for a lunch break. I'll sit behind you so no one hits your rig from the rear."

He idled there, flashers on, protecting me. What a guy.

Three minutes later, a Ram 2500, just like Casper, came up the highway toward me.

"You need help?" the driver asked. A woman sat in the passenger seat.

"Yes, sir. Even in four-wheel drive, it's sliding down the bank."

He pulled over. The calm, methodical way he inspected the situation reminded me of my grandpa.

He nosed his truck up to mine then put on rawhide gloves that'd seen some work. "I'm gonna throw mine in reverse. Steer your tires toward me," he said, as he attached a chain between our matching front tow hooks. "As soon as there's tension on the chains, put yours in neutral and let mine do all the work."

His tires screeched. The engine roared. The truck bounced. I watched this stranger risk his own truck to save my rig. As I gripped the steering wheel, my eyes met those of this kind, capable stranger, and I saw the truth: my fierce independence was quietly held by the kindness of strangers, by the hands of helpers and life's gifts that appeared at just the right time.

His tires caught traction. My truck lunged, and that kind man dragged my whole rig to safety.

Before I could get out, he was unhooking the chains.

"You're a lifesaver," I said, hands together as if praying.

"Been stuck more times than I care to count," he said, coiling his chain. "Road's got a way of humbling us all."

"I want to pay you or give you something."

"No, no. You're welcome," he said, with a wink. "Neighbors helping neighbors."

Warm tingles rippled through my chest. This burly, weather-worn man from the boondocks of Maine considered me a neighbor. I was reminded again that independence and interdependence aren't opposites but partners in a beautiful dance of Life.

460.

December 21 – A text from Samir

> Hey Krissy. So sorry to share this news with you. My dad passed away last Sunday. He had an awesome morning dancing with some neighbors' 10 and 12 yo kids—was teaching them new dance moves! Had a nice lunch after that with Mom and went for his afternoon nap. Never woke up. Funeral is done and we are working on bringing Popo to Canada.

> My heart is with you and the whole fam. What a sweet sweet man. Sounds like he had a wonderful, joyful day and passed in peace. This is the most beautiful last day I've ever heard of. If only we all can be so blessed as your dad. I will miss him dearly. So many will. Please pass on my love and hugs to everyone, especially Popo.

461.

December 25 – Havana, Florida

5:30 p.m. – My family Christmas festivities finished up early and M is already at the beach house, a three-hour drive away. I can't imagine waiting twelve more hours to be together. I go.

9:00 p.m. – I'm in St. Augustine sweating bullets.

462.

The number-one lesson I've learned on the road is to be fluid. When I think I know what's next, that's just an idea.

463.

December 25, 9:15 p.m. – St. Augustine, Florida

M opens the door, and without a word, we fall into an embrace. Ocean waves crash in the distance and my heart is cranking like a snare drum in a marching band. This feels better than I imagined. We fit together like matching puzzle pieces. I'm almost six feet tall, so M's ear rests against my chest, and I am embarrassed by my racing heart. Her dirty-blonde curls catch the porch light, and I catch a hint of coconut in her shampoo.

After a long, quiet hug, we move to the couch and snuggle in side by side. She's wearing a fitted black shirt and jeans that hug every curve. Her arms are solid, her thighs strong, no jiggliness. Oh, *This* is even better than I'd hoped. We become more entwined—not just in body, but in something unspoken and electric.

I want to kiss her, but something she said weeks ago keeps echoing in my mind: "Once we cross this line, we can never go back."

We both want to be in each other's lives, always. I would never do anything to jeopardize This.

A few weeks back, we'd talked about kissing. Since I was still unsure if I'd be physically attracted to a woman, we'd agreed I'd be the one to decide when, or if, that first kiss would happen.

Now, in the quiet of our embrace, my cheek rests against hers. I press my lips to her skin, not quite a kiss. Still hesitant. *What if? What if? What if?*

I've never kissed a woman. It feels like standing on the edge of a cliff with no idea what's on the other side. I trace the shape of her face with mine, the closest thing to kissing without an actual kiss.

"Would you like me to kiss you?" M asks, through a smile and a whisper. "I can feel you want to. I mean, we're kinda making out with our mouths closed." She giggles.

Her giggle drives me crazy. I smile against her cheek and whisper, "Yes."

464.

I've squirreled away experiences and places like a chipmunk whose cheeks burst at the seams. I'm ready to savor each flavor, sink into the soil, listen as if I've never heard a breeze rustle maple leaves. Take long, slow breaths beside familiar faces until all the nooks and crannies of my lungs fill with tenderness.

465.

December 31 – St. Augustine, Florida
We don't leave the beach house for the first two days, don't set foot on the sand. In four days, we haven't been physically apart except to go to the bathroom. Four days of deep being, deep conversations, and almost constant skin-to-skin togetherness. Her hands find mine with a warmth that defies ordinary temperature—a living heat that pulses with its own current. When her fingers trace my skin, they leave invisible trails of fire, as if electricity flows through her veins. The smoothness of her touch contradicts its power; silk concealing lightning. Each point of contact between us becomes a small universe of sensation, dismantling me cell by cell while simultaneously rebuilding something new in its place. When she laughs, it begins deep in her throat before cascading into that impossible sound, part giggle, part squeal, that seems to ripple through the air and rearrange something fundamental inside me. It's the sound of champagne bubbles breaking against crystal, unexpected and effervescent. She is by far the laughiest person I've ever known.

466.

What a wander. Love is love. Welcome to the club of lovin' on souls.

467.

January 1 – Topsail Hill Preserve State Park, Florida
For the last few years, Mom and I have gone to the first official Airstream Club event of the year, the Canopener Rally. It's at a state park on the beach two hours from Mom's house. On the drive, Mom asked how things had gone with M. All Mom knew before I went to St. Augustine was that M and I might be more than friends, but we didn't know yet.

"We're more than friends now," I said, as I drove down a two-lane highway through a pine forest.

"What about the age difference?" Mom asked. "Eighteen years doesn't seem like much now, but there will be a time when it is."

"Jack is two years older than M," I said. Mom loves Jack, and they're still friends. "And they have the same birthday. You didn't seem to think Jack was too old."

Mom's head whipped in my direction. "M's birthday is July 1?"

"Yeah, how'd you know?"

"My dad and Jack have the same birthday, so it's easy to remember." Mom adored her dad. He died six weeks after I was born.

"Well, it'll be easy to remember M's birthday too."

"When are you going to tell your brother?"

"Tell him that Grandpa, Jack, and M have the same birthday?"

"No, silly." Mom shook her head. "About you and M."

"I don't even know what's going on right now. He'll know when he knows."

"That won't go over well."

"Mom, Uncle Charlie has been gay for fifty-something years, and Ben is fine with that."

"Your nieces don't worship Uncle Charlie. They barely know him." My nieces are ten and thirteen years old. "The girls look up to you. That's the difference."

468.

I love this soul in such a clean, all-encompassing way. When my goat got stuck in the fence, it thrashed and bleated because M was a woman. I'd been taught same-sex love was wrong. I'd thought I'd moved beyond that belief, but when it came to me, it was alive.

When M visited Coddi in Virginia (#421), we sat fireside in darkness. Staring into the forest, she'd said, "I love souls." M was speaking to the forest, and to me. She'd read a blog I'd written about Randy: KristyH. com/love-is-love. She was professing something sacred in a way I might recognize. It was an invitation to open up, but my goat was already in the fence. M suspected I was straight. My silence was her answer.

I felt how M saw me, listened, and shared, how she hugged me as if we were one. The truth is, my beliefs almost ripped the rug out from under This before it began. I'm thankful I didn't resist the attraction and had enough sense to see through what I was taught.

469.

What has scared you? Have you ever been in emotional, physical, or spiritual free fall?

In the realm of physical harm or damage/thievery, other than when Casper and Coddi almost slid off the hill in Maine, I can't remember being scared since this journey began. Although, in interpersonal relations, when sharing my feelings or views, asking for help, or about to give a speech, I can get anxious. Some might say that's the same thing as being scared.

As for emotional free fall, other than the bout of loneliness in 2018, nothing else comes to mind. The experience with M was, and is, an awakening. It's never felt like a free fall.

Spiritually, I've let go of tons of beliefs and feel closer to God than I ever imagined. God no longer seems like an entity that has the capability of judging or granting favor. There is no separation. So no, no free fall, simply love and openness.

470.

January 2 – Topsail Hill Preserve State Park, Florida
I've felt a lifetime of feelings and experiences since Christmas. M and I are happy, open, trusting, tickled, and surrendered. Many firsts for both of us. An openness beyond anything I thought possible is the bedrock of This. No yearning, needing, or desire to change her or me. There is an understanding that This will change everything. I am already closer to my essence than ever before. Mom is accepting, but not overjoyed. She says she's concerned about the age gap and how difficult this might be. I want to ask, "If M were a man, how different would your joy for me be?" I'm pretty sure if M were a man, Mom would be thrilled, over-the-top happy.

471.

January 3 – Topsail Hill Preserve State Park, Florida

Mom and I met Jill and John hiking in spring 2021. We stopped, talked for hours, and became instant friends. They travel full-time in their fifth wheel. We've crossed paths four times since we met. They happened to be at Topsail and knew Mom well. I shared about M, and Mom's reaction, and asked for advice. John offered thoughts about getting opinions from others on navigating Mom's hesitancy.

"Scratch that," John said. "Knowing you, I take back everything I just said." We were in the living room of their RV. He straddled a workout bench in jeans and a sweatshirt and leaned toward me, elbows on his knees, eyes focused on me. We'd been talking for two hours. Dumbbells and other workout equipment littered the floor beside him, and a dime-sized piece of cobalt sea glass sat on the carpet between his bare feet.

"Why?" I asked. "What do you mean by 'knowing you'?" I sat on the couch next to Jill.

"What I mean is how you live your life." John's eyes widened and he leaned toward me a bit more. "You don't need permission for *anything*. Nothing scares you. You live your truth like no one we've ever met before." I felt my face flush and noticed I was fidgeting with the zipper on my coat. "Scratch everything I said before." John sat up straight and inhaled deep. "You *never* need to ask for anyone's opinion."

472.

I wasn't mean to kids at school or in the neighborhood, but behind the closed doors of our tiny red-brick childhood home in the pecan grove, I was a world-class bully. My little brother, Ben, followed me everywhere and had looked up to me since before he could walk. I was a year older but wanted nothing to do with him.

473.

This isn't what I imagined. It's beyond love, beyond connection, beyond anything I could ever say no to. This is quiet, free, and full. I don't even miss M that often, though I'd stay right with her forever if I could. I wonder about This love: steady when apart, magic when together, and rooted in acceptance and allowing. *Is this what true love feels like?*

The fact that I almost ran from This, before it had a chance to begin, stirred a vivid memory from when I was fourteen.

"Now you're on all these sports teams with older girls, there's something we need to talk about," Dad said, as he turned down the car radio. We were headed to basketball practice. He sounded serious. I thought it was going to be a pep talk on honing my skills and making the cut.

"Lesbians run rampant in female sports. They try to recruit, and it's easy to get sucked in."

I stared straight ahead. It had come out of nowhere.

"You know ... peer pressure. Same with drugs and alcohol."

"Dad, come on." I huffed, rolled my eyes, and turned toward the window.

"Being romantic with someone of the same sex is a sin. They're all going to hell. You will too, if you let them drag you into their disgusting ways."

This belief was reinforced by church, family, and friends. Over thirty years later, I can still see the exact street we were on when he said it.

474.

Love is the divine energy that is all of existence, an expression of the sacred. How can an expression of the sacred be a transgression against God?

475.

January 5 – Topsail Hill Preserve State Park, Florida
Each morning I venture out of my home on wheels, through a predawn preserve, onto a boardwalk over sprawling dunes, and down to a sugar-sand shore. Each morning is unique. This is the inspiration for this poem.

Dear Nature
Gentle, resilient, elegant, and mighty.
Nature is, without apology.
She does not cry, nor cry out.
Pure and simple, She lives.
I sigh and pick up litter from her shores.
"They do this without knowing, Love,"
She whispers with her wind.
"Don't worry. I am eternal, dear one.
We will all be OK. There is no end,"
She says with brilliant pastels to welcome each day.
"I'll be here long after humans have journeyed on,"
She says with the pitter-patter of rain on starless nights.
"I remember," I say with my meander
of footprints on her sugar-sand shores.
She acknowledges my flash in the pan
by washing away my steps with her tide.
I witness her sun and clouds, and damp salt air.
I acknowledge her breeze
that has traveled round the world to tussle my hair.
Her rough seas whisper truth.
The lure of adventure sends tingles rippling across my skin.
In This, I know everything will change.
Her sunrise brings a quiet knowing:
Like nature, I am.
She and I, we are one and the same.
I smile with shimmering appreciation.
I know no fear.

476.

January 21 – Havana, Florida
"Look, that lady announcer is wearing a rainbow jacket," Mom said. We

were settled in our recliners in her living room, a side table between us, watching a Kansas City Chiefs football game.

"Why did you say that to me?" Mom being all excited about this ruffled my feathers.

Mom looked back with raised eyebrows, her eyes darting from side to side as if to say, *You know why.*

I turned to face her with my whole body. "Mom, I'm not a lesbian."

Mom's brows stayed raised, her eyes on mine.

"I am not gay, I am not bisexual. I am me. Just because I love a human does not warrant a label."

A slight grin graced Mom's face. I was just getting going. This boxing me into a label because of who I loved pissed me right off.

"I am not about to jump onto any rainbow bandwagon," I said. "That's ridiculous. I care about one person a lot, and that person happens to have a vagina. That's it. I am no different than I've ever been." I settled back into the chair, exhaled, and looked at the TV. "Please don't think of me as anything other than your daughter."

477.

There is a propensity for misunderstanding in spiritual understandings. Everything shifted when I stopped trying to "get it" and released the idea that there is a self that needs improving. This is seeking and seeking is suffering. As I embrace life's unfolding without clinging to "shoulds," clarity and peace flood in. In this fearless, regret-free space of wonder, the weight on my shoulders lifts. When I know that life is a game on a grand stage, everything gets stupid simple. I still work, play, interact, and "live responsibly," but I'm not calling the shots. I am free. It's pointless to predict the future and be upset when life doesn't match my forecast. Living without fear isn't a pipe dream.

478.

January 27 – Virginia
I bit the bullet. I left Coddi at Mom's house and flew to Virginia. My

return ticket isn't until February 24. One month with M. My return ticket is changeable, just in case.

479.

Why aren't you scared, especially as a single woman in the forest? Do you put up an energy state that says, "Nobody is going to attack me"?

I don't put out protective energy, nor do I dream up horrible situations that might happen. I am pure consciousness. If I am not afraid of dying, what is there to be afraid of?

480.

January 30 – Virginia

"Oh, look at you, sweetheart," M says, a smile in her voice. "You're growing so beautiful. Look at these new fronds." Sunlight spills through the kitchen window. M is leaning in, one hand hovering over a vibrant fern, fingers tracing the edges of its leaves, the other tipping a glass half-full of water. She's the epitome of love and care.

I know how that fern feels. M's palm against my cheek feels like pressing against a sun that somehow doesn't burn. It just radiates a healing warmth that seeps beneath my surface and unravels knots I didn't know I carried. In the wake of her touch, I am both undone and made whole, torn apart and carefully reassembled into something better than before.

481.

Late-Night Snack

At 8:45 p.m., my lover and I hop out of bed. I fry up goat cheese quesadillas on a cast-iron skillet in the nude and whip up fresh guacamole then top it with salsa. My lover moans at the scrumptiousness of my spur-of-the-moment treat. I drop a clay plate and try to catch it midair. It smacks her hard, square in the face.

482.

In love. Yes, I am in love. I couldn't speak this four-letter word for twenty-five years. It meant too much, cut too deep: L-O-V-E. Now, those letters don't seem all-encompassing enough. What became clear wasn't that I learned to love, but that love is what I am. The apparent falling in love was love recognizing itself. In this is a scent of bewilderment, reverence, and surrender to a divine truth—pouring out, flowing in, bubbling up through cracks I didn't know I had. What I feel begs to be expressed. It is beyond, far beyond, love.

483.

Black-and-Blue

My lover doubles over in pain while she holds her right eye.

"What happened? What happened?" she says, between groans. Splintered glass covers the table. Jagged slivers cling to her hair and nightshirt.

"I'm sorry," I say, while picking shards off the floor around her feet. "I am so sorry."

"It's OK, baby. You didn't mean to," she says, as she holds ice on the huge blue lump on her forehead.

484.

One of the most common questions I'm asked is whether I see myself living this way indefinitely or if I know when I'll settle down. Since 2017, my reply to this question has remained the same. I am open to anything, including having a home base and non-nomadic way of living. As long as I'm drawn to wander, I'll wander. When I'm drawn to something else, I'll do that.

485.

February 12 – Virginia

I hold and I am held, physically, emotionally, wholly, by a soul in a body that feels tailor-made for my soul and my body. Tears stream from my eyes down our cheeks, lips, and necks. Each tear holds an entire ocean of emotions. I thought I was Medusa and better off not loving for fear of losing.

We are lit by the flicker of a candle on the nightstand. Third eye to third eye, drenched in beyond love, all eyes wide open, tangled, embracing, accepting, allowing all of This, all of us, with an intensity, freedom, and gentleness I couldn't have hoped for. This love is beyond the limits of my imagination, and beyond what she's dreamed of all her life. We hold still, except for our breaths. No one turns to stone, no one leaves. What reveals itself isn't love for each other, but the recognition that the apparent two were never separate. We are free.

In this embrace, I know I am made of, and made for, all that I've been most afraid of.

486.

Love.

487.

We are still third eye to third eye. A few delicate taps break the silence and crescendo into a rumble as a downpour of raindrops rattle the jet-black skylight above us.

As the sacred dives into the depths, reaches for the seafloor, and reaches, and dives deeper and reaches, and discovers there is no bottom in this sacredness, even God cries.

488.

The day after Valentine's Day 2018, I met Henry and Sharry in Fredericksburg, Texas. The retired couple had found me through an Airstream group and they were the first of many to love me swiftly and deeply, the kind of love that never lets go. Mixed in with shared meals, sage wisdom, and life experiences, Henry tried to get me to invest in solar for Coddi. The year before, he'd bought a solar setup for $15,000 that powered everything in his Airstream. I thought that was way too much money for some extra power.

"You're buying freedom," Henry said. We stood in his shop, a metal building large enough to hold his four Airstreams. His words were soft, slow, and deliberate. We'd known each other for three days, but he felt like a loving father. A film of fine dust coated the once-shiny silver shell of the Airstream beside us. "I know how you enjoy living and I have a feeling you'll invest in solar sooner or later. This may seem expensive, but freedom is priceless. Why wait?"

I struggled to live and work off-grid for over a year before my frustration pushed me to bite the bullet and listen to my wise old friend. I bought freedom in June 2019. I can live off-grid in perpetuity with my solar setup. Henry was right.

489.

Note to self: Always listen to the words of the wise.

490.

February 16 – Virginia

The first couple of weeks in Virginia were close to magical. We fit together in almost every way. After Valentine's Day, things go downhill. M gets worn down by work. She holds space for beautiful humans in an online community she created, but the company drains her. She loves and counsels people all week, and still answers texts and calls on weekends. Behind the scenes, the company is falling apart, and she's getting her butt kicked by C-suite execs who are clueless about her love and dedication. Each week she says, "It's been one of those weeks." M has also suffered mistreatment from many people she thought loved her most, and this still affects her. Combine that with work frustrations, and it's the perfect storm. The tug-of-war tears her apart daily, affecting every aspect of her life. In moments of utter exhaustion, she snaps at me about things it feels she imagines about me. My insecurities rear their ugly heads too. Being with her through this is harder than I imagined. I don't know exactly how she feels, but all of this seems to keep her from being herself. We both are doing our best to love in the ways we know. She loves through attentive tenderness, conversations, meaningful time together, and touch. I love by inquiring, listening, touch, giving her quiet space, and taking care of the small things: errands, cooking, whatever helps. I care and hope to lift a bit of the burden, but I don't know if I can do this forever.

491.

The saying "hurt people hurt people" feels like a cop-out. Life happened. I was a lonely and hurt little kid who wanted to feel loved more than anything but didn't know how to ask. I popped out of the womb tough. My brother, Ben, arrived a sensitive little fella. My independent nature left no room for tagalongs. Even worse, the more hurt I felt, the more I took out my anger on the only one in the house littler than me. I could be spit-and-vinegar mean. I was smart about it too. I never left physical evidence. Raised by a single mom who worked a lot, I hit Ben with body shots with my hands and beat down his soul with my words. I called him fat and stupid and who knows what else.

Now, I look back and can't imagine being on the receiving end, especially from someone I looked up to and loved. Ben is a great man and a wonderful father. Still, I wonder what kind of man he would have been if I'd been loving and kind. I wonder what kind of woman I'd be had I felt more loved and learned how to express love as a kid. We both made it. No thanks to me.

492.

February 21 – Virginia

"I can feel you're sad," M says. We hold each other in the dark, wrapped in nothing but flannel sheets dotted with blue birds. My heart aches. I am so close to walking away. M's hand strokes my head. In silence, my tears flow. M pulls me in tight, cheek to cheek. Her face is dry. She thinks I'm sad because I'm leaving in a few days. It's much worse than that. I don't want to break her heart, and my heart is already breaking. We both have too much baggage in the life department and I don't have enough experience in the romance department. It's not her fault. It's not mine.

This is what I would say if I had the guts.

My soul wants to be with your soul. Your soul wants mine. My tears are for love found and love lost. I don't know if I can be me in this situation. I wish I were better, stronger, and knew how to help. Maybe we must wait until we meet again, until we've both cast off the shackles of the past.

I've never felt more myself. I am torn. What if we are the loving mirrors we each need to walk hand in hand as we let go of all that keeps us caged? What if being together is perfect for our imperfections? I'm crying because this might be the last time we hold each other in this way, in these bodies, in this life. I'm sad for waiting so long for This, to know you're here and walk away. I'm weeping in your bed because I'm scared I'm losing you before we begin.

493.

Perry's quote about Hebron echoes in my mind. *"You don't know what you're missing, but if you knew, it's something you'd regret for the rest of your life."*

This statement feels truer about This and M than anything. This isn't about a boat ride. This isn't even about M and me. This is about everything, the synergy of an infinite alchemy unfolding.

494.

February 24 – Virginia
M is driving me to the airport. We haven't talked about "us" or what might happen next. We hug and kiss goodbye. I'm flying back to Florida wondering if I'll ever see her again.

495.

March 20 – Querétaro, Mexico
After a few weeks in Florida, I flew to Mexico to visit a close friend, Marina. I hang with her family for a few days before we drive to Acapulco to work on her condo, which was hit by a Category 5 hurricane three months before. In between runs to Home Depot, we worked and relaxed on the beach.

496.

Coddiwompling is allowing. No need to sell everything and move into an RV to do it. It's simple: be open in every part of life. I used to cling to plans and ideas. But life is fluid; opportunities pop up. When I pause and listen without expectations or preconceived ideas, the answer becomes crystal clear.

497.

March 28 – Acapulco, Mexico, day one of yoga
Each morning, Marina does yoga on a grassy patch with a clear view of the sea. Years ago I tried yoga, but didn't enjoy it. Marina invited me. I went.

"How was it?" Marina asked. Drenched in sweat, she sat cross-legged at the end of her mat.

"Painful," I said with a smile. "I'm impressed with your yogi skills."

Marina could tell if my poses needed adjusting without even looking at me.

498.

If someone writes my epitaph after I'm gone, I'd love it to go something like this: *She lived wild and free, followed her heart, and felt it all.*

499.

March 30 – Acapulco, Mexico, day two of yoga
"Do you want to do yoga with me, or walk with Isabel?" Isabel is Marina's best friend, who doesn't enjoy yoga. The three of us stood in the living room. I wanted to walk the beach, but something told me to go with Marina.

Day two was painful, but better. Marina invited me to bend and twist in ways I hadn't thought possible.

"You're like Mr. Miyagi in *The Karate Kid*," I said.

Marina laughed. "Each more difficult pose we do, I prepare five to seven poses ahead to allow the body to get there. The student doesn't have to understand any of that. There's a trust there."

"Yeah, when I see you do things so easily, it helps me know I can, too."

500.

Since 2019, I've loved being a solo traveler. Aloneness has been my refuge. A welcome space, an opening to bloom into, a sacred universe where stars twinkle in the soundless void. My aloneness has provided opportunities for miracles to flood in.

501.

April 1, 5:00 a.m. – Acapulco, Mexico

I pushed a kayak through crashing waves and jumped in. I wore a bikini and a pink long-sleeved sun shirt. The sea and sky were inky black. Each paddle stroke lit a swath of blue-green bioluminescence, which swirled in eddies like underwater lightning. It felt like paddling through a dreamland. Each drip from my paddle flashed blue. Cold water splashed on my arms, a stark contrast to the humid morning air. The bow of my kayak rose slowly and then fell. It felt as if the sea were breathing. Bright-blue water sprayed and rippled from under the bow of my kayak. These wide waves traveled across the Pacific.

Under a crescent moon and thousands of twinkling stars, I paddled toward the sweeping beam of a lighthouse on an island off the coast of Acapulco. After an hour, the sky turned marigold and tangerine, and the island took shape. I'd set out early to finish the eight-mile round trip before the sun turned me into a blister. At sunrise, I hauled my kayak onto the island's sand and walked in flip-flops, paddle in hand. I found a rustic trail through the forest, where tropical birds serenaded me. I bushwhacked through fallen trees to dead ends blocked by tangled branches, damage from the hurricane. Eventually I made it to the top: a lighthouse and observatory. Six guys in green military fatigues raked palm fronds and leaves and cleared branches and trees.

"*Buenos dias*," I said. Small smoky fires dotted the jungle. There was an open-air bunkhouse, an outdoor kitchen, and vibrant turquoise views forever.

"*Buenos dias*," they said, and continued with their work.

Not a bad way to start a Monday.

502.

There's something captivating about a woman traveling solo. People get curious and welcome me into their lives, like Daniele and Fabien, who'd admitted he wouldn't have invited me on his boat if I'd been a man, or not alone.

A few years ago, I'd finished a long hike in Glacier National Park and needed to get to my truck, twelve miles away, so I stood on the side of the road and threw my thumb up. The first vehicle that drove by stopped. Steve in his big red truck.

"Keep this pen," Steve said. We'd made it to Casper, and I stood at Steve's window. "That's my business. Come visit when you're in Wisconsin."

Two months later, I called him. He invited me boating and to camp on his property. Steve said he'd called his wife right after we spoke. "I picked up this girl in Montana and she's coming to visit." His wife had laughed and wanted to hear more.

Traveling (and hitchhiking) as a solo woman has its perks. I've got at least fifteen more stories just like this. Couples adopt me often.

503.

On the grand journey of life, the idea of being a solo turtle who swims through sea after sea and sees the world without someone to breathe in the scents of those beautiful beaches with, and to frolic on the reefs with, and to dive deep with ... now, after This with M, the idea of forever being that solo turtle cracks my heart in two.

504.

April 2 – Acapulco, Mexico, day three of yoga
"Either set an intention or listen for one."

Each morning, as we stood facing the Pacific horizon, Marina began our yoga practice with the same words. I waited and allowed each time. My mind stilled. Within ten seconds, an intention would arrive, like a tender green leaf floating down from the tree of everything. It would land in my hand, with no attempt on my part to catch it. Every time, it amazed me.

Thirty minutes into yoga, I lay on my back, feet planted, knees bent, palms flat on the ground above my shoulders, elbows pointed to the sky.

"Just push up," Marina said.

I looked to my left, wondering what she meant, and saw Marina pop up into a bridge pose with the ease of lifting a feather.

No way.

"Push up, it's simple. You can do it." It was as if she'd heard my thoughts. I hadn't moved but kept my face turned in her direction. She dropped and then popped back up again. "See. Simple. Your turn. Just push up." I did, and like magic, there I was, in an impossible pose.

"How was it today?" Marina asked, after we finished.

"I can't believe I'm saying this, but I'm enjoying yoga."

505.

I'm ready to share life, to slow way down, to let stillness seep into my bones. I will need to leave parts of life I've loved to allow the unimaginable in. I love solitude and having plenty of time to write, read, play, relax, work. During the four weeks in Virginia, I felt the days shorten with the fullness of two lives mixing into one. It's worth it. I'm ready to dive in.

506.

Text M to K:

> It is my great pleasure to invite, inspire, and initiate your allowing. To witness and love the divine miracle that is you. I will love, protect, and nourish that safe sacred space for your full release. With reverence, gentleness, kindness, and all the love that flows effortlessly from my soul. You matter to me. I will catch and hold you in your emancipation.

> My goodness, my goddess, my Beyond Love. What a loving proclamation. Thank you. I love you beyond beyond beyond.

507.

April 3 – Acapulco, Mexico
M wants to give coddiwompling a go. I'm excited she wants to travel with me. She hopes to come on her two-week vacation near the end of April. She just called with a question: "What if I bought a one-way ticket?"

508.

Given the chance to go back in time to 2017, would you change anything?
My first inclination is to say no. After reflecting, being completely honest, I'd get the full solar setup as soon as Henry suggested it. Other than that, I wouldn't change a thing.

509.

Text M to K:

> With you, I am also wanting to release and free myself from the remaining scars of all the "little murders" from the conditioned need to prove myself. To trust more. To be less restrictive with my time and working, which has been my sole companion. To love you fearlessly and with complete presence. I am lighter, more open. This is the Being I want to nurture and expand. I beyond love you and want even more!

510.

I can't read a book on how to get comfortable sitting in an icy stream, or go to a class on it, or watch a video about it. I have to get in and experience the icy stream.

511.

Text K to M:

> I will kiss and love your "little murders" until everything falls away, and with a smile that lights up the universe, you'll take that last tiny step into the undeniable knowing that you are a perfect, complete, undamaged, unbroken, scarless, immaculate, beautiful, miracle of light, and you always have been. The being

> who you want to nurture and expand is the being who is doing the nurturing. The giver and the gift. I will love you as you remember, and every time you forget … just as you do for me in my remembering and forgetting. We are mirrors, the same in the best of ways and opposites in the best of ways. I beyond love you and know much more is coming. There is no limit to how high we will go, in this alchemy unfolding.

512.

I know what to do, but for my ideas, worries, and beliefs that muddy things up. Most people think that following their heart should always feel warm and fuzzy. Sometimes it feels like dragging a tractor tire uphill through wet cement.

513.

Text K to M:

> You are as perfect as this infinite sky, that holds your tiny moon, that will darken the earth's view of the sun, and turn day into night, just for a moment, a few minutes of witnessing a miracle of light and dark, the alchemy of a tiny moon and a fireball 400 times its size, which is 400 times further away, thus the possibility, thus the eclipse of light, light that is still there, except for its shadow, except for what we see, for that moment. Coincidence?
> Or a reminder? … that we are all in the midst of the perfect unfolding, even when life doesn't seem perfect at all.

514.

During our last week in Acapulco, Marina's fifteen-year-old son and four of his friends joined us. The teenage boys were cuddly and snuggly. They'd lie on a bed together, watch movies with their limbs intertwined and heads resting on chests, bellies, and backs. The same thing happened when they were lounging on the couch. They would mindlessly caress each other while laughing, joking, and making fun of one another.

On the long drive back to Marina's home in the minivan, they watched a video on one phone together, cuddled up. These were young men who thought nothing of what I considered affectionate touch. It was a beautiful innocence, not sexual, but intimate and loving. It was unlike anything I'd seen with teenagers in the US. These boys will grow into men who naturally express love. This is our nature, and they have not been taught otherwise. What a gift.

515.

There'll be a moment when I must choose to walk the path not alone and release this way of life that set me free, opened my eyes, and introduced me to so many incredible people. This life that taught me how to be me.

516.

April 7 – Querétaro, Mexico
"I've never loved anyone like this," M says, her voice trembling. I sit on a cold, flat rock at the edge of a raised garden bed. Evening has settled in and the scent of vine-ripe tomatoes hangs in the air. A half-used bar of soap lies face up a few rocks down. The rich, dark earth, still hot from the day, warms my bare feet.

"And I love you," I say into the dark air, into the phone on my thigh, into M's ear half a continent away, into myself, into everything I've ever dreamed of in a lover and a friend.

I see an image of M floating above. She looks down at me overflowing with love, her eyes rimmed with tears. She's wrapped in a white flannel sheet dotted with blue birds. Dirty-blonde curls hang wild and frame her face. I love her, but not near as deep and wide as I want to. I'm not sure what love like that is, or where it comes from. I want to experience this … with her.

We sit in silence together, M in her bed in Virginia, I on a rock in Mexico. I tear up, alone in the garden. I'm as free as the wind, and still my heart aches for that one warm, soft place to lay my head.

517.

Life is lived in the lightness of traveling with as little baggage as possible.

518.

April 14 – Havana, Florida
I'm back from Mexico and at Mom's house again, doing a few repairs on Coddi. M will be here in five days. This coming week feels like the precipice. I straddle the edge, between the way I've lived and the way I'm invited to fall into. Life is living me, and the decision has been made. In This, I choose to leap into the unknown and welcome the unimaginable. I am ready for the next adventure, a grand opening, a shared journey.

519.

As I set off anew, I must remember to linger in wonder and sweet anticipation.

520.

April 17 – Havana, Florida
Yesterday was Mom's seventy-first birthday. Jupiter's moons! How did that happen? In her late fifties she got a bleak diagnosis. At sixty she was told she might be dead in six months, and there was a slight chance she'd make it two years, but not longer.

521.

People often wonder how I know this is the perfect unfolding. The short answer: Because it happened.

If it happened, it couldn't have happened any other way. Even when things are hard or don't make sense, everything in the grand infinite scheme is the perfect unfolding. From the personal perspective, life might seem confusing or unfair. But if I could zoom out and see the full tapestry of existence since the beginning of everything to the edge of forever, the whole thing would make sense.

We are a boundless being. We are love. Love is at the heart of all things, and I can rest easy knowing: it's all OK.

522.

I need little and want even less. Every possession, idea, and loved one remains not by force, but because Life allows it. When something falls away, this is coddiwompling in action. This is love. This is freedom.

523.

The tickles of my soul, my heart's desire, this is the voice of God. Not some fear-driven, finger-pointing, judgment-hurling deity that demands I beg for forgiveness. No, not that guy.

524.

April 17, 2:00 p.m.

Subject: An exercise in full expression
From: M
To: K

My beloved beyond love,

I want to write this out first, then speak with you about it all, if you want to have a conversation. I am coming from a place of love and vulnerability and hopefully it will be received in the intention of honoring our highest good, individually and collectively.

Stating my needs is REALLY hard for me. I am physically shaking while writing this and I hardly slept last night because I knew the time had come to express myself. It is an old wound I am releasing, and I ask for your grace.

...

This trip doesn't feel good to me anymore. I'm trying to fit into a lifestyle I know I don't want.

It has gone from feeling like an open-ended adventure to one big compromise ... I'm choosing to honor myself and what I need right now. I'm choosing to honor you and your life by releasing the need to figure out how to fit me in it. Let us just love each other in the biggest and freest of expressions. I think we wrote a love story way before we had the full picture of reality. I won't be flying to Florida on the 19th to join you on your trip. You are free to coddiwomple to your appointments out west.

I love you with every fiber of my being,

M

525.

I live free of guilt, worry, and silly ideas that rip the joys of life out of my grip. And I'm still surprised by unwritten rules that muddy up the crystal-clear river of truth. I don't know I have these misunderstandings until I slam up against them. And boy, do I have a knack for slamming. If there was such a thing as a spectrum when I was a kid, they would have labeled me as being on it. I'm still learning how to feel, how to respond. Sometimes I don't notice when people are experiencing emotions. I feel for M; it's hard on her. I am hard on her. I want to learn, and become aware of the places where I can be supportive and caring. I want to love deeper, fuller, and freer.

I don't fucking live free. That's a lie. I live in a prison of my misunderstanding. And it's not fair to those I love. Tears are streaming now. Tears of sorrow and love, all mixed up. As mixed up as me.

526.

Back the truck up. I didn't mean to give ideas a bad rap. They're fresh green buds of creativity, the flower still tucked inside, not yet unfurled. There's so much latent potential in an idea. To assume I've got it all figured out would be like claiming I know the shape of every petal that will burst from a fuzzy lime-green bud.

527.

April 17 – Havana, Florida

When I read M's email, my body reacted as though I were being left. My mouth went dry, I shook, and waves of panic hit me. My heart ached for M, and I loved that she trusted me with her truth. I wanted to comfort her. And her change of heart felt as if it had come out of left field. I didn't understand. I'd wanted her to meet Mom, maybe even my brother's family, even if they didn't know she was more than a friend. Being the wise one, she knew it was too soon. We'd been planning her visit to Florida for weeks. I should've asked more, listened, and found clarity with her and what she wanted. Two days before her planned arrival, this. I'd screwed up. I tried to keep going with my day but couldn't. I cried and couldn't stop.

I didn't want to waste the feeling. I needed to write with it. I poured out pages on love and loss, on my longing to be with a soul who loves and is willing to learn to love with me. I wrote about freedom from expectations, abandonment, and old stories. The whole document disappeared into the digital oblivion.

528.

"Aha! You're not as free as you think," Life says. We float in the vast dark void. I don't answer, but wait in the quiet, and remember again how stuck I can get when I forget that my heart always, always, always knows the way.

(*Side note to Farmer Joe in Canada: this is one of those rare times when "always" actually ages well.*)

529.

Now isn't a moment in time; it's a space where my mind is free from fear and memory. This is what allows me to experience what is, without resistance. This is living meditation.

530.

April 17 – Havana, Florida
I lie in bed, door closed so Mom doesn't know I'm crying.

Where am I? What does it even matter? My whole world is dizzy spinning. I'm not where I was, and not where I'm going. I'm in between. I know nothing.

This feels like the moment in the bike crash when an awkward jolt sent shivers up my spine. Time stretches as my body drifts further and further off-center. *In the stillness of free fall, milliseconds last hours.*

531.

Writing, whether it's articles, posts, or now a book, is part of my greatest expression. From the outside, it might look as if I'm motivated and disciplined. But the truth is, the way I live and create is both an expression of my true nature and a way of seeking it. I question everything. I spend time in the wilderness. I experience God, the Universe, the Mystery: in all forms.

Writing is how I share that experience. It's how I tap someone gently on the shoulder and invite them to get curious about freedom, about what's possible, about following the tickles of their soul. The act of writing invites me to pause and check in, to reflect on what I know and what I don't. It's not about effort. It's not discipline. It's desire. I follow what calls me, and I'm called to share.

532.

April 17 – Havana, Florida
M and I talk a few hours after her email. I apologize for not asking her what she wanted and for seeming to disregard her needs. She apologizes for making some assumptions. We cry together, turn toward, and love on each other. M changes her mind. We decide together that she won't meet Ben's family yet and that we'll get on the road as soon as possible after she arrives at Mom's. M wants to coddiwomple to Arkansas and who knows after that. We plan to leave Mom's on the morning of April 21.

Part Six: New Beginnings
Wandering West

As M and I prepared to leave Florida and head west, I realized we were embarking on two journeys simultaneously: one across the physical landscape, and another through the uncharted territory of loving someone this deeply. Both required surrender to the unknown, both demanded presence, and both promised vistas I couldn't fathom. The road west beckoned, and I wouldn't be facing it alone.

The experiences in Newfoundland and Labrador had prepared me for this. The resilience I'd found in the bike crash, the vulnerability I'd embraced through illness, and the openness to connection I'd discovered with strangers such as William, Daniele, and Fabien—these lessons were becoming the foundation of something even more profound.

533.

April 20 – Havana, Florida

After twenty hours together, Mom and M have already ganged up on me. I can see the two of them as great friends. I am in awe of the way M cares, loves on, and gives to all people. She'd felt this was too soon to meet Mom, yet here she is, loving and helping her. And Mom is loving her. My guess is they are each relieved that things are simpler than they anticipated, that they are more alike than different, and that someone they love (me) is cared for.

534.

I'm holding on when I wish to let go. I forget who I am and ask for too much. I have more than I need. I've landed in Life's jackpot and it is no fault of my own. No credit taken. I'm shedding tears of awe—for everything and nothing at all. There's no thank-you card to mail. No need for a god in the sky to tally blessings or demand repentance. These tears aren't for earning or owing. They're simply gratitude. Pure and full.

535.

April 22 – Whitten Park Campground, Fulton, Mississippi
I cried off and on for hours during the drive yesterday. My heart was ripped out and wrung dry. When M and I left, the last visual of Mom was a reflection in the passenger-side mirror. She stood in a pink sweatshirt at the end of the driveway, her right arm raised to wave goodbye. As with each time I leave, I wonder if it will be the last time I see her. A reflection, a tiny image of a woman larger than life, reduced. So small her face, and features are a blur.

M reached across the console and placed her warm hand on mine. "She loves you so much," she whispered. I nodded, unable to speak. What M didn't know was how that simple gesture of Mom waving transported me back to being thirteen again: watching her drive away, feeling abandoned all over again, even though I was the one leaving this time.

As I drove yesterday, it was the first time I couldn't wail. M sat quietly beside me, witnessing this ritual without intruding on it. I felt exposed and cried silently. M was seeing a part of me I'd kept private, this raw ache that comes with loving someone whose time is measured differently than it once was. That was the first time someone held my right hand while my left hand gripped the steering wheel, and my shirt caught all the tears.

M's loving touch said everything: I see you. This matters. You're not alone in this anymore.

I'd learned to carry my grief in solitude on empty highways with only my reflection for company. Now there was a witness, someone to hold space for what had been mine alone to bear.

536.

"Explanation by the tongue makes most things clear,
But love unexplained is clearer."[13] – Rumi

This is what hums beneath everything: Love unexplained. I'm living it when words fall away completely. I hadn't heard of Rumi until I read *The Forty Rules of Love*, a novel based on Rumi's life. In 2018, Marina knew I was hiding and suggested I read the book. She could smell the love that begged to be set free even though I'd thought I'd squirreled it away, packed it in airtight containers in the darkest corners of my heart.

537.

Is that all the love of my life will be, a faceless blur?

538.

April 23 – Whitten Park Campground, Fulton, Mississippi
Oh my God. She's peeing again. What? M has been to the toilet three times, and it's only 10:15 a.m. I want to say, "Get a grip on your drinking, woman." It used to take me close to three days to fill the pee pot. It's at least once a day now. Being hydrated is nice and all, but sheesh. It's bonkers how much urine we're dumping in the frickin' woods.

The mundane realities of traveling together highlight the contrast between my profound grief and these small frustrations, a surreal balance. Perhaps this is what it means to share a life with someone: they witness your deepest pain and your pettiest annoyances, and somehow make space for both.

539.

I've only ever done grief alone.

540.

Reservations and campgrounds aren't my thing. Being in a campground is like living in a sardine can. I'm packed in with glamping divas with fancy LED lights and outdoor TVs. People bring tons of unnecessary stuff for a weekend in the "woods." I prefer living far away from all that excess. As part of our compromise, M and I agreed to stay in campgrounds as much as possible, and that calls for reservations. Here's another tidbit of campground wisdom: Army Corps of Engineers campsites are my go-to when I gotta be civilized. They're spread out, and usually lakeside nestled in the forest. So, M and I became Army Corps camping divas.

541.

I kiss in the safeness of the known. I gaze in wonder at the feeling and desire of the eyes gazing back, and know my reflection is not the same. I am the kid on the diving platform, eager to take the plunge but terrified to jump. I'm wrapped up with and witness orgasms that last for eons. I feel the reverberations and jolts, the aftershocks that linger for many minutes after we've stilled. I wonder what that feels like and if this kind of pleasure will ever grace my shores, as I swirl my toe along the surface, nothing more.

542.

April 23 – Whitten Park Campground, Fulton, Mississippi
M and I are snuggled up in a hammock hidden between two trees, beside a lake near Tupelo, Mississippi, Elvis's childhood home. Early-evening sun reflects off the water and lights tender spring leaves from below. The stark blue background of a cloudless sky contrasting the dancing neon-lime leaves looks too electric to be created by nature. When M laughs at something I say, the quake travels through both our bodies. In this moment, I understand what poets mean about eternity existing in single instances of perfect connection.

543.

I stand at the edge, swirling sweet nothings across the water's surface with my big toe. I'm scared. If I jump in, I might lose myself. I might get battered and bruised. I might uncover something I didn't know was missing, and the life I love might no longer be enough.

So, I love with only the part of me that's tough enough to take a loss.

544.

April 24 – Whitten Park Campground, Fulton, Mississippi

I say the darndest things. While I'm mentoring or during friendly chats, off-the-wall questions and metaphors pop into my head as if delivered for whoever I'm with. I often say them aloud, even when clueless as to whether they relate. This usually works well for everyone. During a recent coaching session, a roller-coaster image appeared in my mind's eye. It seemed unrelated to our discussion. "I'm not sure why, but I'm seeing a roller coaster," I said. My client's face lit up, and she described a vivid memory of standing in line for one. Something clicked. She had a massive realization and big shifts followed.

Another instance: M and I are walking through a forest on a trail.

"Fuck Elvis," I say, and grab M's hand. She doubles over laughing.

After crossing into Alabama and Mississippi, we were careful not to show any public displays of affection. M's idea, because it's not always safe in certain areas for people who love souls. Birds chirp, a breeze blows, my heart is full. I want nothing more than to hold her hand. No ill will toward Elvis. We're close to his birthplace and "Fuck Elvis" popped into my mind and out of my mouth.

545.

April 26 – Pinnacle, Arkansas

A massive thunder boomer blows in. M and I are on the move between campsite reservations. The planned sleeping spot is twenty minutes due west, directly into the storm. I scour my phone for the normal resting spots: Cabela's, Walmart, rest stops ... nothing is close.

"Maybe a church parking lot?" M says. Casper wobbles back and forth in the wind. We just finished a hike and are at a small wooded trailhead. M leans over the center console, craning her neck to see the map.

"There!" I say. "A church two miles away." It's 6:30 p.m. I call and leave a message. Thirty seconds later, my phone rings.

"This is Pastor Jake. I missed your call." Dark-gray angry clouds blanket the sky to the west, and the weather apps on our phones flash red with severe storm and tornado warnings.

"Hi, yes. Thank you, this is Kristy and I'm a full-time RVer." I tell him where we are and that we need a safe place to wait out the storm. "Would it be OK if we parked at your church for the night?"

"I don't see why not. We'll be there at 9:30 Sunday morning, but I'm guessing you'll be long gone by then." A wave of relief spreads out from my chest. My shoulders relax.

546.

Expecting a partner to meet my needs (including comfort or intimacy) is a recipe for disaster. When we both know we're complete and whole as we are, then our life is an expression of Love/God. Intimacy isn't something we need to create; intimacy is found in our shared journey back to our true nature: the love that we are.

547.

"How did you know what I meant by 'Fuck Elvis'?" I ask M.

"I just knew it meant fuck the establishment," she says. "Fuck all the unwritten rules. I don't care what happens. I'm going to be me."

Yup. Live, love, be yourself, and let's all get along. That became our secret code statement. I smile a cute, mischievous smile every time I think about or say, "Fuck Elvis."

548.

April 26 – Pinnacle, Arkansas

Minutes after our conversation with Pastor Jake, we're at the church. An eerie bronze-yellow color tints the sky and everything else. We make a mad dash through wild wind and pissing rain and hunker down inside Coddi. I check the weather and there's a severe hail warning too: *100 percent chance of hail, estimated at 1.5 inches, along with 60-mile-per-hour winds and funnel sightings.* Wind shakes Coddi. Buckets of rain fall so thick I can't see the church. We yell to speak. I pace and fear the worst.

Hail is an Airstream killer. For seven years I've watched the weather like a hawk, driven far and wide to avoid storms. I was enjoying the afternoon with M and missed this one. Now it's too late.

"I gotta move us," I yell. Hail clanking on the roof and walls adds to the heavy-metal concert of thunder, rain, and wind. Coddi lurches side to side. M sits on the front bed, her phone in her hand, looking up at me. "I'm gonna drive up beside the church, get as close as possible to block the wind."

We both jump as deafening thunder cracks and everything flashes purple and white. I snatch my keys and bolt out into the deluge.

549.

Do you reckon your previous life as a firefighter/paramedic has influenced your courage and confidence in living a nomadic life?

What is courage? What is confidence? I don't need courage when I know I'm safe. To me, what we call "courage" or "confidence" is a lovely side effect of having complete trust in Life. It's living without expectation, deeply knowing who we are at our essence, and knowing without a doubt that we are forever in the midst of the perfect unfolding. If I know who I am cannot disappear or die, and is not in danger, then my everyday actions appear courageous. When I live in the grand allowing, I live from love. More often than not, this is the space I live in.

550.

Avoiding emotional storms: that is something I'm great at. For twenty-five years, I didn't let myself feel and avoided love, so I wouldn't have to suffer through heartbreak again. I ran away from conflict. I overachieved in school, sports, and work. If I filled my life and never sat still, the storms could never find me.

551.

April 26 – Pastor Jake's parking lot, Pinnacle, Arkansas
By the time I make it to Casper's driver's seat, I'm as wet as if I jumped into a swimming pool. CRAP! The backup camera is off because I unplugged

Coddi from the truck for the night. I drive along the sidewalk at the front of the church. The wind all but stops, but rain and pea-sized hail are coming down in a deluge. Coddi is still mid-turn. I have to straighten her to get her closer to the church and out of the wind. The windows are fogged and I can't see anything behind me.

Backing up a fifty-two-foot-long rig as a solo RVer is one of the hairier things I do. Except for trained semitruck drivers, most people wouldn't risk backing up a rig this long alone in unfamiliar places. My mom got a backup camera installed on Coddi for my Christmas gift in 2017. That was a useful gift! There are still plenty of risks. When I'm backing up in close quarters, I get out and look several times, even with the camera. In 2020 in New Jersey, I was backing into the driveway of a lady who offered Airstream courtesy parking. I trusted her to watch for obstacles. I hit a cast-iron historical sign with my center awning arm and bent the bracket. It was pure luck I didn't rip a hole through Coddi's aluminum. That was the last time I trusted a stranger when backing up.

552.

Yes, my previous life as a firefighter/paramedic helps me live this nomadic life. When my crew and I showed up at an emergency, our job was to mitigate the problem. There were plenty of times we'd roll up on a scene and think, *How the heck are we going to fix this?* We'd take action and try stuff. We were confident we'd find our way through the challenges and never considered quitting. Sure, we were well-trained in mitigating emergency situations, but we often took our knowledge and flew by the seat of our pants. As we tried stuff, the most miraculous ideas popped up. For fourteen years as a firefighter/paramedic, I honed the skill of knowing the seat of my pants has wings.

553.

As much as I love M and open up with her, more than any other human (personally, spiritually, sensually), I still hold back intimately. Sex is an area I've never been comfortable in, even with Jack and Wade. Now, with a woman, I'm more in my head than ever. To think during sex violates a fundamental law of lovemaking, yet I haven't allowed myself to let go.

As M and I explore the borders of our new connection, I find myself revisiting memories of pleasure and shame that I'd buried. The teachings about what was "appropriate" that had shaped me from childhood suddenly seemed worth questioning in light of this new love.

1986 – Tallahassee, Florida

Before we were latchkey kids, my little brother and I spent each summer weekday at my first-grade teacher's house. Her two teenage daughters made sure we stayed alive. They had a pool. For fun, I learned to float like a channel buoy with a ball gripped between my legs in the deep end. Then I mastered the bounce and balance. As I bobbed, waves of pleasure crashed and ricocheted. I'd never felt such enjoyable tingles and delight. At seven years old, I played my way into pure bliss.

1987 – Tallahassee, Florida

My father passed by the bedroom of his eight-year-old daughter and saw a romantic interlude between the girl and a stuffed animal. The next day he took the girl to an ice cream shop for a treat: frozen yogurt in a waffle cone with rainbow sprinkles. The pint-sized lass picked a table for two by the window for their special date.

He sat down and cut straight to the point.

"That pleasurable feeling is only supposed to be felt between a husband and a wife."

The girl's cheeks flushed. She fidgeted in her chair, licked her treat, and stared out the window.

"If you pleasure yourself," he said, "there will come a time when you're married, and it's time to have sex, but your body will find pleasure too fast and ruin the moment."

Her melting cone in one hand, she fidgeted with a clean napkin in the other as he went on and on. She continued to stare out the window at nothing.

"You must wait to have sex until you are married by a preacher or else God will punish you."

She imagined the sorrow of her future mate when he found out she'd used it all up on a pink-and-purple Popple when she was eight.

554.

April 26 – Pastor Jake's parking lot
"You're soaked," M says. I plop onto the bed next to her without thinking. I pull off my shirt and shorts and snuggle into her wearing nothing but panties. The clanging of hail makes it sound as if we're inside a ginormous, old-fashioned popcorn popper. I panic as I watch ice chunks bounce off the skylight. Hail the size of ping-pong balls is on its way. That will shatter the skylights and destroy Coddi. Worse than the damage, wandering with M will be over. Worse yet, tornadoes are out there too.

555.

My childhood was full of storms. My dad changed churches faster than most people go through shoes. For a little kid, that led to a whirlwind of friendships built and lost, and of varying degrees of religious rules and rituals learned and then preached against. I saw Dad get baptized many times. I half-thought he just enjoyed getting dunked by dudes in capes. Boy was he strict about relationships and sex. No sex until marriage, marry a God-fearing man, even kissing was serious business, and homosexuals were damned to hell.

The irony wasn't lost on me, the hope of riding out a storm at a church with the woman I loved. The thunder outside paled compared to the storm of convictions I'd already weathered, between what I was taught and what my heart knows is true.

556.

I reflect on deeply loving a partner. M is my second taste of romantic love. I've never felt love, been caressed, or experienced companionship like this. We are together all our waking hours and tangled while we sleep.

When I learned to love Wade, he became my first, but it wasn't mutual. That turned into a shitstorm when Wade snuck off to Kansas. He dumped me without emotion, via phone at 1:00 a.m. No avoiding that gale-force storm. That's what started this whole adventure.

557.

April 26 – Pastor Jake's parking lot
The church parking lot is eerily quiet. A few sprinkles of rain tap on the aluminum. I open the door and blue sky peeks between gray clouds. We've made it.

558.

Do you take something with you everywhere you go? For example, a special keepsake?
No, I rarely get attached to physical things such as keepsakes. Although, when M arrived in Florida in April, she brought me a gift: a sterling silver Möbius-strip pendant on a thin chain, as a reminder of our love: infinite and unending. I've worn that almost every day since. And that says a lot because I'm not a fan of jewelry and rarely wear any. Maybe this special pendant will change my answer to a yes.

559.

April 26 – Pastor Jake's parking lot
M and I shower and crawl into bed. We're both spent.

A simple kiss goodnight lingers and grows in magnitude like waves in a stormy sea. I want her. She wants me. Somehow, in the shadow of a church in a small town in Arkansas, all the invented rules, ideas of good and bad, and made-up judgments from God and myself … all that thinking falls away. I let go and make love.

April 27
"Hallelujah! Praise Jesus! And thank you, Pastor Jake!" M says, right after waking up. Giggling and laughing ensues. What are the chances

that the "good girl" would let go in a church parking lot? With all my history and baggage around Christianity, sex, sinning, punishments ... and now this?

I often leave a thank-you note for people who host Coddi and me. Pastor Jake deserves a thank-you, though much of our gratitude is for something he never intended to facilitate.

While sipping coffee and tea, M and I write and laugh and write and giggle. The topic: an ambiguously loving note of appreciation. I wish I'd taken a photo of the note because its ingenuity will never be reproduced.

"Pastor Jake will stand at the pulpit on Sunday morning beaming!" M says. "He will read this to his congregation." On my dark-wood breakfast table is an ivory envelope and gold-embossed Hallmark card lit in a bright swath of early-morning sunbeam.

"Girl, Pastor Jake is gonna have no clue what that note is really thanking him for," I say.

"Can I get an amen!" M tilts her head back and holds both palms toward the ceiling. "Thank you, Pastor Jake!" She slips the card in the envelope and scampers out. I watch from my seat at the table as she skips like a schoolgirl playing hopscotch across a parking lot of puddles up to the front door of the church. She pins the envelope above the door handle and claps her hands twice in a joyous display of enthusiasm.

560.

April 28 – Petit Jean State Park, Arkansas

Halfway through our hike, the trail meets a flooded river seventy-five feet wide. Swollen waters cover the stepping-stone pillars that stretch across. I try crossing while M stays on dry ground, but the water is too deep. The map shows no alternate route: cross here or backtrack to the truck. M isn't keen on crossing. One slip means being swept downriver over rapids.

I remove my boots, string them around my neck, and attempt to cross step by careful step. Once my bare foot lands on dry land, I look back. M is a tiny figure against bright-green jungle; there's a gauntlet of rushing water between us. This feels bigger than a river crossing. *Adventure, or turn back?* Will M choose the unknown, or the known? *Am I OK with whatever M chooses?* Definitely yes. Our relationship has been one long river crossing. So many uncertain steps and emotional currents threatening to sweep us away. *Trust, or live in fear and what-ifs? Will we meet each other where we are and journey together with no judgment?*

I give M the space to decide without pressure. Love is watching someone make their own choice, even when we have more confidence in them than they have in themselves.

561.

Writing on the road is tough. After leaving Virginia two months ago, I wrote religiously, two to three hours in the morning, and another hour or more in the afternoon. We've been on the road for ten days and I've hardly written at all. The beauty of this way of life is the haphazardness of everything. Haphazard isn't the norm for writing a book and routine isn't a state in the coddiwomple way, especially now that my solo journey has become a duet.

562.

April 28 – Petit Jean State Park, Arkansas, flooded river crossing
Barefoot and tentative, M begins her journey across the river with a furrowed and determined brow. At the halfway point, her steps are deliberate and brows soft. Three-quarters of the way across, she sings "Slip Slidin' Away" by Paul Simon. I sit on a boulder at the edge of the river and watch her step closer and closer, dancing, giggling, and blooming. God, I love M. I love This. I love being loving witnesses in this alchemy of a lifetime. I love coddiwompling together, while we both listen to the tickles of our souls, in loving witness of one another. This woman is everything I could ever ask for in a lover and best friend.

And maybe this is how my writing will continue, too: more spontaneous, finding its way like bare feet across river stones. This is a dance. This is feeling my way through the unmundaneness. I will be surprised by how this works, and it will work. These words are proof.

563.

We.

564.

It's so strange, those two letters, *W* and *E*. I haven't used those two together much. *We*. There is a lot implied there: more than one; collaboration; togetherness; a spice untasted by the *I* livers; new scents; the breaking of routines; an alchemy unfolding. Who knows how high w-e will go.

565.

April 29, 9:07 a.m. – Petit Jean State Park Campground, Arkansas
I'm lounging in Coddi's front bed. M is at the front desk. We're both writing. She turns, wraps both her warm hands around my right calf, caresses my entire lower leg, leans down, presses her lips against my shin and kisses slow, like a butterfly's wings, up toward my knee, then returns to writing again. The sensation lingers and sends me into oblivion. The honey heat of her palms and the tickle of her breath against my skin, the love and sensuality, her desire to touch me, my desire for her to touch me, my desire to touch her … A dream I didn't know to dream has come true.

566.

I love Coddi just the way she is. I don't have any planned changes or upgrades for her. As for my lifestyle, I can see changes coming. M and I have talked about finding land to build a home base if we continue doing life together. M loves traveling, and she wants to have a place to call home for the long haul. I'd like that too. We wish for a place with access to a lake, a river, or the ocean. A place in the forest, yet with cleared land for a vegetable garden and at least a partial view of the horizon, the further off the beaten path the better; a space to connect with a community of people that invites everyone to settle and open up. An outdoor area to gather, cook, and commune with nature, places to walk or bike without the need to drive to get there, mountains nearby, a small, simple house, and a covered parking area for Coddi. I'd love to share life with M, and if this place appeared, a lot of things would change.

567.

Ten minutes after the leg-caressing episode, M crawls up next to me, apologizes for interrupting my writing, and asks if she can snuggle in for a minute or two. I set my computer to the side and wrap her up. Her head on my chest just below my chin, she feels different, heavy, sad.

"What's going on in there?" I ask, as I kiss her silky hair. She drapes her leg over mine, her knee bent and firm on my crotch, her hand on my sternum.

"I don't want to get old," she says, as her voice cracks and tears darken my forest-green T-shirt.

568.

These last few days—my letting go in Pastor Jake's parking lot, M crossing the flooded river despite her fears, and now this tender moment—are an expression of love unexplained. We are being drawn, letting go, and taking one step after another, even when we are afraid. This is Life living itself through two people longing, at the heart of it all, to love and be loved.

569.

April 30 – Hemmed-in Hollow Falls, Arkansas
I live rich. Rich in experience, connections, reflections, and emotions. I walk through a lush green canopy serenaded by the chuckling warble of a red summer tanager, like a robin with a sore throat. I am in awe of a strip of afternoon amber sun that glistens on a boulder and sparkles dewdrops on ferns. I am in wonderment with Life, a love story too rich for words.

570.

If Virginia and Wisconsin had a baby, it'd be Arkansas. Mountains, rivers, untouched wilderness, rolling hills, farmland, and good and friendly people. Of all the states in the US, I'd bet Arkansas is the best-kept secret. If I had to pick one state to live in, I'd be happy in Arkansas.

571.

M washes dishes one plate at a time. As in: there is a pile of dirty dishes on the counter and the sink is empty. She holds one bowl under the faucet. She rinses it, washes it, rinses it again, and puts it in the drying rack. Then repeats with every single item. I wash an entire day's worth of dishes with the same amount of water she uses for two bowls and spoons.

I'm lying on the bed trying to read while watching what feels like a water crisis unfold. We're gonna run out of water in three days like this, and we need to make it two weeks. This frustration feels like a rabid rat clawing at the inside of my chest. I want to rip the sudsy blue sponge from her cute little paws and banish her from the kitchen, but I know this isn't really about water. Seven years of solo travel taught me to be efficient with resources. It was just my systems and me. Now I'm learning that partnership means finding a middle way: merging two lives, two ways of being, into one shared space. It's about letting go.

I slip outside to check the air in the tires, giving us both some breathing room. Even this is the alchemy unfolding; learning to understand ourselves, with all our hiccups. This is the true journey.

572.

April 30 – Hemmed-in Hollow Falls, Arkansas
We hike too long and do too much climbing. While trudging our butts up the last hill, there's Coddi at the trailhead looking serene and welcoming, deep in the forest, miles from a highway or any paved roads. So we stay. Home is where you park it.

Best night's sleep in a while. W-e are having a perfect morning. W-e might stay here for a couple of days.

573.

May 1 – Hemmed-in Hollow trailhead, Arkansas
I have thirty pairs of panties. We've been on the road ten days, and my fellow traveler is almost out. I mean come on. She knew I do laundry only

every few weeks. The closest laundromat is an hour away. One might say, "Well, hand-wash a few," but we're in the forest and have enough water for a couple more days (thanks to the one-plate-at-a-time dish-washing). Neither of us has shared panties before, but it's that or she goes commando.

574.

What else is different living in the w-e? Never before have I been the object of such tender affection, and felt so wanted, beautiful, and cherished. I've never had an object of my affection adore me like This. Together we are learning so much about Life and love. We are becoming more ourselves in the unfolding of This.

575.

May 3 – Wichita Mountains Wildlife Refuge, Oklahoma
Hello, Oklahoma! I never dreamed you'd be this beautiful! Wichita Mountains Wildlife Refuge is a jaw-dropping gem: burnt-orange boulders rise from emerald grasslands that ripple like ocean waves in the prairie wind, herds of shaggy bison graze like living shadows, longhorns stand silhouetted against impossibly blue skies, turkeys, wildflowers in full bloom, rushing rivers, waterfalls, and sunsets ... A hiking and biking paradise.

When the Airstream is a rockin', don't come a knockin'. In a week and a half, I've had more sex than in the whole rest of my life. I had no idea women could make love in the ways we have, all natural and exceptionally enjoyable. Morning, midday, afternoon, night, anything goes. We've been so exhausted from hiking that we drag through dinner, shower, crawl into bed, snuggle into each other half-asleep, then BAM! We become insatiable under the sheets.

576.

May 4 – Palo Duro Canyon State Park, Texas
The "Grand Canyon of Texas" is raw country: jagged wind-carved cliffs and sunbaked rust-red stone where light and shadow dance across ancient cathedral peaks and silence runs deep.

Back to the panty calamity. Sharing is caring, and that seems the simplest remedy. "How about these?" I stand in the bathroom wrapped in a tan cotton bath towel and hold up two pairs of leopard-print panties. M is on the front bed in sky-blue Life Is Good pajama shorts and a dark-green Packers T-shirt. Rain spatters on Coddi's aluminum and thunder rumbles through the canyon.

"Cougar panties for your cougar." A smile curls the corners of M's lips. "I'll take 'em."

577.

May 6 – Albuquerque, New Mexico
Rose, a friend of M's, invited us to park in her backyard.

"You're being summoned," M says. I'm writing in Coddi. M has the door cracked open and cranes her head inside. Silver hoop earrings jut out from behind her curls. The way her blue eyes look me up and down warms my center. "Rose's friend, Kate, is here. She's dying to meet you."

Rose and Kate are both in their mid-seventies and remind me of the golden girls, but a whole lot funnier and more intelligent. And they swear like sailors. We chat while they drink old-fashioneds, then we tour Coddi, prep dinner, eat, and finally sit down to play Yahtzee (but never play because we're so deep in conversation).

578.

Something else I get asked is how I meet people and maintain relationships while on the road. People pop up out of nowhere. We meet on a trail or in a parking lot, or through friends of friends, or at a gas pump. You name it. The number and depth of intimate platonic relationships that I've spontaneously formed in the past seven years is mind-blowing. I grew to love being alone in nature: days or weeks wrapped in quiet solitude. In that sacred stillness, something in me softened, opening the way to be with others in a depth few know to touch. On top of that, people are attracted to shiny objects and ask if they can see inside Coddi. I'll give almost anyone "the thirty-second tour."

579.

M is a self-starter. We are true partners in every sense of the word. For example, without my asking, she picked up the responsibility of taking care of the inside of Coddi. Even if she doesn't know how to help with repairs and such, she's right there supporting me. We look out for each other, and keep each other's comfort, happiness, work, writing, and friendships top of mind.

580.

"Maintaining relationships" is an idea. Great relationships aren't great because they've been maintained. Love, peace, and the feeling of coherence that most would define as a deeply connected relationship happens when I let all beliefs, expectations, judgments, and assumptions fall away, and when I remain open to seeing everything fresh and new. Great relationships thrive in openness and curiosity.

In the w-e, M and I are meeting each other's friends. Our circles are wider and deeper than in the "I." Life, friends, relationships: everything is richer when shared.

581.

May 6 – Albuquerque, New Mexico
Rose's friend Kate is quite curious, and our interactions feel familiar. This is so common now: conversations with strangers that begin in a flurry of questions.

"How did you go from a regular life to this?"

"Do you ever get scared?"

"How do you afford it?"

"Have you ever felt threatened?"

They ask one question after another, inquisitive, wide-eyed, and sometimes cautious. These chats are part of the rhythm. It's nice to hear what people are curious about. I answer openly, and barriers drop. The person across from me opens up. We laugh. I listen. We sit in easy silence, share a meal, talk some more. Then, without warning, their tears appear: soft, unannounced, steady, and without apology. Maybe there's a quick swipe of a hand across a cheek, maybe the drops fall onto their shirt like a light rain. But they keep going, as though tears are part of telling the truth. We wander through stories late into the night. And when it's time to say goodbye, we hug slowly and closely, as if we're not strangers anymore, and maybe never were.

582.

I don't enjoy shopping. I don't collect things or need more to be happy. I love simplicity and want to declutter even more.

583.

M's age never registered. I don't think of her as a cougar. Though, if we were into labels, she'd qualify. She was in her twenties when I was still wetting my pants. She graduated from high school before I was born. And damn, she's beautiful. I love seeing the look on people's faces when they hear she's in her mid-sixties. Shock and awe. I get it. I assumed she was much younger, too.

584.

I am with people when I'm with people.

585.

This past year has been beyond difficult for M. Her brother, her favorite person and her soulmate, passed away one year ago May. I can't speak for her and what she's feeling, but I can try my best to describe what I witness. This woman, this caring, beautiful, selflessly loving soul, harbors a grief and sadness that is deep, wide, and raw. She loves in a way that is fuller and more far-reaching than I've ever known. The person she had by her side to play with, learn and laugh with, who held her and loved her like no one else ever had, died too soon. This left a gaping hole in M. This empty space is far greater than I'll ever know. I can't grasp what she's feeling, though I'm doing my best to love her through it. I just wish I could love her better.

586.

Insomnia. I fall asleep easily and quickly, but waking up in the wee hours of the morning has plagued me for years. I'm usually up between 3:00 and 4:30 a.m. No stress. No worries. No wishing life were different. I lie there in emptiness and wait for hours. Often, I get up and write. Sometimes writing puts me back to sleep. Most of the time, I write and continue with my day.

587.

I did more in the I. I live more in the w-e.

588.

The last few weeks have been a tremendous change for me. Yeah, people have visited Coddi, but they've never slept in my bed. And they've never visited with the potential for it to be long-term. Coddiwompling naturally includes the wants and needs of each other. I've gained a mirror, a partner. We bring out the best in each other, even though recognizing our sticky places (which are fertile grounds for letting go) can resemble an emotional bar fight.

Coddiwompling with a partner might seem different, but it's the same. We are being guided together in this interconnected dance. Wandering with M is more of an internal adventure than an external one. "Doing" isn't the only way to experience life fully. "Being" together creates moments that feel more complete than all my solo adventures combined. We are both finding our way home with each other.

589.

In the I, I sent more emails. Now I answer emails when needed. In the I, I had time to peruse Facebook. In the w-e, we sit by a fire under a blanket of stars and discuss Life, lie in a hammock and read to each other, and cook and share meals together. To share Life with someone this special elevates everything. I'll take the w-e over the I any day.

590.

Since high school, I've been surrounded by women who are attracted to women: in sports, engineering, and firefighting. There were moments I thought maybe I had feelings for a few friends, but it was never enough to warrant my attention or action.

591.

Something else that's different: I sleep soundly, often all night. M also had years of interrupted sleep. Together, we sleep entwined, forehead to cheek, holding hands. On our backs, arms tangled, my leg draped over hers, heads on shoulders. On our first night together in December, we woke side by side, hands on each other's hips. We still wake this way. In sleep, we are forever in contact. In this profound comfort, I can only guess we've both relaxed our way out of insomnia together.

592.

May 8 – Albuquerque, New Mexico

In the w-e there are two of us working from home hosting Zoom calls, and both of us need a desk and a quiet space. M was on vacation for the first two weeks, which made things easy. Now, three days into our first dual workweek, it's hairy. I offered my desk to M and worked outside for two days. Today I need the desk, so M is outside. It's 5:00 p.m. and M looks to be on her last nerve.

"How about we sleep on the front bed and convert the back bedroom into your office?" I ask. Coddi was built for this: the back bed converts into a love seat and a solid-wood desk folds out on a piano hinge. Winner! M feels at home in the back office. It's a place to nest and treat as her own.

593.

My favorite humans are old men. I'll hang with them anytime. I haven't enjoyed most older women as much, until this week in Albuquerque. At Rose's place, I've met couples and singles in their seventies, all lady lovers. Down-to-earth, loving, hilarious, and proud lesbians. I don't like labels and don't want that one. But for the first time, I'm really enjoying hanging with older women. Who knew?

594.

I lean in and give M a kiss goodnight. "Hey," I say with a giggle. "You stole my lip balm." Mine is tea tree, hers is vanilla bean.

"I did." She leans in more and kisses me soft and slow. "And now I'm giving it back." Her smile stretches wide against my lips.

M's voice carries the gentle texture of river stones, smooth yet with an edge that catches the ear. A honeyed tone that lingers. Her whispers carry that same delicious friction, like pages of a love story being turned slowly in the soft glow of evening light.

595.

Five months into my "loving on souls" experience, pride celebrations don't resonate with me, though I respect their significance for others. My journey is about releasing labels rather than embracing them. Categories of any kind divide us. I'd rather marvel in the flawless being that we are. M and I both find quiet freedom in the space between labels and definitions. This mutual understanding has been particularly refreshing for us.

596.

Many people I visit plan an unrelenting series of outings. They think I'm on vacation. I'm invi-told to see the best of their area. I'm invi-told to dinner with friends each night, or invi-told on excursions to museums, botanical gardens, and scenic drives. I work, for goodness' sake. It's annoying as all get-out wrapped in a bow of good intentions.

597.

May 13 – Kanarra Falls, Utah
"Do you homeschool your son?" I asked the mom of the sweetest family of three. We stood ankle-deep in a rushing river in a slot canyon. They were from Mexico, and on a one-year adventure sabbatical. Mom was a schoolteacher, Dad a construction worker. Their son, Patricio, was eight. Burnt-orange rock walls at least sixty feet tall towered over us on both sides, and there was a sliver of spotless blue sky at the top. The roar of waterfalls echoed through the canyon. "No, we all took a year off, including him."

598.

No. I am not on vacation. No to the four-hour drive for a ninety-minute hike on a Monday. No to visiting the glass museum at 10:00 a.m. on a Tuesday! No, I don't want to eat dinner, chat, and have drinks *every* night into the wee hours. No, no, and no thank you. I parked my house in your driveway. I am not on vacation.

599.

May 13 – Kanarra Falls, Utah
"He'll learn more out here than any year at school," I said. We watched Patricio as he sat cross-legged on a boulder, head down, playing with a stick. Glossy dark-chocolate hair hung like a fondue fountain and hid his face. He wore black sneakers, which dripped water and darkened the sandstone boulder in bronze streaks. "Does he know English?"

"He didn't know any when we began," the mom said. "I'm pretty sure he understands almost everything now, but he hasn't tried speaking yet."

Patricio looked up at us, a full toothy smile stretched across his porcelain-doll face.

"You know we're talking about you, don't you?" the mom said. "Are you ready to go?" Patricio giggled and hopped from his perch back into the crystal-clear river.

What incredible parents. My parents did their best, but boy would I have thrived in a family like that.

600.

What advice would you give to someone considering this lifestyle?

Have patience. When shit hits the fan, put your goggles on and keep plugging away.

601.

May 15 – Virgin, Utah

"Are these yours or mine?" I say in a whisper, as I wipe the wetness from M's right cheek and my left. We lie on top of the comforter in the dark, she on her back, I on my side, cheek to cheek. Ten minutes ago, M told me she thought it was time to book a flight and go home. Slits of dark-orange sunlight sneak in around the closed blinds along the west side of Coddi. "Mine," she says.

Living in the w-e, in 250 square feet, is tough. In a new relationship, it's tougher. When one person works a nine-to-five job and the other has a flexible schedule with much more playtime, it's tougher still. Then add a tumultuous season at work for M, the approaching anniversary of her brother's passing, and not enough hours in the day, and the breaking point snaps, crackles, and pops.

The cherry on top: M's lease on her cottage in Virginia is up in six weeks. She has two weeks to decide whether she renews or joins me in Coddi full-time, or something else.

"I'm cramping your life," M says, as she stares up at the ceiling. A desert wind shakes Coddi. "I don't ever want to hold you back and I am."

The words sting because they carry a kernel of truth we've avoided. My solitary wandering left room for spontaneity that partnership sometimes can't. Yet sharing this journey brings a whole new depth of joy and the richness of witnessing each other's growth. Not constrictions, but expansions.

In Newfoundland, feeling trapped or injured wasn't limitation but invitation to see what I might have missed otherwise. The bike crash slowed me down. The broken rib made me appreciate breath. Likewise, these "constraints" with M aren't limitations but doorways to possibilities.

"You're not holding me back," I whisper, finding her hand in the darkness. "You're showing me parts of the landscape I would have driven right past on my own."

602.

Resilience becomes indistinguishable from love when I stop protecting the identity I think I am, and rest as what I truly am, inseparable from everything.

603.

"To be fully seen by somebody, then, and be loved anyhow—this is a human offering that can border on miraculous."[14] – Elizabeth Gilbert.

604.

More advice for someone considering this lifestyle: Miracles happen, and often it's when we reach our bitter end. Hang on. The way will arrive. It's OK to cry. Ask for help. Give yourself plenty of downtime.

605.

May 17 – Boondocking near Panaca, Nevada
Desert flowers, sagebrush, and mountain views forever. I've set two chairs facing the sunrise. M is in Coddi making coffee. We are in the wild. M's choice. There's a campground nearby, yet she asked for this: freedom and wide-open spaces. She is coming more and more alive, the deeper we move into nature. Each day, we choose This. We are together after lifetimes or eternity, or for the first time.

606.

In all my life and all my travels, I've never met a more special person than M. I love how deep she feels and expresses, and how true she is to herself. I love her laugh and silliness, honesty, goodness, gentle touch, sage wisdom, her fieriness, strength, and softness. I love her quirks and her gifts. I love all of her. And the miracle is that she seems to love me just as completely—my restlessness, feralness, stubbornness and all. She sees me, not as the wanderer, the free spirit, the unconventional nomad, but simply as me. If I could take anyone on my next adventure, it'd be M. Give us a house with a view and waking up in This and I'm all-in for always.

607.

May 19, 6:30 a.m. – Walker Lake, Nevada, living on public lands
I sit in a folding chair by a campfire. The sun rises over jagged mountains and reflects off a lake. The steam from M's coffee mug warms my right forearm. I sip matcha tea from an olive-green ceramic mug. A chilly west wind makes the fire roar. My bare shins burn hot.

When I remember where I was one year ago today, in the Appalachian cabin with my family, my heart aches and tears prick the corners of my eyes. I miss the six of us, the familiarity of touch, the sweet tone of Mom's voice, the frolickiness of my two nieces, the togetherness that says "I've known you forever. I know all your faults, and I'll always love you."

608.

"If something burns your soul with purpose and desire, it's your duty to be reduced to ashes by it. Any other form of existence will be yet another dull book in the library of life."[15] – Andrea Balt

609.

That week in the Appalachian cabin was a vacation. It wasn't life.

610.

M and I coddiwompled into each other on the great meander. Here I sit, with a sweet soul who I've known for months, who might want to do Life together for a short while, or a longer while, or maybe until one of us takes our last breath.

I will live and love without regret. I will not protect myself or my heart, nor will I play it safe. I will not wait for a week's vacation to live my best moments. Life begs me to exist in a primal space and live in a way that could be judged as reckless. Here, I suck the marrow out of life.

I wish to free the animal of being. If the voice of ego thinks it can sway the wildness from being wild, well, let it try. The moment I cannot be manipulated, I am free. The moment I remember I am infinite and lack nothing, I am wild. In each fresh moment, in this absence of judgment and expectation, I am wild and free.

I wander. And now, I am no longer wandering alone.

611.

May 19, 7:27 a.m. – Walker Lake, Nevada
With the warmth of a windblown fire on my shins, I remember this year: the tears, adventures, new friends; all the laughing, learning, seeing, and love.

612.

This is a life lived. This is possibility. This coddiwomple is one small step and then another, and another. This is knowing I am held.

613.

May 19, 7:30 p.m. – Lodi, California
Three years ago I met an Airstream couple. We spoke for half an hour and they invited me to stay in their mother-in-law suite the next time Coddi was in the shop in Sacramento. We hadn't spoken since, until M and I arrived at their home this evening.

We are in an actual bed, in a room without wheels, nestled in their backyard bungalow. Coddi is parked out front, ready to head to the shop.

Yesterday M said she felt as if she was just along for the ride on my journey. So I gave her the reins. She'll choose the direction for as long as it takes for her to know, deep in her bones, *This is our journey.*

614.

Life is a wander, a never-ending invitation to be, to bathe in experience, and to take a step into the unknown. I never know what will be. There is delicious enjoyment in remembering this. I forget, I remember, and repeat.

615.

W-e will live.

616.

May 19, 8:02 p.m. – Lodi, California

"Have you been to Sisters, Oregon?" M asks, while gazing down at my tattered Rand McNally road atlas spread across her lap. She is propped up next to me, pillows behind her back. The simple act of her finger tracing routes on the map feels like the most intimate gesture—not "your trip" but "our adventure." After years of following the tickles of my soul, our tickles are dancing with each other. A candle flickers on the bedside table, casting soft light across M's cheek.

"Yeah, I was there about five years ago. It's beautiful."

M turns toward me with soft, loving eyes and the hint of a smile.

"I'd love to go again. Together."

Epilogue

Life is one vast journey. A journey that lives us.

There are tours within this journey: stretches of time, space, and connection that seem to have a beginning and an end. The day I hit the road in 2017, I began my tour as a wanderer.

May 19, the day this book began, was the start of another tour. Leaving my family in Georgia to head north felt like the second start of my wander. Discovering the rugged beauty in Newfoundland and Labrador would have been enough, but then came November 4, the day M and I met, which began something else: a tour into love, partnership, and discovering myself while discovering another.

After Lodi, California, M and I meandered north and explored the Canadian Rockies together until mid-July, when she flew back to Virginia. I continued alone through Canada and then in mid-October made my way to Virginia, where I stayed at M's cottage for a month. By Thanksgiving, I was in Florida with Mom.

Just before Christmas, I finished the first draft of *Perfect Unfolding*, much of it from journal entries, raw and unedited. I asked M to sit with me and read it, giving her full permission to suggest edits or deletions. We met in South Carolina on December 26. I brought Coddi and candles. She brought treats and massage oil.

I made a big mistake. There were two journal entries in that first draft, about my doubts in the first couple of months of our relationship, that I shouldn't have shared with anyone. Not even M. Yet I thought it would be okay to include them in the book. I was wrong. My heart broke witnessing M's shock and pain.

We edited the sections together, finished reading, and had several emotional conversations. I told M I'd delete the files, burn the journal, erase the book. M wanted me to publish and pulled out a bottle of champagne. I felt there was nothing to celebrate. Still, she poured two flutes, and we toasted. Her celebratory gesture touched me deeply.

We packed up and shared a tearful farewell, and two more goodbyes after that. M was behind me on the road when I stopped. I saw her get out of the car and I jogged back. One more hug, kiss, and goodbye. *Fuck Elvis*. I called six hours later to make sure she'd gotten home safe. We spoke briefly, then the call dropped, which left us hanging. The silence stretched on.

My gut told me it was over, though my heart wished I was wrong. I cried in front of Mom more in those few weeks than I had in forty-six years combined. Mom had hoped I'd fall in love, and she realized I finally had. I sent M a long email. No response.

On January 13, Mom and I were traveling and stopped at a gas station, where I read an email from M. She wished me well on my life's journey and asked me not to call her or travel to Virginia. Uncontrollable sobs racked me as interstate traffic rang in my ears. I crawled into Coddi, curled up on the bed by the front door, and wailed and shook. It was a grief I'd never felt before, raw and overbearing. I cried for all the love I had lost and for what I thought "being left again" meant about me.

Mom doesn't drive my rig, but she took the keys, moved Coddi out of traffic, and climbed inside to hold me. She cried too. Two grown women grieving in a gas station parking lot. This is love.

When I calmed down, we continued on. M's email had begun, "Happy full moon …" The moon meant a lot to her, and she'd often said the moon shines her love down on me. As we drove east on I-10, the full moon hovered dead ahead above the eastbound lanes, extra large like a peach-colored beach ball. I was a wreck: crying, driving, torn between devastation and the overwhelming depth of our love. One moment I wished I could look away, the next I wanted the moon to swallow me whole. M's moon stayed with us the whole drive.

Journal entry
I'm sad. Sad for our lost dreams, love, and friendship; for my mistake, our misunderstandings, and M's deep hurt; for this sacred soul connection that must now go on without voice, touch, or worldly senses. I'm in full-on love, wrapped in bottomless loss. I hurt for what will never be, not just for M and me, but for everyone. We both have gifts, but the combined effect of our w-e feels like a once-in-a-lifetime gorgeous glitch in the system. Together, we are catalysts for each other's fullest expression, expanding our gifts to help others too ... Perry's words on the ferry in Labrador ring truer than ever: "You don't know what you're missing, but if you knew, it's something you'd regret for the rest of your life."

Even pain is love expressing itself. Had I not let myself fall head over heels into This, I'd have missed it all. Love, like Hebron, is wild, beautiful, and challenging.

I didn't want to publish this book and emailed my editor.

"I'm so torn. Our love is a thread through the entire book ... I'm profess-ing this deep love, and I'm also coming out to the world. Do I want to do that anymore? I don't even know if I could be romantic with other women ... I poured all I have into This ... I am wondering if I should even publish. Do you have any words of wisdom?"

His reply was touching, but one sentence in particular grabbed me.

"It would be a shame to have one devastating loss followed by another."

I cried. Not the same kind of tears, but tears of knowing. Something shifted. I stopped resisting grief or wishing it was gone. I let the tears come anywhere, with anyone.

Two weeks after M's email, another blow struck my family. Mom's PET scan revealed ten tumors in her liver, several in her bones, six in her brain, and more in her lungs. After fourteen years with cancer, this was by far the worst it had ever been.

Mom Gave Me Diamond Earrings
She took the silver studs out of her ears,
plopped them in my hand.
We sat in recliners, two porcelain mugs of tea on the table between us.
"I treated myself to these, and I want you to have them," Mom said.
I wear two fake studs and haven't removed them in years.
She knew I'd do the same with hers.
An offering, that's what the diamonds are.
Tangible tokens of her love, her touch, and this moment,
which will soon be a memory of sitting in the living room,
as Mom checked my lobes to be sure I fastened them to her liking.
I'd give anything for these diamonds to sparkle in her ears,
plump with life, for the rest of mine.

A week later, I rushed Mom to the hospital, where she was admitted to intensive care with severe brain swelling. I wrote this.

Mom is alive, but her mind is gone. I stand, my back to her bed, and look out the window. I swallow my grief and blink into a pink sky where a helicopter rests on a roof. Its rotors droop with sadness. I can't cry—not now, not here. I wish I could call M, or heave and wail while wrapped in a hug with the only one I want for comfort. Instead, I stare out at a limp orange windsock and fight against my tears. My pocket buzzes. I look, and choke back a whimper while one drop drips down my cheek. A text from M. Through the ethers she must have known.

"I'm gonna take a walk," I say to the ICU nurse.

With a dry face, I ride the elevator down. Its doors yawn open. I find a bench outside in the dark. I take a deep breath and look at the green Call button next to M's name. One more deep breath. I tap the button. Two rings and a surprised "Hello."

"Hi," I say. Then the dam breaks, the heaves take hold, and tears and snot and all the colors of my sadness roar.

I Am Love

Love for another is an invitation to love myself anew.

I can't hurt myself any more than a tree can saw its own branches.

When a storm blows through, it doesn't aim to destroy.

It does what storms do.

My heart's been ripped out and pulses in a bloody mess on the floor.

Still, I've never been angry at the weather.

From a distance, M and I have had many tough conversations. We keep turning toward each other, no matter how difficult things seem. Like storms, our challenges weren't personal attacks, they were Life expressing itself through two people learning to love. M felt hurt and scared, and wanted to be loved. We both want to be loved.

As I navigate this uncertainty with M, I'm also living with Mom and holding her hand. My love with Mom has flourished in ways I didn't know were possible. As her brain swelling subsided, her mental and physical symptoms improved. Mom is my first and greatest love. I intend to be fully present and full of love for her until her body takes its last breath on this earthly tour. Even then, I imagine our love will continue to grow. I can't fathom life without her physical presence. We will dive into the unknown together, hand in hand, Mom, me, and my family.

These twin lessons in love, with M and with Mom, feel like the culmination of everything this wandering life has been preparing me for.

The phrase "time heals" gives time too much credit. Understanding, perspective, and insight heals. Suffering comes when I think I need something "better" in order to be OK. That's when life feels sticky and stressful. Suffering is my reminder, a symptom of disorder, an invitation to remember and understand the underlying message—to let go of seeking and wanting, and to realize the truth: I am undamageable, everlasting, and complete.

"It's worth it. You don't know what you're missing, but if you knew, it's something you'd regret for the rest of your life." Boy, do I feel the truth of this, in everything!

Through writing and rewriting these pages, I've learned to boldly share my truth while keeping the tender hearts of others in mind. I've had tough conversations, listened deeply, and understood more about myself and those I love. Writing a book, especially one that breaks writing rules and chronicles a life that kicks societal norms in the nuts, isn't always fun or easy. But like coddiwompling itself, it's absolutely worth it.

When I began writing this book, I thought it was about wandering. But the wander showed me the way, and the way is love.

If you feel that subtle tug toward something unknown, that tickle of your soul urging you toward a life that makes no logical sense, trust it. The most magical journeys often begin with the most uncertain first steps. Whether your wander takes you across continents or simply to a new understanding of your own heart, know that every step, even a painful one, is part of the perfect unfolding.

I befriend where I stand. In stillness, I feel the nudges and the knowings. I take one step, then another, ready to embrace all that Life asks of me. This is love.

In grateful memory of
"Uncle" Emanuel Ibrahim
Antra Boyd
Joas Fox

In gratitude for the warmth and wisdom shared by the people of
northern Labrador, 10 percent of this book's profits will be donated
to support their communities.

CONNECT WITH KRISTY

Thank you for taking this adventure with me.

Has this book encouraged you to explore for yourself? Are you open to getting curious and wondering if it could be true that we are all in the midst of a perfect unfolding, even when life doesn't feel perfect at all? I'd love to hear from you.

Share your experience and help others discover their own Perfect Unfolding within these pages: hop online and post a review.
Thanks!

KristyH.com
Instagram: @Kristy.Halvorsen
Mailing list and offerings: KristyH.com/links

Would you like to see photos of this adventure?
PerfectUnfolding.com/photos

Acknowledgments

Thank you, Mom, for giving me that first big nudge to set off on this wild journey, and for all the nudges and love since the beginning, and into eternity.

Thank you to ALL my mentors and guides. Yes, you. I'm so fortunate that there are too many of you to thank individually. You shaped this expression of who I am. This life and this book exist because of your love and care. With endless gratitude, I love you.

Thank you to everyone who has been part of this journey—to those mentioned in this book and all who aren't. And I mean everyone. No matter how or when we've crossed paths, or the perceived significance or insignificance of our connection, everything would be different without you.

Thank you to my soul sister, Mer Monson. What a journey from the innocent wish to travel the world together to seeing more in each other and our writing than we could ever see on our own. I am forever grateful for your wisdom, countless conversations, keen inferences, suggestions, edits, and most of all: our fond friendship. You have a gift. You are a gift. It's your turn now.

Thank you to Tom Evans and Christine Nochasak (Nunatsiavut Government) and George Rich (Innu Nation) for sharing your time, wisdom, and guidance, and for helping me share about Inuit and Innu history and communities, and their profound connection to the northern Labrador coast.

Thank you to my writing teacher and friend Jules Swales for your tough love and unwavering guidance that allowed me to find my voice and unmute myself.

Thank you to the January 2024 Wednesday Method Writing class. You recognized this book before I did. You wouldn't let me not write this and steered this into being. I am the luckiest.

Thank you to all the writers in all the Method Writing classes. We've all witnessed and taught each other, and we are better writers (and humans) for it.

Thank you to Maria Iliffe-Wood, my book sherpa and publishing partner turned dear friend. Without you, this book would have died on the vine. Your care, professionalism, and unwavering support made all the difference. Thank you for believing.

Thank you to Jennie Linthorst. Woman, you were brave enough to say it. You are the best kind of friend: loving, wise, and bold. May we all be so fortunate. From me, and the readers: thank you.

Thank you to my editors Mark, Maria, Mer, and Rachel for everything, and the editing too.

Thank you to all of my beta readers. Your curious inquiries, promptings, comments, brutal honesty, and suggestions shaped what this book has become.

To my social media friends and followers who responded to my request and asked all those intriguing questions: Wow! Thank you! Who'd have guessed people wondered where I peed? … and all the other stuff, too. This book is what it is because of you.

Thank you, M, for finding me, for allowing This, and for tumbling together in our alchemy unfolding. I am forever grateful for our laughter, tears, giving, receiving, endless conversations, pounces, adventures, and all the uncomfortable bits. This is True Love, in every form.

Questions to Ponder

1. When did you last experience true quiet and solitude in the natural world? Is there a place, near or far, that's calling you?

2. Kristy's mom saw her strength before she could see it herself. Who has served as a mirror for you? What did they help you discover that you'd been blind to?

   Flip it: Who could benefit from being seen and supported by you?

3. What does "follow the tickles of your soul" mean to you? If you *really* knew that following your soul's tickles would serve the whole universe, which tickle would you follow first?

4. Is there a label you've accepted about yourself that might not be true? (For example, "I'm not creative," "I'm too old," "I'm bad with money," "I'm not good enough.") Which label would you most like to release?

5. If you let go of every possession you didn't need, what would having "enough" feel like in your life, in your mind, and in your body?

6. If you weren't afraid of being afraid, what's one new experience you would welcome into your life?

7. Kristy discovered that "home" is a way of being rather than a place to be. What does home mean to you when it's not about buildings or addresses?

8. Reflect on one important relationship in your life. What might

become possible if you allowed yourself to be even more vulnerable, and love without any armor?

9. Have you ever allowed yourself to be completely seen by another person? If not, what stops you? And what might unfold if you were fully seen and loved anyway?

10. If you knew you were in the midst of a perfect unfolding and you couldn't get it wrong, what's the first bold step you would take?

NOTES

1. Ingrid Goff-Maidoff, *What Holds Us: New and Selected Poems* (Chilmark, MA: Sarah's Circle Publishing, 2011), 43.
2. U.S. Environmental Protection Agency, "How We Use Water," accessed March 14, 2025, https://www.epa.gov/watersense/how-we-use-water.
3. Charles Bukowski, "Wandering in the Cage," in *The Last Night of the Earth Poems* (New York: HarperCollins, 1992), 167.
4. Maggie Nelson, *Bluets* (Seattle: Wave Books, 2009), 13.
5. Friedrich Nietzsche, *Human, All Too Human: A Book for Free Spirits*, trans. R. J. Hollingdale (Cambridge: Cambridge University Press, 1996), 241.
6. Sri Nisargadatta Maharaj, *I Am That: Talks with Sri Nisargadatta Maharaj*, trans. Maurice Frydman (Durham, NC: Acorn Press, 2012), 245.
7. Paraphrased from Martha Medeiros, "A Morte Devagar."
8. Jerry Hannan, "Society."
9. Rebecca Solnit, *A Field Guide to Getting Lost* (New York: Viking, 2005), 6.
10. Jalal al-Din Rumi, *Rumi, Day by Day: Daily Inspirations from the Mystic of the Heart*, trans. Maryam Mafi (Charlottesville, VA: Hampton Roads Publishing, 2014), 276.
11. Vocabulary.com, s.v. "Miracle," accessed October 24, 2023, https://www.vocabulary.com/dictionary/miracle.
12. Mary Oliver, "Not Anyone Who Says," in *Felicity* (New York: Penguin Press, 2015), 65.
13. Maulana Jalalu-'d-Din Muhammad Rumi, *Masnavi i Ma'navi*, trans. E.H. Whinfield (London: K. Paul, Trench, Trübner & Co.,1898), 5.
14. Elizabeth Gilbert, *Committed: A Love Story* (New York: Viking Press, 2010), 131.
15. Andrea Balt, "Writing Lab: Advice from Charles Bukowski," Rebelle Society, October 22, 2012. Note: This quote is often misattributed to Charles Bukowski but was written by Andrea Balt, and confirmed by Andrea Balt herself.

About the Author

KRISTY HALVORSEN has been telling stories her whole life. She was first published at fourteen in her local newspaper. Online publications have featured her articles, essays, and life/travel tips. For several years, she has been a regular columnist for the *Blue Beret* magazine.

Kristy began her career as a mechanical engineer and then pursued a calling to be a firefighter/paramedic, which she enjoyed for fourteen years. She founded her mentoring and coaching practice in 2015.

In 2017, Kristy began migrating with the seasons full-time while living off-grid in her Airstream trailer. Since then, work and fun have intermingled. A common thread is helping people realize who they truly are and to live their dreams without sacrificing happiness along the way. Her word to describe this simple, fun, and beautiful way to live is "coddiwomple"—that is, to live in wonder, embrace the unknown, and trust Life while waking up to the complete freedom available to us all.

Perfect Unfolding is her first book.